BIENFAIT:
THE SASKATCHEWAN MINERS'
STRUGGLE OF '31

Against all odds, the miners of Bienfait, Saskatchewan, attempted, in 1931, to change their miserable situation by organizing a union. Exploring the social consequences of capitalist restructuring during the Great Depression, Stephen Endicott focuses on the miners' tumultuous thirty-day strike. Their bid to gain union recognition with the aid of the Workers' Unity League of Canada ultimately failed, and Endicott's in-depth examination of the key factors and players attempts to explain why this was the case and why a similar union drive a decade later succeeded.

Based on a large number of both oral and written primary resources, *Bienfait* offers a new interpretation of the role of corporations, governments, courts, and the police in the events surrounding the strike. In the process, Endicott demonstrates how a militant union leadership helped the workers gain the strength and unity of purpose to challenge the powers of wealth and deep-seated prejudice. *Bienfait* opens a new chapter in the history of Canadian labour relations that reveals much about Canadians and Canadian society during the Depression.

STEPHEN LYON ENDICOTT is a Senior Scholar (retired) in History, School of Arts and Letters, Atkinson Faculty of Liberal and Professional Studies, York University.

Bienfait

The Saskatchewan Miners' Struggle of '31

STEPHEN LYON ENDICOTT

UNIVERSITY OF TORONTO PRESS
Toronto London Buffalo

Reprinted 2002, 2003

ISBN 0-8020-3593-0 (cloth)
ISBN 0-8020-8452-4 (paper)

Printed on acid-free paper

National Library of Canada Cataloguing in Publication Data

Endicott, Stephen Lyon, 1928–
Bienfait : the Saskatchewan miners' struggle of '31

ISBN 0-8020-3593-0 (bound)   ISBN 0-8020-8452-4 (pbk.)

1. Coal miners – Labor unions – Organizing – Saskatchewan –
Bienfait – History.   2. Coal Miners' Strike, Estevan, Sask., 1931.
I. Title.

HD5329.M6152 1931 E52 2002   331.892′822334′0971244   C2002-900723-2

University of Toronto Press acknowledges the financial assistance to
its publication program of the Canada Council for the Arts and the
Ontario Arts Council.

University of Toronto Press acknowledges the financial support for its
publishing activities of the Government of Canada through the Book Publishing
Industry Development Program (BPIDP).

This book has been published with the financial assistance of the
Dogwood Foundation of British Columbia.

To Peter, Nick, and Julian

Contents

viii   Contents

Illustrations follow pages 36, 68, and 116.

Acknowledgments

This is not a work of fiction; it is history. But since history is also shaped by memory and memories colour the facts, some readers, especially those with a personal connection to the events described, may think they are reading fiction. That is inevitable and there is little help for it. Yet somewhere in the back of beyond, there is a telling historical reality. The historian's challenge is to discover that larger, more subtle, objective past which encompasses the experience of individual lives but is not bounded by it. Through this process of discovery, it is my hope that one may be able to recognize patterns of the past, become aware of historical continuities, and achieve heightened readiness for things to come.

In this search I wish to thank the many residents and former residents of Bienfait for their generosity in welcoming me into their homes, sharing memories and thoughts about people and events surrounding the storied miners' strike of 1931, and offering their photographs. Not every interview is actually referred to in the text but they were all important to this book's preparation: Mike and Helen Hitchens/Pryznyk Antoniuk, Tony Bachynski, Mike and Elaine Baryluk, Steve and Gloria Baryluk, William Baryluk, Ann Elchyson Bozak, Amelia Billis Budris, Paul Carroll, Gene Choma, Wrally Choma, Jim Davies, Donald Doerr, Sam Dzuba, Steve Elchyson, Peter and Stella Bachynski Gemby, Stewart Giem, Kenneth Hesketh, Mary-Jo Rohatyn, Tom and Mary Sernick, Anne Billis Thompson, Norvin Uhrich, and George and Olga Boruk Wozny.

Helen Gurski and W.R. Coward, administrators, respectively, of Bienfait village and Rural Municipality No. 4 (Coalfields), located the original council records of 1931. In Estevan, Bob Leslie shared his archives of the Estevan Labour Committee, and Marcel Hoste, Estevan city manager, produced the town's '1931 Strike files.'

Among those in Regina I wish to thank are Malcolm Wake and Bill McKay of the Royal Canadian Mounted Police Museum, the prairie history librarian at the Regina Public Library, Kenneth G. Aitkin, Bill Brennan of the department of history, University of Regina, the research and communications director of the Saskatchewan Federation of Labour, Garnet Dishaw, and the staff of the Saskatchewan Archives Board, all of whom were most helpful and attentive to my requests for assistance in this project. Special thanks to Trina Gillis, archivist of the government records branch, and Tim Novak, archivist of reference and special media in the Saskatchewan Archives Board, for sharing their knowledge and responding to my numerous inquiries over several years.

My thanks to Rose McEwen, of Vancouver, who wrote to the government authorities supporting my request to read the Canadian Security Intelligence Service / Royal Canadian Mounted Police files on her husband, Tom Ewen; to George Brandak, special collections at the University of British Columbia, for drawing my attention to important sources on the Workers' Unity League; and to the Dogwood Foundation of British Columbia for helping to make this publication possible.

I am indebted to a number of archivists at the National Archives of Canada: Ellen Scheinberg and Kerry Badgley for helping me find deportation files; and Sarah Gawman, Jay Khosla, Doug Luchak, and others for arranging access to the relevant Canadian Security Intelligence Service files. I am grateful, too, to Tom Mitchell, archivist at Brandon University, for biographical information about mine owner John R. Brodie.

In Toronto, my thanks to the Thomas Fisher Rare Books Library of the University of Toronto for access to the Robert S. Kenny collection; to the Archives of Ontario for use of their microfilm records of old newspapers; to Miguel Figueroa, secretary of the Communist Party, for access to the records of the party he leads; to Richard Anderson, department of geography, York University, for skilful map work; to York University for support with research grants; to Gladys Fung of York University library for her untiring efforts to track down records through interlibrary loans; to Misha Korol for his knowledge about the Ukrainian Labour-Farmer Temple Association and for help with translations; to Taime Davis for sharing her recollections of Sam Scarlett; and to Jim Buller for access to his mother's papers.

I also wish to thank Garnet Dishaw, Lena Wilson Endicott, Norman Endicott, Andrée Lévesque, and two anonymous readers for comments and suggestions on the whole or parts of earlier drafts of the manuscript. Their advice proved to be of great value to the text and to the author, who, nevertheless, bears sole responsibility for the shortcomings that remain. My thanks, finally, to editors Jill McConkey, Len Husband, Frances Mundy, and Curtis Fahey of the University of Toronto Press for their initiative, understanding, and careful attention in helping to bring the project to fruition in book form.

Stephen Endicott
Department of History
Atkinson School of Arts and Letters
York University, Toronto
November 2001

BIENFAIT:
THE SASKATCHEWAN MINERS'
STRUGGLE OF '31

Introduction

When I began talking to coal miners and their families in the village of Bienfait and in Estevan, some wondered why I had chosen to write a book about the people of this corner of Saskatchewan in the 1930s. 'Did you come from here?' they asked, implying that there could be no other earthly reason for engaging in such a project.

There was a family connection, since Charles Endicott, my great-uncle, was the first Methodist minister in Estevan, starting in 1903, and as a child I had listened to his stories. But as an adult my interest was of a more general nature. It had to do with understanding the social consequences of economic restructuring and, flowing from that, learning more about how people survive in hard times, how they organize themselves to cope with the adversities that restructuring in a market economy brings in its wake as surely as drought brings dust storms. I said that I thought this topic would be of interest not only to residents of Saskatchewan but to Canadians in many other communities as well. After hearing my explanation, the local people agreed in principle that their experience in the coalfields and especially that of their parents fitted the subject. Over the course of several years, about thirty residents of Bienfait and Estevan gradually shared their thoughts for this book.

It was in Estevan, Saskatchewan, during a 1931 miners' strike that a peaceful motorcade from the nearby Bienfait coalfields had been halted by the Royal Canadian Mounted Police (RCMP), and in the ensuing mêlée three young miners were shot dead and many others wounded, making this a sad but storied event in Canadian history. The miners were driven helter-skelter back to the coalfields, their leaders and the wounded hunted down like criminals. In an atmosphere of police terror, the miners stood firm, testified in court, raised $100,000 in property and cash bail for their arrested union brothers and sisters, and appeared before a royal commission to state their complaints and offer proposals to change the rules governing the mining industry; but the strike and Local 27 of the Mine Workers' Union of Canada (MWUC) were turned to ashes. The workers were unable to win recognition of their right to have a union of their own choice. Because of the shootings, the miners' struggle has most commonly been referred to as 'The Estevan Strike' or 'The Estevan Massacre.' However dramatic that single event was, the miners and their families mainly lived and worked and tried to organize their union in and around the village of Bienfait and its coalfields: hence the name and focus for this book.

After the savage repression in 1931, the miners continued to nurture their grievances and their hopes as they breathed black powder smoke and shovelled coal for as little as twenty-five cents a ton in the wet and cold underground mines. Without a union they could be fired at the whim of a pit boss. Many were blacklisted by employers, denied work, and evicted from their homes. Defiant men and women with less than five years' domicile in Canada were among those deported by the state to Great Britain and eastern Europe for offences described in government deportation documents as 'communist offences' – distributing literature, unlawful assemblies, and inciting riot. Some had simply been called 'communist' by an anonymous accuser. But the union-minded persisted. They never gave up and, after several more strikes in the late 1930s and 1940s, the miners' union was reborn in Local 7606 of the United Mine Workers of America. A rival company-sponsored organization, the Saskatchewan Coal Miners Union, took root as well, ensuring that the struggle over who could share in the benefits of a natural resource and to what extent would run deep and bitter in this community.

The election of the first Co-operative Commonwealth Federation (CCF) government in Saskatchewan in 1944 rapidly brought changes for the better. New labour legislation required the owners to recognize trade unions of the employees' choosing and also obligated employers to make a sincere effort to conclude collective agreements on the issues brought to the negotiating table by the union;[1] and a new Coal Miners Safety and Welfare Act raised from fourteen to sixteen the age at which boys could be employed in mines. After the start of the rural-electrification program and the formation of the Saskatchewan Power Corporation by the socialist premier, Tommy Douglas, a large and stable market for coal opened up and the workers succeeded in bargaining with the companies for better living standards. By the end of the twentieth century, the union contract negotiated between Local 7606 and Luscar, the giant Alberta-based mining corporation which had become the sole operator in the area, provided year-round employment for almost three hundred workers. Wages reached over twenty dollars an hour. A forty-hour week and paid overtime, a dozen paid statutory holidays as well as three weeks' paid vacation after one year's service, sick leave, and dental coverage became part of the contract. There were procedures for settling grievances and a pension plan.[2] Unionized miners supplying the Saskatchewan Power Corporation had gained a modest share of the prosperity that had come to this resource-rich corner of Saskatchewan.

How were these transformations achieved? How did the people in Bienfait, Roche Percée, and the former company-owned mining camps at Taylorton, Coalfields, and Shand cope with the years of insecurity, the hard times, and the poverty? Where did they gain the strength and unity of purpose necessary to challenge the powers of wealth and the deep-seated prejudice of their day? Where did they get the courage to struggle against the seemingly overwhelming social forces and ever-changing industrial practices that stood between them and a better life? Were they justified in the militant stance they adopted? These matters, hinted at here and there in previous accounts, are the pith and substance of the struggle of social underclasses of every age and in every country for dignity and the power to change their condition.

Like the vast coal seams still waiting under the prairie, the answers to these questions lie buried beneath layers of memory but fortunately not yet beyond the reach of the lived experience. For one thing, the Saskatchewan Archives Board sent young people armed with tape recorders into the coalfields in the 1970s to interview old-timers about their experiences in the bitter Thirties, and these interviews provide the historian with many valuable clues. The provincial archives has also preserved thousands of pages of evidence concerning the coal miners' unrest in the 1930s – records of royal commissions on the coal-mining industry, transcripts of the trials of those arrested during the 1931 strike, microfilms of the *Mercury* weekly newspaper in Estevan, and photographs and other documents of provincial politicians and government departments. The National Archives of Canada has kept the RCMP files made during the 1931 strike as well as some of the deportation orders; the National Archives and the Archives of Ontario have the records of the Communist Party of Canada that pertain to the strike. There are unpublished academic theses. All these are valuable, indispensable even, in seeking to answer our questions. But they are not enough. The lived experience of the miners' distress, the lines of cleavage within the village and the company mining camps at the time of the 1931 strike, and the role of the miners' families, of the village merchants, church members, legionnaires, political parties, members of the two Ukrainian halls – one religious, the other secular – have not yet become readily apparent. Young couples who have moved to Bienfait in recent years detect this gap. 'Do you notice that older people around here are tight-lipped,' one of them said to me. 'They seem to know something they don't talk about.'

It is perhaps natural that people wish to avoid painful memories and prefer to remember the happy times. This was shown at a reunion of alumni who had attended now-vanished 'Black Diamond' schools in the Bienfait coalfields from the 1920s to the 1950s. In a book produced in 1988, many of the alumni recalled the whist drives, concerts, and dances at the community halls, sleigh-rides down Sugarloaf hill and skating on the Souris River in winter, ball games and soccer matches in summer. Lorna Hassard Friess, of Regina, wrote: 'We still consider the Mine area and Bienfait home. Some of my fondest memories are of friends who lived at the Mine as well as Sports Day at Black Diamond. To this day, the smell of the lilacs remind me of my walk to school each day in June. Who among us could forget the "East Pits," Halloween or our Grads. The list seems endless and whenever I think of the Mines, I smile.'[3]

But some of the alumni also recalled the harsh conditions of the 1930s where work was 'not work, it was close to slavery.'[4] Lorna Hassard Friess was also one of these and when she went to university she wrote an essay on 'The Unionization of the Estevan Coal Miners.' Her essay examines 'the anti-labour attitude of the mine operators, their action against organization and the rights of employees, as well as the poor pay, long hours and desperately hard conditions in general' which were 'the main ingredients of the resulting explosion' of strike action in 1931.[5] There are other ways in which the local people showed their wish to have their work experience truthfully recounted. On the fiftieth anniversary of the 1931 strike, in 1981, the Globe theatre company from Regina went to Estevan to perform Rex Deverell's play, *Black Powder*. The play was based upon the testimony of workers and employers to the Royal Commission on the Industrial Dispute in the Coal Mines in the Estevan District in 1931, and its dialogue and re-enactments moved people greatly, helping them reclaim their history; the large audience crammed into a school gymnasium gave the performance a prolonged, standing ovation.

But still, newcomers to Bienfait notice that there is 'something people know but don't say' about the past. One of the things that remains repressed in memory, barely acknowledged, is the role of the Workers' Unity League (WUL), which was the catalyst in helping the miners organize themselves in the summer of 1931. This was the organization which responded to the miners' calls for assistance and whose organizers and affiliated union, the Mine Workers' Union of Canada (MWUC), shaped the strategy and tactics of the resultant thirty-day strike. The tragedy of 'Black Tuesday,' when the police opened fire on the miners in Estevan, and the subsequent repression of the union by the provincial government have all but obliterated the reputation of these organizations and of their supporters in Bienfait and the coalfields. They have been accused of plotting riots; they have been dismissed by historians under the heading 'red scare'; there has arisen 'a collective, psychological mind set that instinctively associates the word "communist" with something adverse,' as author Larry Warwaruk noted in his book, *Red Finns on the Coteau,* and 'the word cannot be approached without emotion.'[6] Yet, without knowledge of the role and participation of these socially conscious, militant people, the course of events can hardly be understood. The RCMP seem to have fathomed this point, putting their entire file on the strike under the heading 'Sam Scarlett, communist agitator.' This was an exaggeration. But the account that follows intends to give a more sympathetic hearing to the WUL, its program and policies, its organizers and supporters among the men, women, and children of Bienfait during the summer and autumn of 1931. They were a critical ingredient in channelling the miners' explosion of anger, grief, and determination to forge a better future. And there is a surprising continuity between the struggles of the Thirties and those of the decades that followed.

Chapter One

The Bienfait Coalfields

I consider the conditions ... very excellent. I do not think there is anything in Western Canada to surpass it.

– J.R. Brodie of Winnipeg, owner of the Bienfait Mine, 8 October 1931[1]

I have been disappointed with them, they start grumbling and trying to stir up some kind of trouble with the other men, they are continually talking about how they do in the Old Country and expect us to alter all conditions of working to suit them.

– A.C. Wilson, manager, Manitoba and Saskatchewan Mining, Bienfait, February 1930[2]

The village of Bienfait sits low on the prairie. It is a fine district for mixed farming, with a supply of water in the nearby Souris River. In 1931 the village was sandwiched between the now disappeared station grounds of the Canadian Pacific Railway (CPR) and Canadian National Railways (CNR). It had eight short streets, bisected by Route 18, the east-west provincial highway connecting it to the town of Estevan, eight miles to the west. As in many prairie settlements, the centre point was Main Street, only two blocks long but twice as wide as the other streets, lined with shops, businesses, and vacant lots; along Railway Avenue, grain elevators of the Saskatchewan Co-operative Elevator Company (known locally as the 'wheat pool elevator') and the privately owned Lake of the Woods Milling Company stood sentinel. By then, it bore no memory of the French-language origins of its name;[3] the local residents pronounced it Bean-fate.

The hundreds of rural municipalities into which Saskatchewan is divided have a regular shape: square boxes. These squares, each subdivided into divisions and subdivided further into townships (running east-west) and ranges (running north-south), form the grid lines within which are the sections of land, subdivided yet again into quarter-sections, many of which were given to the CPR as part of the contract to build the transcontinental railway. Since then, many sections have been sold to private landowners, speculators, farmers, and mining companies or are still held as crown land. The Rural Municipality No. 4 (Coalfields) is no different from these. It sits on the United States border, fourth over from the Manitoba boundary, where all the numbering begins.

With the village of Bienfait as its administrative centre, Coalfields, as its name implies, encompasses many of the rich seams of the Estevan coal bed. A large community pasture, over 40,000 acres and with several corrals, covers about 20 per cent of the land area on both sides of the winding Souris River, while almost 200 widely spaced farmhouses are sprinkled around the landscape. The municipality, whose territory is crossed by both major railways, also has within its boundaries the villages of Roche Percée, North Portal, and Frobisher and the remains of the hamlet of Hirsch, famous as an agricultural colony founded by Jewish immigrants escaping the pogroms of tsarist Russia in the late nineteenth century and for a time the parental home of Eli Mandel, one of Canada's best-known modern poets.

Responding to the efforts of CPR recruiting agents in Britain and in Europe, the population in this area grew substantially after the First World War. Some of the new immigrants came from England, Ireland, and Scotland, while others came from Germany, Scandinavia, Lithuania, western Ukraine (under Polish rule after the war) and other areas of central and eastern Europe, bringing with them their languages and cultures and adding Greek Catholic, Greek Orthodox, and Lutheran to the existing religious mix of Anglican, Baptist, Methodist, Pentecostal, Presbyterian, Jewish, and Roman Catholic faiths. It was a population divided and fragmented in many ways except for a common desire and a mutual competition to build for themselves a more prosperous, secure life in this unfamiliar environment.

All the arriving immigrants had their tales of adventure or hardship about the long journey out from 'Old Country,' of the high expectations and disappointments, the gradual adjustment to new realities. The migrants who travelled alone, without family and without knowledge of the English language, possibly had some of the more poignant experiences to shape their entry into Saskatchewan. Peter Gemby was one of these. His recollections illustrate the poverty, illiteracy, drunkenness, and ill-health on the one hand, and the family solidarity, cultural awakening, self-reliance, and collective, union psychology on the other, that together formed the coal-mining workforce:[4] 'My brother and I became homeless when our mother died after the war in 1919,' he began. It was in western Ukraine and the two brothers moved from one uncle's home to another, never having enough to eat. Eventually, in 1922, his father was able to send some money from Taylorton, Saskatchewan, for one of them to come to Canada, and Peter, the eldest, was chosen. He could not read or write 'because our school system closed down in the war.' So he hired a tutor to learn to write his name in order to sign the papers to immigrate to Canada. As the fifteen-year-old made his way westwards across central Europe, he became self-conscious in his baggy peasant clothes. At the first opportunity he spent some of the travel money his father had sent to buy a western suit for three thousand marks. 'That wasn't much – inflation was so bad in Germany.' Once aboard the transatlantic liner he tossed all his old belongings overboard, including his birth certificate. 'Time to forget the past,' he said. 'Begin a new future!' He hoped to live in a Canadian city like ones the train passed through in the eastern provinces and Manitoba. But in Saskatchewan he found his father living in a mining camp, a few miles south of Bienfait where the highest building was a grain elevator. The Gemby 'house' was little more than a shack, the back portion of which was dug into the side of a ravine. There were twenty or thirty single miners living this way, squatters on the property of the Western Dominion Collieries where they worked. 'My father, who was not a healthy man, got me a job in the mine opening and closing doors for ventilation at twenty cents an hour,' Peter recalled, and with enough food to eat he soon grew accustomed to the new surroundings.

The most popular activity during the men's free time was making home-brew. At the beginning of the week, his father would take a bunch of potatoes, sugar, and yeast and create a mash in a barrel. By Saturday it would be ready for the distilling process through heating and on Sunday the 'vodka' was done. All day the men would visit each other, sampling their results, socializing. By evening there were often heated arguments, sometimes fighting, as the inebriated bachelors argued, usually about politics in the Old Country. Next morning, sobered up, they would go off to work together, friends again. 'There was no time to hold grudges down in the mine.' Periodically the RCMP would make a raid on the illegal stills. But, according to Peter, the officer would warn them in advance of his visit. 'When he arrived we handed him a bottle and that was the end of the inspection.'

Less than a year after his arrival, Peter's father, barely forty, passed away in the shack where they were living. His body lay there for two days before burial since it took that time to dig the grave in the cold and snow. In the little cemetery on the hillside at Taylorton, there are scores of graves, some unmarked, of men, women, and children who died before their time. Peter returned to the shack, living alone, sleeping in his father's bed and having nightmares. Soon he found it too difficult to get by on his meagre wages and he moved in with his cousin across the ravine. During the next several years, with the help of friends, he learned to read and write in Ukrainian and in English. He joined the Ukrainian Labour-Farmer Temple Association in Bienfait, took out sickness and life insurance offered by the Workers' Benevolent Association for one dollar a month, and subscribed to the *Ukrainian Labour News* of Winnipeg. With this orientation he quite naturally became one of those agitating for a miners' union, and was blacklisted, but he survived by operating his own little mine for a few years. He went on to marry and raise a family, becoming a community leader and serving eleven terms on the Bienfait village council. Throughout, he was a staunch advocate of a miners' union.

With the influx of new immigrants in the decade after the First World War, Bienfait itself doubled in size to 500 – or about 100 families. Yet even when these numbers are added to the larger surrounding rural municipalities of Estevan and Coalfields, the census of 1931 showed a local rural populace – men, women, and children – not much in excess of 4,000 people.[5] Still, it was of sufficient size to provide a plentiful supply of labour for the mines in the winter months.

The head of the Bienfait community, A.H. Graham, commonly referred to as the overseer,[6] liked to boast that the village was the most prosperous place of its size in Saskatchewan. For five months of the year, there were plentiful signs of activity: four men working full-time in each of the railway yards making up train-loads. On average, during the winter months, they shipped out one hundred cars of coal per day. Even though the yards were virtually empty during the rest of the year, an annual payroll from the mines, amounting to $400,000 in 1930–1, provided the material base for a score of more-or-less successful business and community enterprises. As signs of Bienfait's vitality, the fledgling village Board of Trade cited the presence of a garage, a hardware store, five groceries, two butchers, a barber-shop, a pool room, a drugstore, several cafés, an electrical service shop under construction, a lumber yard, a machine shop under way, two amusement halls, and football, baseball, and other organized sports, including a hockey team 'that had figured in the provincial play downs.'[7]

Perhaps the crown of this bustling community was the King Edward Hotel, a two-storey frame building on the corner of Main and Railway Avenue. It advertised itself as 'the best equipped village hotel in Saskatchewan' – Simmon's beds, Slumber King springs throughout, hot soft-water baths at all times, four first-class billiard tables, three bowling alleys, a first-class two-chair barber-shop, and electrical refrigeration. The proprietor, Gordon White, had his motto written large: WHITE HELP–WHITE SERVICE.[8] The village elite – mine managers and office staffs, pit bosses, the school principal, business people, and others largely from the Anglo-Saxon and north European majority – gathered at the bar for smoking, relaxation, and socializing and took their privileged standing for granted.

Other places that played an important part in village life at the time were two Ukrainian halls and Boruk's Bakery and Boarding House. These were the gathering places of the 'foreign born,' in the parlance of the day, immigrants from eastern Europe – Lithuanians, Poles, Ukrainians, Czechoslovaks, and others who made up about 30 per cent of the population. It was the men of these families who did much of the bone-and-muscle work down in the mines and who, according to Mervyn Enmark, a mine foreman in the 1970s, 'were treated as Indians are treated today.'[9]

A few miles south of Bienfait were the largest mining camps. Perhaps the most important of these in the 1930s was Taylorton, a company-owned place that was home to hundreds of miners and their families until it was abandoned in the 1950s. A general store and the Black Diamond School, not far from the gate of the mining property, and a deep well operated by a windmill, stood on a large flat area. The store was made of granite rocks and cement, built and owned originally by Robert Hassard, pioneer miner in the area. Today, even after local people carted the granite away for building purposes, parts of this ruined structure remain. Farther to the east was the post office, an overcrowded boarding house, thirty small- to medium-sized houses for miners with families, and a community hall. Behind the miners' houses were fenced areas which the company ploughed for vegetable gardens. 'It was not too bad,' says Norvine Uhrich, son of Elizabeth Sloan Uhrich, who ran the boarding house for many years.[10]

To the south, not far from the general store, the flat area drops off into a draw or coulee which has two distinct valleys, east and west. They were variously called Klymyk, Dzuba, or Pryznyk valley, named after some of the newly arrived Ukrainian families who dug their homes into the sides of the valleys and lived as squatters. Of these two dozen or more ramshackle structures, scarcely a trace remains; there is nothing in the area now but a couple of rusted 1930s automobiles and the verdant grasses and scrub trees which dot the valley slopes. These families often kept livestock, supplying milk for themselves and their neighbours. Some were industrious and self-sufficient. 'Mother looked after everything,' recalled Joe Pryznyk. 'She had two thousand cabbage plants, two or three cows, pigs, ducks, geese. We didn't buy much – sugar, salt and flour, but we had food, we had cheese, bacon, hams and sauerkraut.'[11]

Outside the mine-property gate (later moved inside) was the United Church, the only church building in the area and used by other denominations as well. Near the church, on the side of the coulée, was the graveyard, later preserved by the provincial government as a heritage cemetery. A few hundred yards farther south, Sugarloaf Hill, highest point in the area, overlooked Taylorton Bridge and the former wagon road from Bienfait to North Portal and the United States border, which crosses the meandering Souris River at this point. The most important feature of community life was controlled from the mine office: a long whistle at night meant there would be work in the morning; a short whistle, no work.[12]

Seams of lignite coal in an area seven miles square lie beneath the prairie at Bienfait, spreading down to the border of the United States and into North Dakota. Geologists call this the coal-bearing Ravenscrag Formation. The coal beds in southern Saskatchewan are in relatively horizontal seams that gently dip to the southeast at twenty-five feet per mile. Sometimes the coal stretches for several miles in uniform thickness, a welcome contrast to the often steeply inclined and faulted seams in the foothills of the Rocky Mountains to the west. Test boreholes established nineteen coal zones, fourteen of them 'deep coal zones' and five of them 'shallow coal zones.' The readily accessible coal in the shallow coal zones, called by such names as 'Boundary,' 'Estevan,' 'Souris,' and 'Roche Percée,' lies near the surface, covered by relatively light layers of glacial silt, sand, clay, or weak rock formations. The thickest zone, the twelve- to fifteen-foot 'Estevan' seam, had within it two thin layers of bone or impure coal, sometimes called 'black jack' – usually one or two feet from the top of the seam and the other a similar distance from the bottom; these two beds of bone were taken as natural boundaries to work to. Although considerable quantities of coal were wasted, the part remaining on top provided a safer roof than the clay immediately above it; the coal on the floor was left so that the impure bone bed would not get mixed with the middle coal of first grade.

The Souris River, which cuts the plain to a depth of about one hundred feet, exposed to the naked eye the easily recoverable coal twenty to one hundred feet below the surface of the earth and led the Indians and European fur traders and early settlers to the discovery of the mineral. All these geological features greatly influenced the subsequent patterns of mining and settlement in the Estevan–Bienfait area.[13]

In the off-season, using their hand tools and with the aid of horse-drawn carts, the farmers singly or in groups dug slopes down into the prairie soil to reach the coal. Once a mine was established, it could go on producing for years, providing a welcome source of supplementary income to struggling settlers. The product of these unlicensed operations on their own lands served to provide the settlers, their neighbours, and villagers with heating and cooking fuel which was picked up or delivered along prairie trails by horse and wagon. The prairie coal soon attracted wealthy and powerful entrepreneurs, but even after the mining operations financed by the CPR and the Hudson's Bay Company (HBC) took hold, the labour-intensive 'gopher hole' mining by local, small-scale entrepreneurs continued for decades without interruption. There are more than 130 known producing and abandoned mines in the Estevan/Bienfait coalfield. Although only a dozen or so of them ever shipped coal greater distances by railroad, the persistence of these small operations demonstrated their niche in the local economy; accounting for only 5 per cent of production by 1930, they nevertheless provided welcome back-up and a haven to men blacklisted for trying to form a union in the large mines.[14]

By common account, coal mining began in Saskatchewan in the 1890s along the banks of the Souris River at Roche Percée. Some of the product was transported by barge to Winnipeg and the rest was sold to local settlers. Large mine sites with headframes – structures built over the mine entrance to house hoisting equipment, weigh scales, coal-cart tipping machinery, sorting screens – railspurs, and bunkhouses located in company towns were established on the prairie at Taylorton, Coalfields, Shand, and near and within the village of Bienfait in the first decade of the twentieth century. In 1915, as part of the war effort, the government of Canada built a charcoal carbonizer near one of the mine sites to produce smokeless fuel briquettes. This plant, which, it was hoped, would provide steady employment, was gradually enlarged and upgraded to manufacture by-products such as creosote, coal tar, methane gas, and lignite char for barbeques.

The output of the Saskatchewan coal mines progressed from 100,000 tons, in 1906 to six times that, or almost 600,000 tons in 1931 after the government of Canada offered freight subsidies so that western Canadian coal could compete with American coal in Winnipeg and northern Ontario. As lignite coal began to be used extensively for generation of electricity in places as far away as Ontario, production through strip mining soared until, by the 1990s, it reached a steady volume of 10 million tons a year, with royalties to the provincial government of over $14 million annually. Unless environmental concerns enter the picture, coal in Saskatchewan is an industry with a long horizon.[15]

Before the Second World War, most of the commercial mining was conducted underground using the 'room and pillar' method of excavation. After digging a slope through the sedimentary overburden, and later sometimes sinking a vertical shaft, miners cut drifts (tunnels) and rooms into the coal faces, leaving columns of coal to support the overlying roof. The larger mines used what was described as the 'panel system' of operation, the panels being four or five hundred feet in width and consisting of rooms extending two hundred or two hundred and fifty feet into the coal seam. The rooms, which could be up to twenty or twenty-four feet wide, had to have their ceiling shored up with timbers.[16]

Ventilation to get rid of blasting-powder smoke and poisonous gases, and to provide fresh air for the men and horses, was created in various ways. A fire at the bottom of an air shaft, causing an updraft which drew clean air through the underground passages, was one way. Another was to have a large fan running twenty-four hours a day. It either pushed fresh air into the mine or acted as an exhaust system which drew new air from down shafts on the prairie at the far ends of the mine and expelled the old through the shaft for hoisting coal on the slopeway into the mine. Within the mine a series of doors, partitions, and crosscuts was supposed to direct the flow of air along the haulage ways into the rooms where the men were working. In the busy season, some of the mines employed young boys as trappers to open and shut the ventilation doors. It was not easy to have an air current reach the coal faces in rooms that extended a distance of two hundred and fifty feet.

Water was a problem in many of the mines. They all had a full-time pumpman and electric motors to remove water from the sump. But in certain places the men still had to cope with water twelve or eighteen inches deep and would come in early, before hoisting operations started, to remove the water by dipping or with hand pumps. 'In some of the rooms,' said a miner at Crescent Collieries, 'they had to load a car of coal and a tank of water, turn about ... You pump a tank full of water and the horse draws it away out.'[17]

Mechanization advanced through various stages and at different tempos depending upon the mine. After the early pick and shovel, blasting powder, and manually operated drilling methods, the first advance, according to veteran miners, was a compressed air punch used to undercut the coal seam, allowing the coal to fall down after blasting.[18] When the mines began to generate their own electricity, an electric coal cutter was used. 'This consisted of an endless chain armed with small picks which cut under the seam.' The other great improvement was steam haulage: 'Full cars were hauled up the slope by a two-inch cable which rolled on to a revolving drum. Horses still brought the full tubs to the bottom of the slope and did all the hauling in the underground roads.' Later, electric-haulage locomotives powered from overhead trolley wires operated on the main roads underground while horses continued to haul carts out from the coalfaces. In the 1920s some of the larger mines sank a vertical shaft to replace the slope. Steam from a boiler house drove hoisting machinery allowing loaded cars to be lifted from the mine bottom to the part of the headframe known as the tipple. There, a weighman passed the loaded cars over a scale, crediting each miner for his tonnage before tipping the coal out for screening and sizing prior to shipment. The inter-war years thus saw great improvements in underground mining methods. Diggers continued to load the coal into carts by hand and horses were still in use but modern coal-cutting machines, electric-power drills, shearing machinery, power shovels, and conveyor belts greatly increased productivity per man per day. In this development Saskatchewan was keeping pace with other western Canadian coal-mining areas.[19]

Lignite coal has its special characteristics. It is a soft coal with a higher moisture content than the harder bituminous coals in the neighbouring Alberta or in the Nova Scotia or Pennsylvania coalfields. As a result, it produces less heat per ton and therefore commands a lower price in the market. Another drawback is that it decomposes when exposed to the air and so cannot be mined and stockpiled for later use: it needs to be shipped to its markets as it is mined. A social consequence is that for many years the industry provided only seasonal winter employment for most of its workers. On the other hand, lignite coal's lower sulphur content makes its combustion less harmful to the environment and thus in some ways it is more desirable than other coal. Because it produces little ash, it was much prized for home cooking and heating in the early decades of Western Settlement.[20]

The most prominent entrepreneur in the Bienfait coalfields was the highly successful but shadowy figure of John R. Brodie. He was not well known to the local people, which is not surprising since he lived in Winnipeg and conducted his various business interests from Brandon, Manitoba. In Brandon he chose to use his wealth to endow the university with its J.R. Brodie Science Centre. Born in 1879, and raised in a devout Presbyterian family in Montreal, Brodie had started out in the grain and milling business. But at the age of twenty-nine he joined the westward tide and entered lignite-coal operations in Alberta and Saskatchewan.

Through Great West Coal, which he incorporated in 1908, Brodie became involved in various mining ventures in Alberta and Saskatchewan. His investments kept shifting. In the 1920s he was co-owner of Crescent Collieries Coal with William L. Hamilton and Alexander C. Wilson, and together those three men made up a formidable management team in the Estevan district of Saskatchewan.[21] At that time he also bought into Bienfait Mine, which he and several partners leased from the CPR. He felt able to say of the Bienfait mine in 1931: 'I do not think there is anything in Western Canada to surpass it.' He rated Robert J. Hassard, company president and a member of a pioneer family in the area, as 'about as able a man as I ever met in the mining industry.' The mine was still referred to locally as the 'Hassard's Mine,' and under the leadership of Joseph Bembridge, mine manager, the conditions in the Bienfait mine, according to Brodie, were 'excellent' and 'efficiency' was 'very good.' Brodie had reason to be cheerful since, in spite of the enveloping economic depression, the Bienfait mine had paid a 20 per cent dividend in 1930 on top of an 18 per cent dividend the year before.[22]

Nevertheless, John Brodie's coal business in Saskatchewan was not without its problems as the 1920s shaded into the 1930s. Apart from the general downturn in the Canadian economy associated with the Great Depression, there were too many lignite mines competing for a market which extended only as far as Regina and Saskatoon to the north and Brandon and Winnipeg to the east. While many of the so-called mines were merely 'gopher holes' where farmers hired a couple of people to help them dig surface coal, there were also six large deep-seam mines whose three million dollars of investment required a fairly extensive market to be profitable.[23] The investment in these mines included rail-

TABLE 1.1
Production and profit at Bienfait and M&S mines, 1929–31

Mine	Year	Net tons produced	Profits or loss ($)	Profit per ton (cents)	Capital	Profit as % of capital	Dividend paid
M&S	1929	100,605	+18,137	18.13	$1,201,500	1.5	nil
	1930	92,179	+ 7,871	8.54	"	0.7	"
	1931	105,478	+ 7,098	6.72	"	0.7	"
Bienfait	1929	76,281	+23,301	30.5	$100,000	23.3	18%
	1930	75,933	+18,650	24.6	"	18.6	20%
	1931	74,016	+ 9,685	13.3	"	9.8	nil

Note: The profits of the M&S are after payment of interest on $201,500 worth of 6 per cent bonds outstanding but before allowing a reserve for depletion of its coal resources. Mine managers' salaries were $5,000 to $6,500. Workers' wages amounted to $450 to $600 per annum. Bienfait Mines had made adequate depreciation and depletion allowances. M&S had 130 employees, of whom 45 were miners or loaders; Bienfait had 110 employees, of whom 75 were miners or loaders.

Source: J. Raffles Cox, 'Confidential Report on an Inspection of Part of the Saskatchewan Lignite Field, with Special Reference to: THE COST AND RATE SITUATION,' Exhibit C27, Wylie Commission, 1931; Inspector F.W. Schultz, RCMP, 'Strike Conditions, Bienfait, Sask.' (Secret), 20 Sept. 1931, H.V.–7 file, Canadian Security Information Service (CSIS) RG146, National Archives of Canada.

way spur lines, underground rails and coal carts, horses in some cases, electrical wiring and tunnel-support timbers, hoisting mechanisms, screening and loading platforms, ventilation systems, surface buildings for housing or boarding the miners, company stores, and smithies and other repair shops for the mining equipment. Unless the market could be extended or controlled it would not be easy to make an attractive return on invested capital. Brodie attempted to regulate the market by forming Souris Coal Distributors. Taking an 8 per cent commission to act as a selling agent for a handful of the most productive mines in the area, he tried to drive the smaller mines from the market by excluding them from his cartel. However, this tactic proved unsuccessful since the CPR and CNR were eager to haul coal from whatever source.

If Brodie was little known in Bienfait, the same cannot be said for his former partner, Alexander (A.C.) Wilson. Moving from one mine to another after his arrival from the Lancashire coalfields in 1904, first as a digger and then as a manager, Wilson became a legendary folk figure who dominated the local scene in Bienfait, inspiring either awe or fear, loyalty or intense dislike. Years later no person was more discussed by the miners and their families than this man, nick-named 'Happy Wilson' because he was always so grumpy.[24] Wilson liked to act as if he was a law unto himself, even referring to himself as 'Outlaw Wilson.'[25]

By 1931, Wilson was the manager of Manitoba and Saskatchewan Coal (M&S), the largest of the six deep-seam mines, and he was fiercely proud of his achievements. He had introduced cutting and shearing machines, thus reducing the black powder needed for shooting and so making for cleaner air in the mine; he was also experimenting with a mechanical shovel to speed up the loading work and reduce the number of men required, making M&S, he claimed, the most modernized mine in the district.

From Wilson's payroll journal for the month of December 1931, a season when the mine was busy, it is possible to get a more detailed impression of the structure of the underground work in the mine. At the top of the heap were the shotfirers. These four men and a couple of helpers bored eight-foot holes to employ black powder to loosen the coalface. It took experience to know how much powder to use – enough to loosen the coal but not so much as to blast it into tiny pieces or, worse, to bring down the roof. The shotfirers were paid the best rate, about $280 for the month. Next were four teams of machine men who did the mechanized work, cutting the coal at the bottom to give it a chance to drop down, operating shearing machines at the coalface and a mechanical loader.

They could make around $200, sometimes more. Then there were the diggers or loaders – sixty-three of them. They loaded the coal by hand into carts for 27½ cents per ton, averaging just under two tons an hour. Wilson thought that a man should load a two-ton cart each hour and set up roof-support timbers in between. 'Any man that cannot do that I always considered him lazy,' he said. Most of the diggers spent 147 hours loading coal that month and, at an average of 46.14 cents per hour, they grossed around $67; some made up to $100 while others, working fewer hours, got $50 or less. Apart from the pit boss, who netted a salary of $140, there were thirty-five support workers, known as 'underground daymen,' who received between 33 and 41 cents per hour. These daymen included such categories as hoist operators, lightmen, tankmen (who removed water from the mine), trackmen, timbermen, stable managers, and drivers as well as a cohort of general labourers, helpers, and 'a boy.' The most numerous category, the dozen men who worked with the horses, averaged $54. These pay scales included the 10 per cent gains made as a result of the thirty-day strike in the autumn of 1931.[26]

Wilson's was the only mine in the field that provided hot-water showers for the miners and their families. In return for this and other amenities, he demanded a high level of discipline and loyalty from his workforce. But, as closer investigation will reveal, his arrogance, favouritism, greed, and bullying fostered instead resentment and revolt. Most galling to him was the attitude of the British miners, of whom he had hired quite a number in the previous two years, giving them preference of the work available. 'In nearly every instance,' he wrote, 'I have been disappointed with them, they start grumbling and trying to stir up some kind of trouble with the other men, they are continually talking about how they do in the Old Country and expect us to alter all conditions of working to suit them.' More than once he shouted at them, 'You are in Saskatchewan. You are not in Scotland!' hoping they would forget their militant British union tradition.[27]

After M&S the next largest mine was the Western Dominion Collieries, with seventy men and five horses. In due time John Brodie would gain control of this operation, but for the moment it was owned by British capitalists and headed by a hard-driving American engineer from New York, C.C. Morfit. Located across the tracks from the M&S mine at Taylorton, Western Dominion had an experimental plant to produce 'smokeless fuel' in the form of briquettes and other by-products such as coal tar, creosote, pitch, and methane gas. Its strategic plan for manufacturing products was such that, if successful, it would lead to year-round operations and full utilization of the coal mine. But for the moment it had not started making much money. Next in size was Robert Hassard's Bienfait mines, with sixty-eight men and nine horses, in which Brodie had a major share, and William Hamilton's Crescent Collieries, with fifty-two men and six horses. They were followed by Eastern Collieries, an under-capitalized mine owned by Herbert Wallace of Estevan, which had twenty-nine men and four horses, and, finally, National Mines, with twenty men and four horses. This was an old mine which was being reconditioned and managed by Harry N. Freeman, an experienced mining engineer from Vancouver Island, on behalf of British Columbia capitalists who were prominent in the Conservative Party of Canada. These were the major players on the operators' side of the bitter struggle which erupted in the coalfields in 1931.[28]

To this ever-shifting configuration should be added an ominous irritant for the operations of J.R. Brodie and his companions in the form of a recent interloper. An American company, Truax-Traer Coal, had come across the border from North Dakota in 1930 to acquire expired coalfield leases. In spite of some questionable connections to the Chicago underworld, Truax-Traer was able to hire a vocal and vigorous manager, Eleazer W. Garner, the former mayor of Estevan. Garner immediately began surface strip-mine operations, a type of mining which made it possible to ship coal at a cost 42 per cent lower than that of the deep mines. Brodie muttered darkly that, with a few bulldozers, electric shovels, trucks, and only fifty men who were not even miners in the traditional sense, Garner could double shift and put out 5,000 tons per day, enough to supply the whole market and at a lower price. If this went on, Brodie warned, and 500 deep-seam miners were thrown out of work, it would cost the government $5,000 in relief. He appeared before a royal commission complaining of Garner's underhanded tricks, which included selling coal below cost to put the other mines out of business. He demanded a tax on Truax-Traer to level the field. This rearguard action went on until finally Brodie himself bought out Truax-Traer and proceeded to change all of his operations into strip mines. The restructuring of the coal industry and its transformation to strip mining was still half a generation in the future, but already the presence of the new Truax-Traer operation was an important complication in the deep-seam coal strike of 1931 (see appendix 1).[29]

It had been a hot, dry spring in 1931. Instead of the gentle rains that aid germination, arid winds blew steadily day after day in June, sweeping up the top soil into swirling dust storms. A professor from Saskatoon touring southern Saskatchewan that month wrote:

> Within the past three days ... the elements loosed themselves upon us with demonic fury. The day before yesterday the heat mounted to 104 degrees in the shade and was driven upon us with a high wind which felt like a blast from the Inferno. Yesterday the wind veered and churned up the dust from fields that had been baked to a fine powder and today the wind is still more violent with a dust storm raging which blackens the heavens so that it seems like midnight. These last three days have put the finishing touch upon a situation which was serious enough.[30]

For a third year in a row, many western farmers were heading into extensive crop failures, failures that were especially heavy in that part of Saskatchewan which lay to the southeast of the provincial capital, Regina, including the area where many Bienfait miners normally tried to make ends meet by working part-time on farms.

The plight of the rural population in southern Saskatchewan is reflected in an investigation made by the United Church of Canada at the time. Worried by the fate of its membership, leaders of the church headed southward in the first week of July 1931. Leaving Regina by automobile, the group, led by the Right Reverend Edmund Oliver, moderator, and the Reverend Charles Endicott of the Missionary and Maintenance Fund, drove four hundred miles to assess the situation and make recommendations to the national church.

To pass through 'the garden of Saskatchewan' from Regina to Weyburn and not to see a single field of grain but bare stretches of sand was a most distressing experience for the churchmen. When it was recalled that 'this was in the famous Regina Plains and along the Soo Line, in the most fertile part of the entire Province,' they wrote, 'one can see how desperate the situation has been.' The group's observations, gathered first-hand and in meetings in the Estevan, Assiniboia, Weyburn, and other presbyteries, were enough to convince them that the situation was beyond the imagination of anyone who had not seen it with their own eyes or heard it with their own ears. The area that was 'the finest wheat producing region of Canada is now a veritable desert,' they reported. 'One can drive mile after mile without seeing a single green blade.' The moderator criticized eastern financial institutions for building palaces for offices yet refusing to provide debt relief by means of credit to western farmers. Drought, unemployment, low grain prices, and high mortgage rates had 'reduced the people to the verge of poverty, if not of starvation.' The clergymen feared that they would lose some of their 'best people through this discouragement' and fretted that 'their places will be taken by Germans and Mennonites and Doukhobours who will stick to it until they come through triumphantly.' At the same time they praised the 'magnificent spirit of the people' and were pleased that 'there was no Bolsheviks talk [sic] in Southern Saskatchewan'; so far as that existed, 'it was in the North or in Alberta.'[31]

Most of all, though, it was a depressing experience for the church leaders and they resolved to mobilize support for government action and for relief efforts from eastern Canada. By the end of 1931, they had established a National Emergency Relief Committee that shipped 165 tons of clothing and 159 freight carloads of fruit, vegetables, and salt fish, most of it going to Saskatchewan. Without the hope of immediate, 'direct Government Relief,' the clergymen warned that there was 'only the prospect of starvation' in some quarters and intense suffering in others. The Saskatchewan Conference of the United Church went further and began debating and passing resolutions demanding new standards to govern the social order in keeping with a Christian economic order whose features included the socialization of banks, natural resources, transportation, and other vital services to replace the existing cut-throat, private-property, capitalist system.[32]

It was in this desperate situation that the operators of the deep-seam mines in Bienfait announced general wage reductions for the miners. A cut of 10 to 15 per cent was necessary, they said, to compete with the lower price of coal being put on the market by the Truax-Traer strip mine. The miners would have to load coal for twenty-five cents per ton. The secretary-treasurer of the village of Bienfait, Arthur Nelson, predicted 'a lot of trouble' in the coming winter. The average income for the miners had been 'from $9 to $25 per month,' he said, 'the latter figure being the exception,' and now it would be worse. Nelson wrote to warn the provincial government that the miners had good grounds for complaint.[33]

The coal operators no doubt worried about the economic outlook but they were also accustomed to having their own way. For over thirty years, since deep-seam mining had begun in the Souris River valley, they had a short answer to any worker bold enough to express an opinion, air a grievance, or complain about wages or conditions in the mine: 'If you don't like it here, pick up your tools and get out!' And the owners often had the provincial mine inspectors in their pocket as well – inspectors who were charged with enforcing the mining laws of the province but who made the most cursory of tests into safety conditions in the mines and then wrote skimpy, uninformative reports about their visitations.

Three times during the early years of the century, the coal miners tried to remedy their situation by collective action. The first time, in 1907, they appealed for assistance to the United Mine Workers of America. This union was organizing the more numerous coal miners in Alberta and British Columbia. However, it was unable to overcome the opposition of the Saskatchewan operators to unions and withdrew from the area after several years, leaving the miners to continue sporadic, largely unsuccessful, struggles on their own.

When the Bienfait miners sought outside assistance again, in 1920, they turned to the militant, syndicalist One Big Union (OBU). This union was also active in Alberta and had played an important part in the Winnipeg General Strike of 1919 as well. But the coal operators were ready to block another attempt at unionization. When the OBU organizer, P.M. Christophers, came to Bienfait, five members of an employer-sponsored vigilante committee dragged him from his room in the King Edward Hotel in the middle of the night, drove him over the American border, and, in Ku Klux Klan style, threatened to tar and feather him if he ever returned. The vigilante group included the president of the Estevan branch of the Great War Veteran's Association and an officer of the Saskatchewan Provincial Police. The group was acquitted of kidnapping in a subsequent trial. The large contingent of provincial police sent into the area effectively prevented the OBU from taking root.[34]

Early in 1931, in response to the wage cuts, someone in Bienfait contacted the newly formed Conservative provincial government, asking the Department of Labour to send someone down to help the miners organize a union to negotiate with the operators. This request, was ignored. Others contacted the Trades and Labour Council in Regina, making the same request, and received no answer.[35] From these stirrings a third attempt to raise the banner of the union in Bienfait was about to commence – from a seemingly unexpected quarter.

Chapter Two

John Billis and Family

MINER: *Another thing I want to explain ... we start at seven and work to six. Last winter Mr Kushner [pit boss] says, 'You come to work after supper.' I said, 'I not stay.' And he say, 'No, if you go home you don't come back,' and about three or four days we work until eleven o'clock.*

. . .

JUDGE: *Did you make any complaint about these troubles before the strike?*
MINER: *No.*
JUDGE: *You did not say anything about that?*
MINER: *Well, because you can't tell nothing before the strike ... if you tell anything else he [Mr Pierce, the mine manager] say right away, 'Take the tools out right away.'*
JUDGE: *And you did not have any committee of the men in your mine?*
MINER: *No.*
JUDGE: *You have now?*
MINER: *Yes, we have now.*

– Judge Edmund R. Wylie, chairman of the royal commission on the
Estevan-Bienfait coal-mining Dispute, 1931, and John Billis,
coal digger at Eastern Collieries, 14 October 1931

According to the records stored in the Saskatchewan Archives Board, one of the strikers who testified at the royal commission on the Estevan-Bienfait mining dispute in 1931 was John Billis, aged forty-one, a coal digger in the Eastern Collieries of Bienfait. Given in broken English, his testimony, lasting perhaps half an hour, was clearly that of a bold, defiant man who did not wish to live on his knees. It made a strong impression. Through a chance conversation at the Saskatchewan Archives, I learned that his two daughters still lived in Bienfait and I decided to try to find out what sort of human being this outspoken miner was by interviewing his descendants. The experience was quite overwhelming.[1]

When I contacted Anne Billis by telephone from Regina, explaining that I was reading her father's testimony to the royal commission and that I wanted to know more about him, she hesitantly agreed that I could come to Bienfait for a talk. The following week, when I called from my lodging in Estevan to fix a time, Anne gave me a blast: 'You should know I don't like to be reminded of those days.' She continued:

> They were not good days. Our family suffered. We had nothing. And as a result of the strike it was worse. My father was blacklisted and he could never get a job, a decent job, after that. He didn't know how to keep his mouth shut. He had no business sticking his nose into things the only result of which his family suffered. My sister, Amelia, had her husband killed, shot during the strike. She was only sixteen and she had a little son. She had to move back in with us. Nobody did anything to help. The union didn't help. And my father put up $500 for bail for someone that was arrested and never got it back. Why hasn't the United Mine Workers Union paid it back? It's a big wealthy union! The lawyer hadn't been fully paid so when the bail was returned he just took it and left. My mother had sold milk for five cents a quart to raise that money and it was all lost. Years of work. It wasn't fair. My father had no business offering it to the union. Our family had nothing. No, I don't want to be reminded of those years.

I was stunned into silence by this outpouring. After a long pause and expecting total rejection, I asked awkwardly, 'Since I've already come down here do ... do you think it would still be possible to meet you and your sister?'

'Yes,' she replied immediately. 'Come.'

I felt relieved. The time was fixed for 10 A.M. the next morning.

That evening in my hotel room I made other phone calls to Bienfait arranging appointment times for other interviews, but mostly I thought about Anne and Amelia and the Billis family. More than sixty years after the strike, Anne, seventy-seven, and Amelia, eighty-two, were still hurting. I abandoned my plan to cycle the seven miles to Bienfait in the morning. I would hire a cab and go via the florist shop. Whatever the result of our meeting, these people deserved to be honoured. I would buy the best two flower baskets available in Estevan, not silk ones, real plants. I prepared a photocopy of their father's testimony at the royal commission to leave with them. I looked up the list of those who had given bail for the eighteen strikers arrested and committed to trial; the Billis name was not there.

When I arrived at the little house on Railway Avenue, a flower basket in each hand, Anne exclaimed, 'What's that for!'

'I'll tell you later,' I said, depositing them on the kitchen sink.

'My sister isn't here. Do you want to meet her?'

'Yes.'

'I'll call her then. She lives just around the corner.'

When Amelia arrived, we sat at the kitchen table. 'Anne has told me how bitterly she feels about those old days,' I said to Amelia. 'Do you feel the same way?'

'Yes,' she replied, nodding her head several times. 'It's the same with me.'

I did not ask for more detail. Instead I began talking about their father, offering the copy of his testimony and commenting on how, from this evidence, he struck me as a courageous, even if sometimes impetuous, man. I said that I supposed that he was one of the leading group in organizing for the union. In every enterprise of this kind there has to be a leading core; in this case, I said that I thought it was the Communist Party unit in Bienfait.

The best way to approach this sensitive topic, I had decided, was to be quite matter of fact.

'I have evidence,' I said, 'that Sam Carr, the national party organizer, came through Bienfait in the summer before the strike and established such a unit. I figure John Billis was one of the communists.'

There was a long pause. Both women were looking at me intently now, eyes keenly alert, but they said nothing in affirmation or denial. I sensed that in some way they were sizing me up.

I changed the subject. 'What I hope to know,' I continued, 'is what John was like. Was he a kind or stern father, did he have a sense of humour, what was family life like, how did he get to be the way he was?'

Amelia smiled. 'Of course he was a kind father. But he always got into trouble!' She returned to the main theme. 'My mother was not a cranky person but she was always mad at him. Because of his activities they couldn't get the naturalization paper. After he died she was denied naturalization for many years, and without it no pension. Later Wally Lynd, the Estevan lawyer, helped her get it. She lived to ninety-four. Her name was Ursula.'

'How did your parents happen to meet?' I looked at Anne.

Anne deferred to Amelia, who began to unfold the family history.

Their father had gone from Lithuania to the United States as a young immigrant before the First World War. He worked in the Pennsylvania coalfields where he came to know the militant American miners and received his first exposure to socialist ideas. There, too, he met Ursula, a Lithuanian like himself, who was a few years older, and they married. Then John did one of his crazy things. 'He insisted they go back to Old Country to see the relatives.' After they arrived in Lithuania in 1914 the war broke out. 'He talked too much. Pretty soon he found himself kneeling down in front of an execution squad. They were ready to shoot. But he talked his way out of that too. Boy was my mother mad at him!'

The family had to remain in Lithuania for ten years, during which time both Amelia and Anne were born. After the war, Canadian immigration agents came around looking for miners and so John left for Canada by himself, promising to send for them when he had enough money. Five years later, in 1924, after a short stay in Winnipeg, they joined him at Taylorton mining camp near Bienfait.

The family became members of the Ukrainian Labour-Farmer Temple Association, which had a hall in Bienfait. There the girls learned singing and dancing. John subscribed to a Lithuanian paper, 'more on the left side,' from the United States which was called *Laisve* (Freedom). He could read in different languages – Lithuanian, Russian, English. He had lots of stories and jokes to tell. 'He seemed to know more of the world, he'd been around and people listened,' said Amelia. Presently the mine boss at Western Dominion Collieries, Sam Holley, learned of John's views and fired him. The family was forced to move from the mining camp at Taylorton.

In 1929 John was able to get another job at Eastern Collieries, located a mile west of Bienfait. That year he said to Amelia, 'You are fifteen now. It's time for you to be married.' He said that he knew a good young Lithuanian miner, Peter Markunas, who worked at M&S, and he would introduce them. Amelia agreed. 'That's the way things were arranged in those days,' she said. Peter and Amelia were married, lived in the mining camp at Coalfields and within the year, when she was sixteen, a baby boy, John, was born to them.

Then came the big strike of 1931. Both Anne and Amelia were at the meetings; they remembered seeing Sam Scarlett, Annie Buller, and the other organizers of the Workers' Unity League, but the experience did not leave any lasting impression.

'We were just kids,' said Anne and I sensed again how much she wished to distance herself from that painful period of their lives.

I felt unable to ask for details about the miners' motorcade and the tragic September afternoon in Estevan when Peter was killed by a police bullet. Amelia blamed her father.

'Didn't Peter want to go on the parade?' I asked.

'Yes he did, but he knew little about it. It was my father's influence. Peter went because he was a miner.' And she blamed him a little too. 'He was hot headed! Why did he have to be at the front of the parade!'

'What happened to you afterwards?' I asked. 'What did you work at?'

'I never worked in my life,' she replied. 'At least, not for money, not a paid job. I had to move back with my parents. I lived there and ate there and brought up my little son. I got $10 a month from the government for relief. Five years later I remarried to Mr Budris. He was a bartender at the White's hotel. He adopted my son as his own. When Mr Budris died I was already too old to work and that's how it's been. That's my life. Now my son lives in Victoria and I'm a grandmother ...'

Anne, too, is a grandmother.

She and Mac Thompson, a miner, were married at St Giles Anglican Church in Estevan on 24 July 1938, when she was twenty. After the war began, in 1939, he continued working in the mines as his war-service assignment. At the end of the war, after little more than five years of marriage, he died as a result of an accident in the mine that ripped open the side of his body. Anne had one daughter and another was born shortly after Mac's death. She worked for the Whites as a chambermaid at their hotel and in their café. Later she got a job at the Bienfait post office, eventually becoming postmaster. She remained at the post office until she retired. She never remarried.

At this point I returned to one of the deep resentments of Anne – the bail money. I handed her the list. She looked at it in amazement. Was one of the family legends about to be shattered? The names of Tekla and Alex Boruk, Elizabeth Brooks, Kostyn Martynuk, and other friends but no Billis. Impossible! Both she and Amelia insisted that the money had been given and that it had not been returned. They remembered the meeting of miners in their kitchen and talk of having to raise $100,000 in property bonds and cash to meet the court's demands. An incredible sum! John had taken Ursula aside, to the bedroom. He said that he needed the five hundred dollars she had saved from milking the cows. He pleaded and she protested, but finally he prevailed. He had assured her that it would be returned since the arrested miners were not going to run away. They did not yet know about lawyers. In all likelihood, the three of us concluded, the bail money was registered in someone else's name, since the family, often on relief when John was between jobs, was not supposed to have any capital.

I asked Amelia if she ever visited the cemetery where Peter is buried.

'Yes, I visit every year,' was the reply.

'Would you go there now and allow me to take a picture?'

'No,' she shook her head slowly. 'No. Once on some anniversary a TV crew came. I didn't like what they did. No pictures.'

'Would you and Anne allow me to take your pictures here in the kitchen?'

Both women declined. Did they have a picture of their father? Again no. 'Do you have your parents' wedding picture?'

'Yes,' said Amelia, 'but it's not here. It's at my house.'

It was arranged that I call around at Amelia's place at the end of the day after my other interviews were over. She would be waiting for me and I could take a snapshot of it.

Before taking leave I stood up to present my flower baskets and I made a little speech to these two gracious, independent-minded women. I said that I wanted to honour their parents who braved much and participated in the struggle to make a better day. I wanted to salute Amelia's husband Peter, who is a martyr of the labour movement, known throughout Canada and honoured by all who fight for worker's rights. Finally I wanted to pay tribute to two grandmothers who had come through all this and who continue to hold their heads high. By now we were all blinking back tears.

In the late afternoon I called around to the little four-room house on Walsh Street, surrounded by a pretty garden, where Amelia lives alone. The cozy furnishings create a warm, welcoming feeling. Her house is near the place that her parents leased from the village when she was growing up. At that time her mother had kept two boarders to help pay the nine-dollar monthly rent. According to the Public Health inspection, the 1931 house, with six adults and two children, was 'very much overcrowded,' it was cold in winter, had insufficient air space for so many people, and the kitchen leaked. Next door was the large house that belonged to A.H. Graham, a man of English descent, who was village overseer in the 1930s. Graham also happened to be manager of the

Lake of the Woods elevator and it was he who controlled relief payments to the villagers. When he felt they deserved it, he supplied his immediate neighbours, the Billis family, and other impoverished villagers with flour from his elevator, paid for by the taxpayers.

During our second encounter Amelia seemed more relaxed, even pleased to see me. As I walked through the living room I noticed reading glasses resting on John Billis's testimony to the royal commission into the 1931 coal strike which I had given her. They were on the page with these passages:

Q (Lawyer Perkins): You say you had to stay on from three o'clock in the morning to seven o'clock and when you finished your digging you were all wet?

A Yes.

Q And still you had to stay the extra four hours?

A Yes.

Q Did you tell the pit boss this?

A Yes, and he has told us, he says, 'You no stay on the job, all right, you go away out and somebody else come on the job.'

. . .

Q You are one of these men that want to stick to an eight hour day?

A Yes.

Q And you don't want to work either before you start in the morning or after you finish?

A Yes.

Q You just want to work eight hours?

A Yes.

Q Whether the mine is busy or not?

A Sure.

. . .

Q You told Mr. Lynd a moment ago that you would have to take from early morning to dinner time for pumping water [out of the mine]. Did you get paid for this?

A That's what I say. We spent one month a hundred hours on the hand pump and get [paid] twenty four or twenty six hours.

Q I see. All right.

. . .

THE CHAIRMAN (Judge Wylie): Now that tells us all your troubles?

A Yes.

Q Did you make any complaint about these troubles before the strike?

A No.

Q You did not say anything about that?

A Well, because you can't tell nothing before the strike ... If you tell Mr. Pierce [mine manager] anything he say right away, 'Take the tools out right away.'

Q And you did not have any committee of the men in your mine?

A No.

Q You have now?

A Yes, we have now.

As Amelia handed me her parents' wedding picture she said matter-of-factly, 'My father was a communist. He was for the working man. What he wished for himself he wanted for others. There he is, dark like a Mexican.'

It was a picture of a good-looking man but a large white blob decorated his forehead. When I exclaimed that this was too bad, she was a little amused at my distress. 'Well, one day when we were redecorating the house some white paint fell on him.'

Then she brought out four more photographs. 'Here,' she said, 'I want you to have these.' The first was a beautiful little picture of Ursula and the two girls when they came to Canada in 1924. Then one of Peter Markunas, her first husband, and his Lithuanian friends in their miner's helmets and work clothes. Next a photo of twelve young people, some of them with mandolins and violins. As she handed me this she said, 'These were the young communists. We distributed the miner's paper, sold the *Worker* and other papers of the youth league; we raised money for the strike. We helped make sandwiches and delivered them to the pickets.' I was spellbound. The history and some of the families at the inner core of the worker's movement were beginning to unfold before my eyes.

'Do you know the names of these young people?' I asked.

'Sure I do.'

'Can you tell them to me?'

'No. How do I know that they want to be identified?'

Amelia had sound instincts, I thought, but she exasperated me. What is the use of anonymous photographs? Sixty years and more have passed. I told her that there are many pictures of the lawyers, judges, government officials, police officers, and mine operators to choose from but almost none of the miners and their families. Yet this book is centred on their lives. If I do manage to get a few photographs but everyone has to be anonymous, without the dignity of a name, what message does that send out about the justice of workers' struggles? Should officials, judges, mine operators, police, and others in high places be recognized but not the working people? Is there not something absurd, unhistorical about that?

Gradually she saw my point. 'I think you're right,' she said reluctantly, they deserve recognition: Germann, Billis, Elchyson, Kytrusik, Bachynski, Konopaki, Boruk, Scribialo. These were all members of the youth group at the Ukrainian Labour Hall in Bienfait.

The last picture was of Stella Boruk and her sweetheart, John Elchyson. Stella was the organizer of the group. Her parents, Tekla and Alex Boruk, had a bakery and boarding house on Railway Avenues; it was there that Sam Scarlett and the other organizers stayed; it was there that the Communist Party unit often held its meetings.

As I bid goodbye and we shook hands, Amelia said that her mother always used to say, 'If I could only write, I'd write a book about my life.' 'And we, her daughters, would say, "Mother, there's nothing so special. Many people have lives like ours." She would reply, "Not like mine!"'

'I want to tell you,' said Amelia, 'my mother would be happy to know that her picture and her name are going to appear in your book.'

Chapter Three

Boruk's Boarding House

For the average mind to follow the trend of events is confusing ... The sum and substance of the commotion is that a very far reaching revolution is under way in Canada. It involves a measure of abandonment of the individualistic preference and a partial acceptance of the principle of communism.

    – Donald C. Dunbar, editor, the *Mercury*, Estevan, 2 July 1931, after learning about the federal-provincial decision to finance relief work for the single unemployed.

It must be observed, while individual liberty is being restricted for the time being, the Soviet objective is plainly the ultimate equalizing and multiplying of material wealth and physical enjoyment.

    – ibid., 26 March 1931

One evening in mid-July 1931, about the time a devastating cyclone hit the Bienfait area, a dark-haired man, of medium build and not yet thirty, got off the train, his travelling bag and portable typewriter in hand. Before leaving the CPR station in Bienfait he took a minute to look around since it was here that a famous armed robbery and murder had occurred a few years earlier when the Bronfman interests were running liquor illegally into the United States. After satisfying his curiosity he started walking westward on Railway Avenue, passing the King Edward Hotel, crossing the wind-blown top of Main Street, past Hawkinson's Hall until he came to the Saskatchewan Wheat Pool elevator. Looking across the street he saw a large, ungainly flat-roofed building, white clapboard on one half, unpainted plain boards on the other with 'Rooms & Meals' written on its upper wall. He went over and knocked on the door.

The proprietors, Alex Boruk and his wife, Tekla Scribialo, were expecting him, for this was Sam Carr, national organizer of the Communist Party of Canada. Carr had a reputation that preceded him and the Boruks welcomed him warmly. Within a month the Ontario government and the federal government of Prime Minister R.B. Bennett would arrange to arrest Carr along with Tim Buck, Tom Ewen, Matthew Popowich, Tom Hill, and several other leaders of the party. Bennett famously attributed social unrest not to hard times but to foreign agitators and other troublemakers and his answer to public dissent was an iron heel.[1] The men were tried on a charge of sedition in Ontario, found guilty under section 98 of the Criminal Code, and sentenced to five years in Kingston penitentiary. The court decision in effect outlawed the Communist Party.[2] But for the moment that was still in the future and Carr had arranged to stay with the Boruks during the Bienfait leg of a national organizing and public-speaking tour.

The Boruk's home, occupying a double lot, was spacious compared to many in the village. The previous owner had used part of it for a theatre and pool hall. The hosts, a couple in their late thirties, with four children, showed their guest around the establishment. Half the ground-floor space on the east side was taken up with a bakery, ovens at the back, and a shop opening on the street. Above this were eleven rooms for boarders – one of them a large room with three double beds. On the west side upstairs was the family dwelling with rooms for Alex and Tekla and their children: Stella, the eldest daughter, aged seventeen and a talented musician; her two brothers; and little sister Olga, who was just two. Tekla's widowed mother, Kathleen Scribialo, lived with them and there was a guest room that was offered to Sam Carr on this occasion. Downstairs, the living room occupying the front section was furnished with two sofas, chairs, a dining table, a radio, a newspaper rack, and a gramophone. Here, at different times, the Boruks put on dances and plays and conducted a workers' school. Beyond the living room was the kitchen with a large table where the boarders always ate first. Outside, to the west of the house, was a vegetable garden with a deep well equipped with an electric pump and at the back of the lot was a storage shed for hay, a coal shed, and a small barn for the cows.[3]

The Boruks impressed Sam Carr as a busy household. 'My family did not have much time to be sociable,' recalled Olga years later.

People came visiting us but my parents never reciprocated. My mother couldn't understand people who had nothing to do but sit around visiting.

She was very hard working. Running a boarding house she had to get up at 4 A.M. every morning to get the breakfast ready, and to prepare lunches for the miners before they left for work. Then in the evening she had to provide supper. This was seven days a week. She also did the washing for the roomers. She used a scrub board to wash the clothes. We also had three cows and they had to be milked. Other women in Bienfait were in similar circumstances. They also took in boarders to help make ends meet. My father, who had been a miner until his legs gave out, ran the bakery with several helpers. He had a very even disposition. During the depression when young unemployed men were riding the freights they would catch the smell of the fresh bread coming from the bakery and came over offering to do some work in return for bread. My father told them he already had enough people to do the necessary work but would give out bread and tell them to share it with the others.[4]

As for bakery and boarding house, perhaps its reputation was summed up best by James Cuddington, whose father owned a rival bakery and grocery store on Main Street. Disparaging the Boruks, Cuddington claimed that they 'held a number of questionable meetings in the other parts of the building' of which 'the police would have knowledge.'[5]

The morning after Sam Carr's arrival in Bienfait, Stella Boruk and her boyfriend, John Elchyson, who were on summer holidays, took him for a tour of the village. They walked past Cuddington's and then went into the stores of Sol Adler and Son, Sam Lischinsky, and Jake Lishinsky, all of whom had moved to Bienfait from the nearby Jewish settlement at Hirsch when the mining village expanded in the 1920s. These storeowners were popular among many of the mining families who hailed from Europe. The young people were pleased to introduce 'Mr Sam Carr, of Toronto,' and to announce that Carr would be addressing a public meeting that evening at the hall. Everyone knew that 'the hall' referred to the premises of the Ukrainian Labour-Farmer Temple Association on Main Street, a building and an organization which played a vital if not central role in the miners' strike a few months later. In view of the focus of this book, therefore, the Ukrainian community in Bienfait, its strengths and weaknesses, cohesions and divisions, deserves some close attention.

The original Ukrainian hall in Bienfait was built by the Taras Shevchenko Society in 1921 and was a place where people celebrated the poetic works of the great bard of Ukraine and conducted other social and mutual-aid activities. But as news of the experiment of building

Bienfait miners in 1930 wait to descend in the cage, carrying home-made dinner pails and wearing cloth caps with detachable lamps. Little of this headframe is enclosed, which would have made it unpleasant for the surface crew in wet or cold weather.

Fully loaded coal carts still underground.

The 1931 miners' strike began with a two-day shutdown at Crescent Collieries (in background) after a miner was fired for signing fellow workers into the union. The 1924 Chevrolet touring car, a popular model in rural Saskatchewan, is being driven by Lena Scribialo.

The M&S Coal Company's mine in the 1930s was located about four miles south of Bienfait. A leading member in 'The Group of Six,' it was owned by Winnipeg businessmen and managed by A.C. 'Happy' Wilson.

The M&S mining camp. Families who rented a company house had priority for work in the mine.

The headframe and tipple of Eastern Collieries. By the 1930s, the underground workings of this mine spread out to an area 400 by 800 yards – about the size of thirty-two football fields.

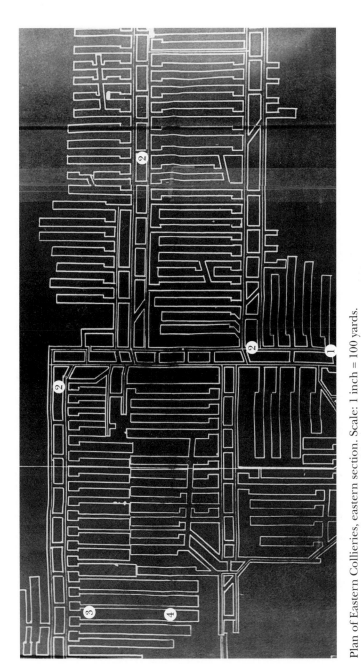

Plan of Eastern Collieries, eastern section. Scale: 1 inch = 100 yards.

1. Location of headframe, tipple, and railway spur line.
2. Underground tracks and air passages.
3. An entry to a room.
4. A room.

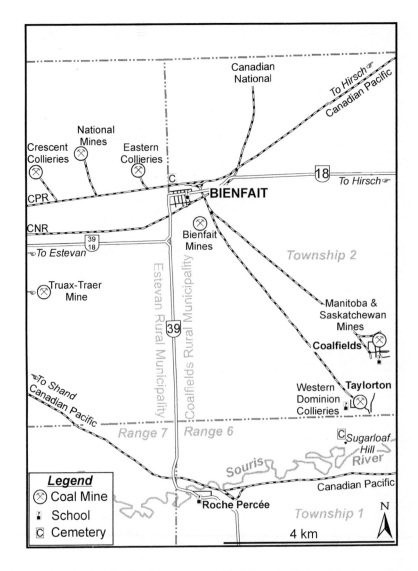

Large mines in the Bienfait/Estevan area, 1931. Map by Richard Anderson, York University.

Sources: for mine locations, report of Robert J. Lee, Dominion mines inspector, Wylie Commission, 1931, v. 11, 1–6; for road locations, National Topographic Series 1:50,000, Estevan 62 E/2 West Half, 1st ed. 1949/1953.

A.H. Graham: Bienfait village overseer.

W.W. Lynd: Estevan lawyer.

John R. Brodie: one of the most prominent operators in the Souris valley coal-fields in the 1930s.

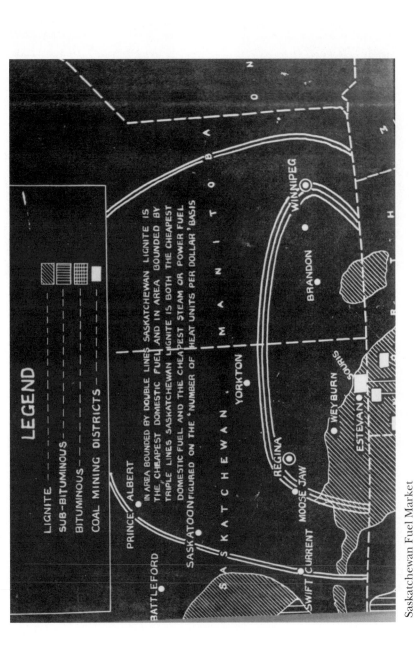

Saskatchewan Fuel Market

The King Edward Hotel at the corner of Main Street and Railway Avenue, Bienfait, in 1934. The owner, Gordon White, advertised it as 'the best equipped village hotel in Saskatchewan.'

The bar and saloon of the King Edward Hotel, now called the 'Coal Dust Saloon,' in 1998.

Bienfait village, circa 1920 (photograph taken from the grain elevator looking west along Railway Avenue): 1. Hawkinson's Hall, corner of Main Street and Railway Avenue (later the site of the Legion hall). 2. King Edward Hotel. 3. Home of R.J. Hassard, mine owner. 4. Jake Lishinsky's store. 5. Telephone exchange. 6. Adler's Store. 7. Sinclair's warehouse (later the 'Red Hall'). 8. Livery stables.' 9. Fire hall and village well. 10. Home of A.J. Milligan, first village overseer, in 1906. 11. Lumber yard.

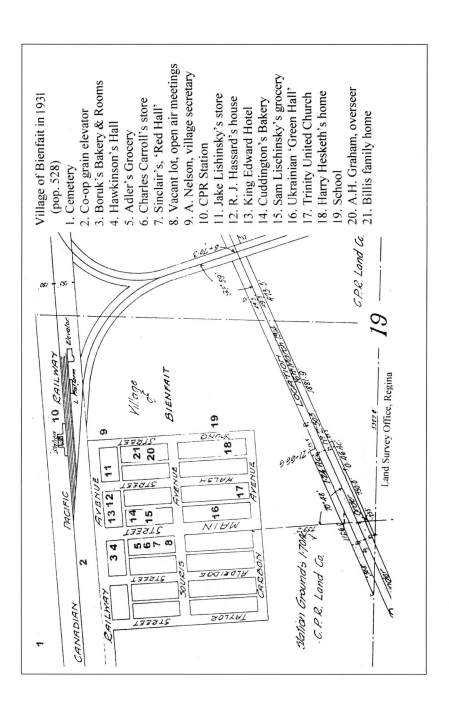

Village of Bienfait in 1931
(pop. 528)

1. Cemetery
2. Co-op grain elevator
3. Boruk's Bakery & Rooms
4. Hawkinson's Hall
5. Adler's Grocery
6. Charles Carroll's store
7. Sinclair's, 'Red Hall'
8. Vacant lot, open air meetings
9. A. Nelson, village secretary
10. CPR Station
11. Jake Lishinsky's store
12. R. J. Hassard's house
13. King Edward Hotel
14. Cuddington's Bakery
15. Sam Lischinsky's grocery
16. Ukrainian 'Green Hall'
17. Trinity United Church
18. Harry Hesketh's home
19. School
20. A.H. Graham, overseer
21. Billis family home

The brick schoolhouse was the most impressive building in Bienfait. The teachers offered classes from grade one to grade twelve for 146 students in 1930.

The 'Green Hall' on Main Street.

socialism in the Old Country filtered into Bienfait, following the Bolshevik revolution, the members of the society became divided politically on how to view the world in general and Soviet Ukraine in particular. The majority, led by miners in the Bachynski, Bortnick, Konopaki, Germann, Antoniuk, Moroz, and other families, were socialist-minded. They voted to change the name of the hall to the Ukrainian Labour-Temple and welcomed people from other nationalities to join in their activities. They also decided to affiliate with the Ukrainian Labour-Farmer Temple Association of Winnipeg and to subscribe to the newspaper, *Ukrainski Robinychi Visti* (Ukrainian Labour News), whose editor was the magnetic communist leader Matthew Popowich, himself a talented musician and married to a former singer in the Metropolitan Opera of New York. The minority, led by Harry Kaik, a mine foreman, and Anthony Sashareski, a CPR section foreman, favoured Ukrainian nationalist organizations and they stopped coming to the hall except to demand the building. Two of the three registered owners were in the nationalist grouping. In their protest they were supported by Harry Kupchenko, a well-educated and influential farmer who ran a successful dairy business on the outskirts of the village. A bitter lawsuit over the ownership of the building ensued, sparked by Kupchenko and a determined Greek Orthodox priest from Brandon, Manitoba, who wanted to run religious classes in the hall. The legal battle divided the community further. Eventually, Judge John Embury of the King's Bench Court sitting in Estevan in 1926 awarded the building, with costs, to the nationalist, anti-communist group. From then on it was called the Ukrainian Library, also known as the Green Hall.[6]

John Bachynski, secretary of the Ukrainian Labour Temple in Bienfait, summed up the situation for the losing side: 'We were then without a roof. But we were not dumbfounded. We rented a modest premises and carried on. In the summer of 1927 we organized a branch of the Workers' Benevolent Association. Also a Ukrainian workers' children's school and a Youth Section. We hired a teacher and sent him to a course for higher education ... The enemy thought to smash us but they mistook our will.'[7]

With the court costs gradually paid off, the socialist-minded group rebounded and grew to seventy members, encompassing more than half of the Ukrainians in the village.[8] In a little-used pool hall on Main street that had been a warehouse for the whisky runners during prohibition in the United States, they built up a womens' section, a mandolin orchestra, and a drama and folk dance troupe, and on Sunday evenings they were able to present live concerts showcasing their Ukrainian heritage as part of their cultural and educational activities. Stella Boruk led the youth section. She was an outgoing person, talented musically and in drama, who wanted to become a teacher. She played the violin, mandolin, and piano. Matthew Popowich gave encouragement and recognition to her program when he visited Bienfait on organizational tours from Winnipeg and this was no small thing in Stella's life at that time because Popowich, like Sam Carr, was an unusual personality and in many ways an inspiring model.[9] His effect on an audience is vividly described by a reporter from the *Winnipeg Free Press*:

> He has the type of face that you notice in a crowd; there is something about it; he has 'the look'; when you get your eye on him his presence holds it; he is self-possessed, quiet of speech, very determined in his politics, and his politics are revolutionary socialism ... Popowich is an excellent speaker. His voice is pleasant, he has it in control, he is persuasive, he is appealing, he explains, he elucidates, he orates, he gets to his audience ... He made them laugh; he made them chuckle; he made them applaud him. He smiled a lot, wise smiles, saying – 'You know how it is yourself'; and smiled more brightly when he got his response on the faces of the audience. He never shouted, but he spoke with force and conviction and beat the air a little with his anger.[10]

Even the secret service of the RCMP, which was following Popowich constantly at this time and writing almost daily reports on his activities for the prime minister, paid him backhanded compliments: 'a powerful agitator'; 'his influence is greater than that of any other member of the Society to which he belongs'; 'a menace to the good order and public safety of Canada.'[11]

To Popowich and his colleagues, the greatest menace to the good order and public safety of Canada was the enveloping crisis of capitalism, specifically, the failure of the 'free market system' to provide jobs, security, or incomes for hundreds of thousands of workers and farmers. People from one end of the country to the other were hungry, homeless, unemployed, and broke. There was no unemployment insurance and other relief was scarce. In these circumstances, Popowich urged the branches of the Ukrainian Labour-Farmer Temple Association to turn their attention to the mines and factories, to the desperate farmers, to the unemployed, and to participate more actively in the class struggles that were unfolding before their eyes. Plays and songs and music should be chosen for their class content and closely tied to the working-class movement; in these times marching music should take the place of folk songs.[12] For various reasons, these were not easy demands to meet. But in Bienfait a start had been made in the spring of 1931 with the circulation of a petition to the government in Ottawa by members of the Ukrainian Labour Temple demanding non-contributory state unemployment insurance. This was part of a memorable country-wide effort which resulted in Tom Ewen, national secretary of the Workers' Unity League, leading a delegation to present an unemployment insurance petition with 94,000 names to Prime Minister R.B. Bennett in April. Not unexpectedly, the millionaire Tory prime minister angrily rejected the petitioners: 'Never,' he told them, 'will I or any government of which I am a part, put a premium on idleness.'[13] But the petition began the process of highlighting the plight of the unemployed that would lead to Bennett's defeat in the next general election. It also spurred a process whereby the Ukrainian Labour Temple on Main Street in Bienfait became known as 'the Red Hall.'

As already mentioned, an important matter that distinguished members of the Red Hall from members of the Green Hall concerned their respective attitudes to news from Soviet Ukraine, attitudes that complicated their ability to cooperate on local issues in Bienfait including whether or not to join the union. Where members of the Red Hall saw a vision of hope and a welcome alternative to capitalism in the Union of Soviet Socialist Republics (USSR), the supporters of the Green Hall saw despair and suffering under socialism. Feelings ran high. Since people in Bienfait argued so passionately about the topic (and the editor of the *Mercury* even wrote philosophical editorials about it), a short reminder of contemporary events in the Soviet Union may be in order.

In 1931 the Soviet Union was in the midst of Stalin's ambitious first Five Year Plan to industrialize and 'build socialism in one country' instead of promoting a world revolution as Trotsky had wanted. Critical to the success of this plan was the need to export surplus agricultural products and other natural resources in order to pay for the import of metals and machinery from Germany and other advanced Western countries.

Government planners calculated that, to boost the grain surpluses for export and to feed the growing industrial workforce in the cities as well as meet military requirements, the small hand- and animal-worked private farms would have to be replaced by large, mechanized state-run collective farms. To this purpose, the government ended private farming and, not without resistance especially from the well-to-do peasant or *kulak* class, brought close to eight million peasant families into collective farms by 1930. In the course of this hurried collectivization campaign, hundreds of thousands of peasant families were deprived of their farms, and when they objected many were deported to distant regions.[14]

Blessed by exceptionally good weather in 1930, the farms reaped a bumper harvest and the Soviet government deluded itself into thinking that the agricultural revolution had been won. This belief was contradicted by wave after wave of peasant protest against grain requisitions and claims for tax arrears and collectivization itself; over the next few years, relations between the state and the countryside degenerated into a condition of hidden and not so hidden warfare. There were thousands of disturbances in Ukraine alone: mass arrests, deportations, executions, banishment of priests, closing of Orthodox village churches as centres of resistance to government orders, murders of collective farm cadres, widespread terror, and upheavals involving millions of people. It was a continuation, according to historian Andrea Graziosi, of the intermittent peasant wars that had engulfed Russia since the decree that freed the serfs in the nineteenth century. Under the government's extraordinary measures, which were combined with several years of poor weather, the farm sector failed to deliver according to plan. Some peasants burned their crops and killed their farm animals rather than have them put into the collective farms. Then there was no food. 'Peasants, who hated the new system but had learned to fear the cold-blooded treatment of open defiance, resorted to passive "resistance" of unprecedented proportions.'[15] The result by early 1933 'was a disastrous famine and social violence and persecution on an unimaginable scale,'[16] with many dying from hunger, disease, or the harsh conditions of remote places. Some people responded to the collectivization program by fleeing abroad and it was from these well-publicized sources that members of the Green Hall framed their understandably negative views of socialism.[17]

Members of the Red Hall were aware of the disturbances in the countryside but considered that their scale was exaggerated by critics of the Soviet experiment and that, in any case, they were really growing pains of a society that was refashioning itself along untrodden ways. They chose instead to pay attention to well-publicized examples of new collective farms that were mechanizing their production and working well. These were seen as the harbingers of a better future.[18]

The Ukrainian Labour Temple in Bienfait had raised some money to help send a women's delegation from Canada to the Soviet Union in 1930 and now, in 1931, they had done the same for a group going to see conditions in Soviet Ukraine. From reports these delegates brought back, members of the Red Hall gained an impression of optimism and dynamism under socialism that contrasted greatly with the news received by the Green Hall. Were they mistaken in their optimism? In retrospect, it is instructive to learn that many of their favourable impressions are validated by such American and Russian historians as J. Arch Getty and Oleg V. Naumov, who have begun working in the now declassified archives of the former Soviet Union with care and objectivity. Their conclusion about industrial (as distinct from agricultural) development in the USSR, written almost seventy years after the fact, is that:

> the first Five Year Plan was a resounding success. Production indexes in mining, steel, and chemicals increased several fold in four years. Factories and mines materialized everywhere, and the country was proud of the new giant dams, plants, and railroads whose construction contrasted so sharply with the industrial doldrums of the Great Depression in the West. Unemployment disappeared and although real wages actually fell (another casualty of capital accumulation), education, opportunity, and mobility were available to everyone willing to work. In the lives of the rapidly increasing urban masses, on the factory wall charts of production, and in the rapidly growing network of educational institutions, everything was onward and upward.

And further:

> The period of the first Five Year Plan (1928–32) was one of exuberance and excitement. Millions of workers went to school and moved into management. Millions of young peasants escaped the villages and flocked to new lives in construction. Young people volunteered in large numbers to work for the common effort, to help with collectivization, and to improve their work qualifications ... The enthusiastic upward mobility for plebians looked much like the fruition of the revolution; the workers were taking power and building socialism![19]

During intermission at the Sunday evening concert in Bienfait, in July 1931, Sam Carr painted a similar picture of socialist achievement; and, like Matthew Popowich, he could do so with great effect and authority. He had recently returned from the Soviet Union where he was a student at the prestigious Lenin School in Moscow. Studying Marxism there for several years, he had opportunities to travel about the country and had many first-hand experiences to share.

Bearing in mind his audience, Carr talked about the coal mines he had visited. Some of them were modern mines with the latest cutting and loading machinery imported from the United States and supervised by American engineers; others were still using pick-and-shovel methods. No matter which kind, the miners were among the highest-paid workers in the country. Under *socialist* modernization and rationalization of industry, the welfare of the workers, he emphasized, was the basic governing principle. Typically, the miners had a one-day rest period in five and worked a seven-hour day, six hours for underground workers portal to portal. There was an enormous extension of social insurance against unemployment, sickness, accident, and old age. Underground miners received a one-month holiday with pay each year while surface workers received two weeks. Union committees had a large share in determining working conditions and, because of all these things, miners worked hard in the USSR: industry was in the hands of the working class, and they were working both for themselves and for their country. This information and interpretation appealed greatly to the applauding crowd that had packed itself into the Labour Temple.

Carr contrasted the social position of Soviet miners with miners in *capitalist* countries. There, the mines were in the hands of individuals who ran the industry for profit, and as a result, wage-cutting and cost-cutting practices more often than not put miners and their families at risk, condemning them to subsistence living at best and endangering their lives at worst. In his confident style, Carr referred to the struggles of miners to change their miserable situation in Alberta, in Nova Scotia, and especially in the United States, where in Harlan County, Kentucky, Pennsylvania, and West Virginia 45,000 miners were currently engaged in a desperate strike battle with the coal companies. The *Worker* wrote that 'the strike is in progress as a protest against starvation wages, poor working conditions, rotten living conditions in the company towns and the employment of scab check-weighmen.' Company police were using tear gas, blackjacks, even machine guns to smash the strike. Strikers were determined to win the right to picket.[20]

At the end of Carr's speech, the crowd rose to its feet singing the *Internationale*: 'Arise ye prisoners of starvation, Arise ye wretched of the earth ... The earth shall rise on new foundations, A better world's in birth.' People were deeply touched; there could be a different world for miners. It helped to strengthen their determination for the struggle that lay ahead. Sam Carr's visit to the Ukrainian Labour Temple in Bienfait and the songs that were sung are still remembered by veteran miner Peter Gemby and his wife Stella Bachynski when I talked to them sixty years later.[21]

After Carr left Bienfait, he was able to write to Tom Ewen, a senior Communist Party colleague in Toronto, saying that he had formed a party unit there.[22] This had been a prime objective for his visit. Among those who came to Boruk's Boarding House to meet with Carr (some of whom joined the party) were, apart from Alex and Tekla Boruk, their daughter Stella and her boyfriend John Elchyson; the already mentioned John Bachynski and his, wife Mary; Maria Germann, a miner's wife and womens' leader; Harry Michalowski at the Bienfait mine; the brothers Alex and Fred Konopaki, who worked at National Mines; and William Choma and John Billis of Eastern Collieries. In addition, there were Martin Day, from Fyfeshire, Scotland, a miner there for twenty-one years and now working at Crescent Collieries; John and Mary Harris, a Welsh couple with thirty-three years' mining experience; and Fred Booth, a coalminer in England since the age of thirteen. Booth, a veteran of the First World War, was one of those British miners A.C. Wilson complained about at the M&S. Besides their long experience in coalmining, the Day, Harris, and Booth families had something else in common: they had all migrated to Bienfait three years earlier after the defeat of the miners' general strike in Britain. Lacking five years' domicile in Canada, they would all be blacklisted and, according to available information, deported back to Britain after the Bienfait strike. The reason for identifying these people is not to embarrass their descendants but to put a human face on a group of people who, in the depths of the Great Depression when hopelessness was widespread, took the lead in fighting for workers' rights and a better life.

It is unlikely that Sam Carr had to spend much time explaining to the miners the Communist Party's ideas of class struggle, the exploitation of labour by capital, the polarization of wealth and increasing poverty, or even the party's program for a worker's government which would nationalize the means of production along the lines existing in the Soviet Union (and, incidentally, along lines suggested by the CCF in its Regina Manifesto two years later). The group gathered in the Boruks' living room knew all this. What they desperately needed at the time was practical help in dealing with the misery being created daily by the workings of capitalism in Bienfait. Carr came with suggestions. From his suitcase he produced the constitution of the newly formed Workers' Unity League and explained the revolutionary nature and program of this trade-union organization.

The league's major objectives were: to fight for the defence of the Canadian working class 'against the bandit raid of capitalism' on living standards; to organize workers into industrial, rather than craft, unions, 'with widest rank and file control'; and to organize Canadian workers 'for the final overthrow of capitalism' and for the establishment of a workers' and farmers' government. The WUL was proud of the fact that it was linked to militant workers all around the world by virtue of being the Canadian section of the Red International of Labour Unions, head-quartered in Moscow (in contrast, other Canadian trade unions were connected to counterpart organizations in the United States, to the Second International in Amsterdam, or, in the case of Catholic unions, the Vatican). The main practical tasks of the WUL were to organize workers in the *unorganized* industries, to mobilize the unemployed to demand *non-contributory unemployment insurance* from the state, and, lastly, to establish left-wing groups *within* existing craft, patriotic, or business unions with a view to transforming them into revolutionary industrial unions.

All this was rather general, but Carr was also able to give the Bienfait miners encouraging news from Alberta. Two months earlier in a referendum, the coalminers there had voted three to one (1,727 in favour, 641 against) to have their union, the Mine Workers Union of Canada, affiliate with the WUL. It is probable that he also shared with them, as a practical guide, the contents of a key document on strike strategy and tactics adopted at an international conference sponsored by the Red International of Labour Unions in Strassburg, Germany.

The Strassburg Resolution, which summed up the recent experience of European workers, was a kind of primer for strike action. It strongly warned against any conspiratorial approach by militants: the important decisions should be made by all the workers in a potential strike situation. Clear and understandable economic demands arising from the concrete situation in the mining pits 'must be discussed by all workers.' In the case of favourable conditions for a strike, the resolution stressed that a strike committee should be elected by all the workers: 'workers of all beliefs and affiliations must be able to participate in these elections, the organized as well as the unorganized,' otherwise the strike would fail. These were strong urgings for democratic participation by all involved. That was the most important point. The Strassburg Resolution also pointed to other concerns. Consideration should be given to the offensive of the bosses, the diversionary tactics of the reformist, business-as-usual unions, and how to paralyze these efforts in the course of the struggle. How were the unorganized, the unemployed, the youth, and women workers going to be drawn into the struggle? How was the whole working class and its sympathizers in the wider community to be mobilized to aid the striking workers in achieving their demands?[23]

These were the challenging questions that the newly formed party club in Bienfait began to ponder as Sam Carr took his leave for the next leg of his tour. The implication of his instruction was that they should try to include both Green and Red Hall members and their families on the union committees, they should make special efforts to involve both the British and 'foreign' sides of the village, and, while being on guard against agents of the bosses, they should open the door to people holding different beliefs and of all religious faiths. They should concentrate on what the miners had in common and set aside past disagreements and differences. This seemed to be the meaning of the ringing phrases with which Marx and Engels had concluded their famous *Manifesto*: 'Workers of the world, unite! The proletarians have nothing to lose but their chains. They have a world to win.'

Chapter Four

August: Gaining Momentum

Saskatchewan is cursed with a swarm of yelpers, crepe hangers, organizers of despair, clamoring for jobs, doles and hand-outs. The whole world is hearing the wail of distress from Saskatchewan, where there is no real distress. The time and emergency call for apostles of faith to restore sight to the blind and put new guts in the faint-hearted.

– *Mercury*, Estevan, 12 March 1931

The unemployment problem will disappear before snow falls and there will be no dole or unemployment insurance in Canada.

– Senator Gideon Robertson, minister of labour, quoted in *Mercury*, 30 April 1931

The deplorable wages and working conditions in the mines are the worst in Canada.

– James Sloan, president of the Mine Workers' Union of Canada, 26 August 1931

By 6 August 1931, the WUL district office in Winnipeg heard that 'the miners and unemployed at Bienfait, Sask., are in revolt,'[1] and Joe Forkin, area organizer in Regina, hurried down to Bienfait to carry on where Sam Carr had left off three weeks earlier.[2]

Martin Joseph Forkin, thirty-one, the eldest of seven children in a Brandon, Manitoba, family, was an even-tempered man, tall, and slight of build but with abundant energy and possessed of a keen political sense. Although he was not an orator, he was persuasive and his direct manner inspired confidence. As a three-year veteran of the Canadian Expeditionary Force in the First World War, followed by a year's service in the RCMP and then ten years of participation in the labour movement in Winnipeg, Forkin had a solid fund of background experience. Before long the *Mercury* would, with good reason, be calling him 'the generalissimo of the strikers' forces.'[3] Within a few years this man would be elected to Winnipeg city council where he served for almost two decades.

On his arrival in Bienfait, Forkin discovered that half the employed miners had already signed lists stating their desire to join a union. He immediately contacted the MWUC in Calgary and requested that they send an organizer and bring union cards and membership books. In the meantime, to dispel gossip and hostile rumours, he decided it was important to make the presence of the WUL publicly known in Estevan. For this purpose he organized an open-air meeting at the fair grounds on Sunday, 16 August 1931 that was attended by about 140 people. There was a good deal of interest. After his address, poorly paid workers employed in a CPR construction gang, workers in a clay-products company and a brickyard, and some unemployed workers – about one hundred in all – joined the General Workers Union, the Lumber and Agricultural Workers Industrial Union, or the National Unemployed Workers Association – all of which, Forkin explained, were affiliated with the WUL. An unemployed miner, John Loughran, now farming, was chosen as president of the General Workers Union.

Loughran, a boastful type who had worked around the mines for thirty-three years and now volunteered for all kinds of activities, turned out not to be entirely reliable, from Forkin's point of view, but at least he was enthusiastic and, as a farmer, out of range of the employers. Perhaps not wanting to expose any of the coal diggers active in forming a union to employer retaliation at this early stage, Forkin also put Loughran forward as pro tem, acting president of the still-to-be-announced miners' union. It was a protective façade.

In the next two weeks, events moved swiftly. On Tuesday, 18 August, the union cards and books arrived from Calgary and the committee men in the mines started signing up the miners. Two days later, Crescent Collieries fired a worker by the name of John Adams, who, according to the local paper, was 'organizing the foreign workers' in the mine. Martin Day, head of the pit committee there, promptly led a small delegation to call on owner William L. Hamilton and his mine manager to see if they would reinstate Adams. They refused to give any reason for Adams's dismissal or to reinstate him. The next day, all fifty workers at Crescent Collieries walked off the job and the workers in the other mines expressed their willingness to call a sympathy strike if necessary.

The following Sunday, Forkin and the committee men from all the mines organized a family picnic down at Taylorton Bridge near the largest mining camps. Twelve hundred men, women, and children turned out. After games and sporting events, the crowd heard speeches by Forkin and George Wilkinson, a veteran English miner employed at Western Dominion Collieries for eight years. Wilkinson was a meticulous, plodding sort, thorough and thoughtful, but he was not comfortable with the militancy of the WUL. Perhaps the most important event for building up enthusiasm was the introduction of Sam Scarlett, 'a ruddy-faced square-built worker with a husky voice' who had come from Saskatoon to give Forkin a hand.

Sam Scarlett was a legendary working-class leader, so much so that the RCMP headed their file on investigations into the Bienfait strike under Scarlett's name.[4] A talented football player and skilled machinist who migrated from Scotland to Canada and then to the United States at the turn of the century, he had soon become involved in some of the epic struggles of the miners in the Mesabie Iron range in Minnesota, along with William D. Haywood, Joe Hill, and other famous figures in the Industrial Workers of the World (IWW). Framed on a murder charge and accused of over one hundred separate crimes, Scarlett was imprisoned for a number of years, released in a general amnesty, and then deported back to Scotland. He returned to Canada in the early 1920s as a harvester, organized for the IWW again, and later joined the Communist Party. Such a man inspired awe among fellow workers.

Scarlett was an accomplished public speaker, someone who could hold his audience spellbound. He used to rent a theatre in Saskatoon on Sundays when no film showings were permitted. He would have a sandwich board outside, announcing his topic, and there was always a good audience. He would walk around as he spoke, approaching the front of the stage with his eyes seemingly shut, putting everyone on the edge of their seats lest he fell off the platform. At first he was opposed to the Soviet Union; he thought it was a betrayal of good ideas. But around 1929 he bought a little shack in the Porcupine Plain district northeast of Saskatoon and lived there for a year reading everything he could get his hands on about the USSR. As a result of this prolonged period of reflection and soul-searching, Scarlett changed his mind, bringing to friend and foe alike all the fascination of a person who has switched sides to join a cause. He decided that the proletariat had within it the power to transform a haystack revolution into a smokestack revolution. The central theme of his speeches was that society is divided into two classes, 'the exploiter and the exploited,' and 'between them there is nothing in common'; he would then go on to trace the pattern of another and better tomorrow based upon the public ownership of the means of production. He brought these ideas and manners with him to Bienfait. Although he was in poor health at that time, thin and somewhat emaciated, his convictions were contagious, and he could move people to laughter or to tears in rapid succession. Older people in Bienfait still speak of Sam Scarlett with respect.

The picnic at Taylorton had its desired effect on the management at Crescent Collieries. Adams was rehired the next day. Meanwhile, James Sloan, MWUC president, arrived from the Calgary headquarters to address an open-air meeting of a thousand people at Bienfait and another one in the Estevan town hall. Sloan, who had also emigrated from Britain, was a self-confident man, short of stature, neatly suited with shirt and tie, who drove an old model-A Ford. Having made some investigations into the local situation, he declared that conditions in the Bienfait mines were 'the worst in Canada.' He was able to announce that one hundred per cent of the miners had signed up for the union.[5]

With Sloan presiding, all the mine committees met together for the first time and Local 27 of the MWUC was born.[6] Provisional local executive officers were elected but for the moment their names were not made public for fear of employer retaliation and firings. Dan Moar, a bachelor and ex-serviceman working in Crescent Collieries and living in a company shack, was chosen president, while John Harris, from the Bienfait mine camp, became vice-president. Harry Hesketh, a proud miner of the British Independent Labour Party tradition, married with a family of seven, who also worked in the Bienfait mine, was elected secretary-treasurer. The Heskeths had lived and worked in the area for almost thirty years, and although they owned their own home in the village, they were forced to seek municipal relief from time to time to feed their family. These men were all from the British element in the mines, and their promotion to leadership was a calculated effort by Sloan to forestall critics who would claim that the union was the product of 'foreigners' and 'un-patriotic.'

The following week both the workers and the coal operators were frantically busy. In each mine the union began collecting information on wages, working conditions, housing, prices at the company stores, and other complaints preparatory to drawing up contract proposals for presentation to the operators.[7] Topping the list of concerns was the wage rate, especially the cuts that the operators had imposed that spring. Since the industry had a minutely differentiated scale of wages depending on where the person worked and on the level of skill involved, the rates required much attention.

Best paid, after the managers with salaries between $4,000 and $6,500[8] and pit bosses at around $1,300 to $1,500[9] per year, were the surface workers – engineers, firemen, carpenters, blacksmiths, electricians, tipple dumpers, teamsters, box-car shovellers – who received fixed monthly or daily wages which in some cases matched that of the pit boss. Most of them had year-round employment. Then there were the contract miners, the shotfirers (who drilled holes into the coalface and then ignited charges of black powder in the holes to loosen the coal), machinemen, diggers, and loaders, who were paid by the lineal foot or ton with different rates for such jobs as undercutting the coalface and shearing it with machinery, pick mining, loading by fork, loading by double fork, loading by shovel, and so on, all rates adjusted according to the size of the entry or room in which they were working and whether or not the coalface had been broken up with an explosive charge of black powder. And finally these were the other inside workers, also called company or daymen – timbermen, track-layers, electric-motor drivers, pumpmen, haulagemen, one-horse drivers, two-horse drivers, track cleaners, boys under eighteen years – who were paid by the day.

The union aimed to represent all the employees but it was the underground workers who did the heaviest and most dangerous jobs and who were the most pressured and generally less well paid. The contract workers, especially those whose incomes depended upon getting the tonnage out, were the most vulnerable to the whims and manipulations of the pit boss. Not surprisingly, the diggers were among the strongest supporters of the union.

Because of the intricate rate schedules and intermittent operations of the mines, with their busy and slack seasons, the creation of a reliable, comparable, and meaningful profile of the annual incomes of the miners is not a simple matter. A mining engineer with the Dominion Fuel Board of the Department of Mines, J. Raffles Cox, made such an attempt by examining mine payrolls over a four-year period from 1928 to 1931. From the Bienfait mine, he found that the four-year average for a group of underground contract miners was $79.22 per month compared to a $95.86 average for day and salaried men. This split demonstrated the high overhead for the amount of tonnage produced by the mine. At the M&S mine, the average monthly wage over the period 1928 to 1931 was $79.32 for underground contract miners, $76.52 for underground daymen, and $107.71 for surface labour. The average for both surface and underground daymen was $92.11. At Western Dominion Collieries, a different sampling was taken involving a group of 'efficient miners' and a group of 'inefficient miners,' a group of higher-rated day labour, and one of lower-rated day labour spread over an eight-month period in 1930, January to August, half of which was in the busy season and half in the slack season. The results of this sample were as follows: 'efficient miners' averaged $70.16, 'inefficient miners' $56.39; the higher-rated day labour received $96.82 and the lower-rated $73.64. Cox concluded that 'over a period of years, wage rates, averaging figures approximating those given, cannot be considered altogether unsatisfactory.'[10]

The Dominion Bureau of Statistics offered two widely different amounts for the miners' average incomes in that period. Information collected from individuals and summarized in the *Census of Canada, 1931*, indicated that average earnings of coalminers in Saskatchewan from June 1930 to June 1931 were $14.12 per week employed or $477 for the year.[11] But in *Coal Statistics for Canada*, based upon company reports, the bureau said that the average wage of Saskatchewan miners in 1931 was $3.83 per day employed or $750 for the year.[12] The second report was possibly closer to reality but for the miners the most pressing fact was that on average they were getting $100 (13 per cent) less in their pay envelopes than a year earlier. And some of the miners suffered even larger reductions as the deep-seam mines cut wages in order to compete with the strip mine.[13]

Those who fell below the average income, as many did,[14] and who lacked access to farmland or a vegetable garden or better-off relatives, faced severe privation and had to rely on charity from the village overseer, A.H. Graham, to feed their families. Even for those who did have gardens or farmland, the drought made it difficult to compensate for their drop in purchasing power by growing their own food. The Reverend H. Gordon Tolton, minister of Stirling Baptist Church, the only minister from seventeen churches in Estevan to express sympathy with the miners' cause in public, made his own investigations in the coalfields. He discovered that between 22 and 32 families in Bienfait were living on village relief all summer, an average of 125 people out of a total population of 532. Tolton said that only Harry Freeman, the National Mines manager, 'had the decency to keep his men in the summer, let them have the houses free of charge for rent.' Robert Hassard, president of Brodie's Bienfait mine, on the other hand, told Graham that he was 'too soft.' 'Don't treat these men too well,' he said. 'I'll be wanting a lot of cheap labor this fall. Starve them a bit, so that I can get them for 20¢ an hour.'[15]

Another of the major complaints of the men was that they were not paid for all the coal they loaded. The crushed coal or slack which was the result of blasting to loosen the coalface was subtracted from their weights as dockage. They had to load it to keep their entries and rooms clear. And yet the companies burned the slack in their boilers and sold it on the commercial market for a lower price. The M&S mine, for example, shipped 20,887 tons of slack in the 1930–1 season – about 30 per cent of the total production of the mine – for which the miners' labour was unpaid. At the Bienfait mine, the dockage was 950 pounds for every loaded cart carrying 4,000 pounds.[16] When the union organizers arrived in the coalfields, the dockage there suddenly dropped to 600 lbs.[17]

The miners were also suspicious of practices of company weighmen at the tipple. This was especially true at the Brodie/Hassard Bienfait mine. There, the weighman was W.C. 'Shorty' Enmark, a member of Hassard's trusted circle. Years later it was still common knowledge how he cheated the miners of their tonnage.

'As for grievances, I'll tell you something,' said the son of a mine manager who prefers to remain anonymous. '"Shorty" Enmark was the weighman at the Bienfait mine. There was a system of brass tags, numbered for each miner, which the miner would hang on each loaded coal cart before it was sent up to the tipple. "Shorty" would "lose" some of these tags, so that at the end of the day many miners found themselves short several tons of coal on the tally sheet.'[18]

'If a miner complained,' added Donald Doerr, a mining engineer who remembers himself as a child of six or seven carrying coal briquettes and water to Hassard's house for five cents a bucket, 'he was told he could pick up his tools and get out! It was through this kind of shady practice that Bob Hassard became a millionaire. If "Shorty" Enmark had not cheated he wouldn't have had a job.'[19] The men wanted the right to appoint and pay for their own check-weighman.

The catalogue of the diggers' complaints about dishonest practices and unpaid labour was a long one. Some workplaces were damp and when water accumulated it was the job of the company pumpman to remove it. If the pumpman came late or his machinery broke down, then the digger would have to take the water out himself or lose his tonnage while waiting. For this work the pit boss had the option to give something, perhaps 25 cents an hour, but there was no recognized payment. It depended upon his generosity. Often he paid nothing or only for a fraction of the time required to do the job. At Crescent Collieries, a notoriously wet mine, the diggers were given the miserly sum of one cent extra for each ton of coal for removing water.[20] Pit bosses could pick and choose whom to reimburse; they had their favourites, the 'loyal' men. The same was true for track-laying and timbering, which were supposed to be 'company work' but frequently became an unpaid burden on the diggers. 'You have to lose money, to get your bread, you got to lose that to put this timber up, to secure the place,' said John Harris.[21] Harris prepared careful notes on all the incidents and irregularities for the coming confrontation with the mine operators.

Other sundry and grievous wrongs came to light especially in the course of investigating the controversies that swirled around the head of A.C. Wilson, the nimble-minded, fast-talking, cigar-smoking manager of the M&S mine, a man whom the RCMP, in their confidential reports, secretly believed was 'responsible for most of the grief' the miners experienced.[22]

In the beginning, though, a man of Wilson's accomplishments was not without supporters and admirers among the miners, and no one was more impressed than Sam Davies and his sons. Like A.C. Wilson, Sam Davies had migrated from Lancashire. He came to Canada with his family in the 1920s to escape wartime taxation and because he did not want to be part of a union. He had a fruit tree, crops, and chickens and worked in the mine along with two of his sons. His wife, Elizabeth Sherratt Davies, ran the boarding house at the M&S mine. Davies Sr was in charge of the stables, receiving a higher than average salary, and he did odd jobs for Wilson around the mine. It was a comfortable life. 'He was very quiet,' said his son Jim. 'He minded his own business and he kept separate from his radical in-laws, my mother's family. My mother's family, now, they were quite different. Give them a beer or two and they knew how to run the mine. This was a radical town. There were communists. They came from Europe. We lived out of town at Taylorton and didn't know of them. I didn't want to talk of that, but yes it's part of the picture alright.'

Jim Davies preferred the example of his father and the mine manager. 'Alex Wilson was a tough boss,' said Jim, 'but there was nothing wrong with him. He was a spur-of-the-moment person. He would fire a man one minute and hire him back in the afternoon. To me he was a good boss. If you did your job he left you alone. I always forged ahead. I looked after myself. I did alright ... People who go hungry bring it on themselves. They could help themselves if they wanted to. The radicals have an attitude about people who get ahead. They say, who do you think you are? They want to keep everyone at the same level.' After the strike in 1931 the Davies men helped Wilson keep the miners' union out of the M&S mine for a long time, with Jim acting as secretary for a company union.[23] Elizabeth Sherratt Davies, on the other hand, became a passionate supporter of the drive for a miners' union.[24]

'It never mattered what you'd done,' said one of the Bachynskis, 'it was never right. If Wilson caught you standing still, you were fired. He'd say, "Go home, you're fired!" An hour later he'd be over at my house. He realized that he needed an experienced loader. He'd say, "I'll give you five cents an hour more than the others." One summer I was fired seven times.'[25]

Wilson's nephew recalled a common saying about his uncle's intimidating, bullying tactics with his workers: 'He always had three crews on hand – one coming, one working, and one going.'[26] For the workers there was an air of perpetual anxiety and insecurity.

Wilson was good at thinking of ways to make the social amenities of the mining camp self-sufficient. There was the symbolic case of the hot-water showers. The showers were much appreciated but Wilson subtracted fifty cents a month from every miner's pay for this amenity even though it was no direct expense to the mine since the workers supplied their own soap and towels. This 'small' amount was the equivalent of 4,000 pounds of loaded coal every month for every digger. Nor was the hot water from the mine's boilers a cost to Wilson because it was heated by screenings from the tipple that the miners were forced to contribute. But Wilson was adamant. 'It goes back to the same old story,' he said in one of his oracular pronouncements. He called it 'making everybody "toe the mark."' And did he not have to pay someone to keep the showers clean? This amounted to a minor expense, with one man working an hour or so each day for fifty cents. Not surprisingly, the showers turned up on the mine's financial report as a profit item.[27]

The company general store was one of Wilson's pet projects. He got a personal discount there, everything at cost, including cigars once or twice a day. But he wanted to make sure that the store paid its way. Although Wilson denied it, miners who lived in the company houses somehow had the strong impression that they had to patronize the store to keep their jobs and their housing even though prices there were considerably higher than the prices in Bienfait stores and those asked by neighbouring farmers and itinerant pedlars. Wilson said that he had never 'taken undue advantage of anyone.' In a moment of candour he conceded that, people 'were more or less afraid of that "Outlaw Wilson"' but he claimed that, until complaints were made during the strike, he had 'no knowledge whatever' that employees thought their jobs depended upon their patronizing the company store. 'I never told anybody that they must buy at the store,' he said. He had only 'discussed with them several times' how they should patronize the store a little.[28] That was how A.C. Wilson stretched the truth. When the mine employees saw a fence go up to encircle the housing area and the general store, they might have been forgiven for thinking that the two were closely linked.

This impression was reinforced by Wilson's habit of posting notices around the mining camp. Several of these related to the new fencing. One notice ordered tenants to stop getting their milk from outside. Anyone buying milk from Mrs Molyneaux, it said, would be 'disobeying the wishes of the Management ... and will be inviting trouble for themselves. Signed: A.C. Wilson.' Another notice forbade 'pedlars' from coming on site and actually named several Bienfait merchants including Jake Lishinsky and Sam Lischinsky. To enforce this rule, Wilson posted his son-in-law, Tom Cuddington, at the gate with instructions to check on vehicles entering the mining camp. Cuddington was a member of a merchant family that ran a grocery store by that name in Bienfait.[29] Even miners' wives who bought goods from Eaton's mail order were hassled.[30] And Wilson required the fourteen families who kept cows to buy hay from him on the excuse that this would keep noxious weeds from entering the premises.[31] In the words of veteran miner Peter Gemby, 'the company store was a dictatorship. One couldn't buy goods any other place but at the store. And even if goods were cheaper elsewhere the miner had to deal at the store because he didn't have cash.'[32]

Much of the company housing for the miners was substandard, unsanitary, overcrowded, and in poor repair, with leaking roofs and ill-fitting doors and windows through which the wind blew.[33] Repeated requests for repairs brought little response. In a much-cited appearance before the royal commission, Anne Baryluk, a sixteen-year-old who lived in the Bienfait mine camp with her family, described their housing in unforgetable terms:

We have only got three beds and there are eleven of us. I think we need a bigger place than that ... When it is raining the rain comes in the kitchen. There is only one ply of paper, cardboard paper nailed to about two inch wood board ... It is all coming down and water comes in when it is raining. The roof leaks ... The kitchen isn't any good. When the weather is frosty, when you wake up in the morning you cannot walk on the floor because it is all full of snow, right around the room ... And in the kitchen the chimney is too low. When you start a fire in there the house gets full of smoke.[34]

For this accommodation the Baryluks had to pay nine dollars a month.

In spite of the overcrowding, many families took in boarders during the busy season to boost their meagre incomes. A.C. Wilson saw this as an opportunity for some windfall profit and required that families get his permission. His standard fee for the privilege was one dollar per month per boarder. Needless to say, Wilson's demand did not go down well with his tenants. To make matters worse, Wilson was inconsistent, demanding up to three dollars in some cases and nothing in others. In one instance, he charged a couple for boarding their own grown-up son on the grounds that he was working across the tracks at Western Dominion Collieries.[35]

Several miners related how Wilson engaged in bootlegging. This was around Christmas time. For concord wine that cost $2.50 at the government liquor store in Estevan, the only legal outlet for selling spirits, they paid Wilson $4.50 at the mine. Others bought cases of beer from him. Wilson asked them to spread the word for other customers: 'Tell them I have got wine in the house.' The miners were prepared to swear to this information under oath and did so but the authorities never pursued the matter. Perhaps they were not anxious to have the liquor laws strictly enforced. Earlier in 1931, the mayor of Estevan, David Bannatyne, had complained to higher authorities that the local RCMP detachment was insisting on 'getting the names of the purchasers of the quantity permits' and thus interfering with the tourist and liquor business in Estevan.[36]

One day Wilson thought of a new idea to improve work discipline. His mine had a double-compartment hoisting shaft for bringing out the coal and by its side there was an enclosed shaft with zig-zag ladders for the men to travel on, known as a 'travelling man-way.' When the mine was hoisting coal, the miners travelled to and from their work eighty feet below the surface on the ladders. This day he posted up a notice announcing that the door to the ladders in the mine shaft would be locked at 7:00 A.M. No one would be allowed to go up or down until noon. Anyone turning up late would forfeit that work time. This news was astounding to the miners. Was it not illegal under the Mines Act to block egress from a working mine? Next day, when sixty miners began climbing up the ladders to exit at noon hour, they could not budge the door. Wilson had forgotten about the men down in the mine. He and Sam Davies were out mending a hole in the fence where Mrs Molyneaux was still smuggling her milk into the camp. For once, the swift-talking Wilson had to climb down from his high horse, admitting his mistake in a letter to the provincial inspector of mines and promising that it would not happen again. His man Davies took the blame for neglecting to open the door.[37]

Next to firing employees who irritated him, Wilson liked to fine them, taking them by surprise. He did not warn them, he said, because 'telling them is like pouring water on a duck's back. It rolls off pretty fast.' Mike Kresko was fined for standing in the wrong place when the coal carts went by; Joe Slenka because his cow got through the fence while he was working in the mine; William Stalene for knocking some timbers down, causing a clay fall. The targets were usually immigrants from eastern Europe, the men doing much of the bone-and-muscle work. When these diggers came to the office to pick up their sealed pay envelopes and due bills, which arrived once a month from the Winnipeg head office, Wilson would state his complaint, break open the envelope, and remove $5 or $8 while the dumbfounded worker looked on. Wilson, in the miners' eyes, was a tyrant, a law unto himself, someone who could lay a charge, decide on guilt, apply a penalty, and put the proceeds of the workers' labour in his pocket.[38]

As the results of investigations by union activists piled up, mass meetings were held among the miners and their families in the last week of August and the first week of September in preparation for the possibility of a strike. Joe Forkin and Sam Scarlett explained how unions worked in other coalfields. James Sloan answered questions asked by the miners and their wives. He told them that they had the sympathy of the people, and 'not to spoil this sympathy by violence.' His promise of the moral support of the Red International of Labour Unions, which he said had twenty-eight million members, including fifteen million in Soviet Russia, was highlighted in the *Mercury*'s reports of these meetings.[39]

The managers of the six deep-seam mines had also been busy. Faced with the growing unity and militancy of the miners, they formed the Southern Saskatchewan Coal Operators' Association. C.C. Morfit, the American manager of Western Dominion Collieries, was elected president.

The coal operators led by Morfit went to Regina in the first week of September and were received by the government at a special cabinet meeting. The meeting took place shortly after a visit of Prime Minister R.B. Bennett to Regina. Given a copy of the *Worker* containing reports of the union drive in Bienfait, Bennett, who had recently shown his determination to crush radical organizations, is reported to have joined discussions about the labour unrest in the coalfields.[40] The conversations with the operators centred on their request first for RCMP reinforcements to deal with a threatened strike, which they predicted would be violent, and second for political help to neutralize the miners' union. The cabinet readily agreed to send police reinforcements and four RCMP officers left immediately for the Weyburn subdistrict to await developments.[41] On the second point, the cabinet was wary and decided to dispatch Thomas Molloy, deputy minister of labour and former president of the Trades and Labour Council of Regina, as a commissioner to investigate the situation.[42]

Meanwhile, the government already had an agent in Estevan who was working with an ambitious and clever young lawyer, W.W. 'Wally' Lynd, to undermine the union. The two of them approached John Loughran, still ostensibly provisional president of the miners' union, and they developed the line that Sloan, Forkin, and Scarlett were outsiders with 'no right to be here' interfering in disputes, and that their union was unpatriotic because of its association with 'the Red International of Labour Unions in Moscow.' They proposed that Loughran split from the newly formed miners' union to become a member of a government conciliation commission on behalf of the men. Loughran was flattered by their attention and expressed enthusiasm for what he termed the 'heart and soul' mediating role of the provincial government. But having no real authority, he worried what Sloan would think and hesitated to act. He passed Lynd and the agent on to Sloan who told them to mind their own business.[43]

Thomas Molloy followed up with three days of shuttling between civic leaders, the police, union members, and the coal operators trying to find an opening for government intervention. On one of these days, Sloan had invited the operators to a joint conference at Estevan town hall for the purpose of reaching an agreement on wages and working conditions, but the big six operators did not come. Molloy turned up at the conference instead and sixty-five surprised, disbelieving men from the miners' committee listened to him say that he was a card-carrying union man and that he had been told it was 'red' but the detractors could not make him excited, 'they could not pull any red herring over him.' 'What you want is to get organized,' he said. 'The government can do nothing until you are organized ... Stick to it boys. I'm with you.'[44] The mine workers' union already had all 600 men signed up! What more did Molloy want? When Molloy returned to Regina, all he could report to the government was what it already knew, namely, that the operators would have nothing to do with the MWUC because it was part of an international revolutionary party; that they would meet a committee of miners composed only of men actually employed in their mines; and that the men appeared to be solidly behind their union and wanted it to represent them in negotiations.

James Sloan persisted on behalf of the executive committee of the union, sending a second letter to the coal operators proposing another joint conference at the town hall on Monday, 7 September 'for the purpose of reaching an agreement covering all the mines in the district.' The letter added that, should the companies fail to be represented at this conference, 'your employees will cease to work on Tuesday morning, September 8th.'[45] This was not the kind of talk the operators or the provincial government wanted to hear.

The minister of labour, J.A. Merkley, made a flying Sunday visit to Estevan in an attempt to influence the troubled situation. Local politicians brought the proxy president, John Loughran, and several of his friends in the General Workers Union to meet the minister. Merkley asked Loughran what position the unemployed would take in case the miners walked out. From this discussion Merkley felt reassured and concluded that a strike would be broken quickly since 'there are a thousand men ready to take the miners' places.'[46] Satisfied with this information and unable to arrange a meeting with James Sloan, whose car had broken down some miles out of town, the minister returned to Regina early Monday morning without contacting the miners' union directly.

As a further reality check and perhaps to mollify the operators, the government had dispatched a detective from Regina RCMP headquarters to join the two-man detachment in Estevan. His instructions were to investigate 'the alleged violence that was to happen at the mines of this district.' After spending a couple of days making quiet enquiries Detective Constable G.A. Sincennes wrote a report that would not surprise anyone who knew anything about the local scene except that he mixed the Bienfait mine with the M&S mine. It read:

fyle [*sic*]: *Sam Scarlett – Communist Agitator (Secret), Sept. 7, 1931*

The Bienfait mines are situated about ½ mile south of the hamlet of Bienfait,

Sask. There is no road other than a prairie trail leading to the mine or the houses. The miners live in small houses, about 35 of them, unpainted, which are owned by the mine owner. The company operates a store and the miners are obliged to buy at this store, if not they are threatened to be fired. The store prices are above any of the private merchants in the district.

The miners claim that they have to dig between 2,500 and 2,800 pounds of coal for every ton.

On one instance one of the operators opened a parcel addressed to one of the miners, and told this miner that if he ordered any more merchandise from Eatons he would be fired. The difference between the Eaton price and the Company's price was deducted from his miner's pay ...

These are some of the grievances the miners have to put up with, and as there is no leader amongst them, President Sloan was certainly welcome in this district ... It is my firm belief that there is, so far, no cause to worry, and that the miners will abide by Sloan's word who has so far told them that no violence must be used if they wanted to get somewhere with their newly born union.

In view of this analysis, it is understandable why the head of the Estevan RCMP detachment, Sergeant William Mulhall, a veteran of the force, was cautious about acceding to the wishes of C.C. Morfit and the Southern Saskatchewan Coal Operators' Association for action against the union organizers. 'There is a noticeable feeling of sympathy in favour of the miners throughout the district,' he told his superiors in Regina, and therefore 'our investigation must be carried out with care and patience ... I am satisfied that there is no immediate necessity for alarm.' The majority of the miners were not in favour of communism, he went on, 'though they believe that they have had unjust treatment and need a leader to guide them and air their grievances.'[47]

Sergeant Mulhall knew that Morfit, who would not negotiate a contract with the Bienfait union because it was indirectly affiliated with Moscow through the Red International of Labour Unions, was himself a principal in a firm of consulting engineers and efficiency experts of New York City, Stuart, James and Cooke, which held six contracts to operate Soviet mines and enterprises in Tomsk, Kharkov, Leningrad, and Moscow.[48] It was seemingly acceptable for the bosses to have connections in Soviet Russia but not for the workers. The hypocrisy did not pass unnoticed.

Even more damning, Mulhall believed that Morfit was using his influence with the mine owners in 'purposely avoiding a meeting with the miners' in order to force a strike. According to Mulhall's information, the engineering firm that Morfit represented had advised British financial interests to invest about half a million dollars in machinery and other improvements in the briquette plant of Western Dominion Collieries. Since the installation of the machinery, the plant had proved a failure and had suffered extensive financial losses for which the engineering firm would be blamed. Morfit was going to have to report a loss of $33,000 and wanted to save his neck. 'It will be seen that if the plant is forced to close down through strike conditions,' said Mulhall in a report that was passed on to the attorney general of Saskatchewan, 'it will form a loophole of escape through which the above mentioned engineers might "get from under" without exciting severe criticism from the investors.' Mulhall warned that, if the situation did lead to a walkout, 'the miners will not be wholly to blame.'[49]

On the evening of Monday, 7 September, the coal operators failed to show up for the conference at the town hall. Twice the union had invited the operators to a conference to reach an agreement on wages and working conditions and twice the operators refused to attend. 'We will not meet with the representatives of the Mine Workers' Union of Canada,' reiterated Morfit, president of the operators association, 'because they are communistic' and the union 'is an emissary of the Third Internationale.'

That evening the miners' union threw off the façade of John Loughran being president. In final preparations for the strike, Dan Moar (Crescent Collieries) was revealed publicly as president of the local union and Harry Hesketh (Bienfait mine) as secretary. The other most prominent men on the committee, beside Vice-President John Harris, were Fred Booth (M&S), George Wilkinson (Western Dominion Collieries), Martin Day (Crescent Collieries), John Billis (Eastern Collieries), and Alex Konopaki (National Mines). The men elected a strike committee of twenty-eight members who would act as picket captains. That same evening over in Bienfait, fifty women attended a meeting in the Ukrainian Labour Temple to form a womens' auxiliary of the miners' union and they elected Mrs A. Eddy, wife of a machine operator and shotfirer at the M&S mine, as president.[50] Everyone was aware that sometime the next morning, at a pre-arranged signal, the men would lay down their tools and walk out of the mines, leaving only maintenance men to prevent flooding.[51]

Chapter Five

September: On Strike

The miners have a perfect right to strike for better conditions.
– H.N. Freeman, manager, National Mines, Bienfait, 19 September 1931

If this was in the States it would soon be settled ... the strikers would be mowed down with machine guns if they carried on the way they do up here.
– C.C. Morfit, president, Southern Saskatchewan Coal Operators' Association, 16 September 1931

I am of the opinion that the operators wish the Police to start something.
– RCMP Inspector F.W. Schutz (secret), 20 September 1931

The strike got off to a solid beginning. Bouyant with expectation, the miners and their families turned out in near unanimity and with great determination. The local paper observed that 'the streets of the village seem to have become the meeting place of the strikers,' in 'the first strike in the history of the Coalfields.' The strike was widely recognized in the province with a banner headline on the front page of the *Leader-Post* – 'Six hundred Estevan mine workers quit' – and in the telegram that the Southern Saskatchewan District of the RCMP sent to the Commissioner, General J.H. MacBrien, in Ottawa: 'President Sloan of the Mine Workers' Union called strike of all miners in Estevan District this morning. Stop. Approximately 500 miners laid down tools. Stop. No disturbances have yet occurred.'

Twelve of the small mines owned and operated by town councillor Harry Nicholson, Thomas McLean, Sr, and other prominent citizens of Estevan agreed to recognize Local 27 of the MWUC. Initial strike-relief pay came from the union headquarters in Calgary – five dollars for every married miner with an additional fifty cents for each child. Declaring that no pregnant women, mothers, or children would be allowed to go hungry, Joe Forkin sent out telegrams from the WUL to the Farmers' Unity League in Saskatoon, and to affiliated unions as far away as Port Arthur, requesting supplies of food and funds.[1]

Knowledge of the miners' grievances and support for their redress was so overwhelming in the community that the provincial attorney general, M.A. MacPherson, ordered the police 'not to take any aggressive measures' or 'take up quarters at the various mines.'[2] This order, which allowed the strikers to hold their meetings and to picket peacefully, would have a significant impact on the first ten days of the strike. RCMP Inspector F.W. Schutz, sent down from Regina by the government to find out what the situation was, had paid special attention to two local observers. One was A.H. Graham, overseer of the village of Bienfait:

> Mr. Graham ... informed me that he has been at Bienfait for twelve years. That the conditions under which the miners work at the M & S and Dom. Collieries and the Bienfait Mine are very bad and that the miners have a real grievance. He claims that if a man made a complaint he was given his time. That these mines had always more men around the mine than could be employed. That they were not paid for the full amount of coal dug. That they were compelled to purchase from the Company stores. That the men did not average any more than sixty dollars a month. That the company claimed that they spent there [*sic*] money as soon as they got it on things other than necessities, while it was perfectly plain that on the wages earned it would keep them guessing to make sufficient to live. That the present strike had been forced on the miners.[3]

The other informant was Harry Freeman, manager of National Mines, who told Schutz that the conditions under which the miners had to work in other mines 'have been a disgrace' and that they had 'a perfect right to strike for better conditions.' He confirmed that miners at the Taylorton area mines, especially the M&S mine, were 'compelled to buy groceries and clothing etc. from the company store at very high prices' so that by the time the miner had paid for his powder and the store bill 'he had nothing left.' As a contribution to his own employees' welfare, Freeman had not given the twenty-two families living on company property notice to vacate the premises during the strike as the other operators had done. Here was an apparently model employer but he, too, had his conditions and schemes. He claimed that he was perfectly willing to recognize a miners' union provided it had 'no red tendencies.' To this end, Freeman was quietly making arrangements to weaken and divide the workers by making use of ethnic divisions in the mining community. He gathered sixteen former soldiers (mainly of British origin) who had served overseas in the First World War, urging them 'to disown their present Union' and start a union of their own.[4] Given these appreciations of conditions in the coalfields, the provincial government decided to pursue a wait-and-see policy as the strike drama unfolded, while keeping the forces of 'law and order' close by in the wings.

On the side of the union, there was from the start a serious problem stemming from disagreement over the choice of strike strategy. One strategy was centred on the views of President James Sloan and on his placement of 'recognition of the MWUC' as the primary demand for negotiations with the employers. His battle plan was not to reveal other demands until recognition was granted: without a union to enforce them, he reasoned, any other gains would merely remain on paper, unenforceable, subject to the whims of management as hitherto. Sloan was a tough, experienced, able negotiator and had acquired a solid reputation for his leadership of the coalminers in Alberta, where wages were considerably higher than in the Saskatchewan coalfields. He held the confidence of the strike committee. In addition, to bolster morale at mass meetings, Sloan referred to the international affiliation of his union, through the WUL, to the Red International of Labour Unions, which he presented as an organization with unlimited funds that could come to the support of any section of the WUL engaged in a strike.

Against Sloan's strategy was the position argued without success by Joe Forkin and the WUL's national secretary, Tom Ewen. It was that, while union recognition should be an important demand, it ought not be made a precondition to negotiation on wages, working conditions, and the recognition of pit committees in the mines. The WUL urged that the bargaining process be an open one, with the union's demands fully publicized and union members kept informed of the progress of negotiations by means of a daily strike bulletin. This would keep the strike committee in close touch with the rank and file of the miners and prevent the operators from spreading stories to divide the workers. It would lay the basis for the continuing strength of the union whether or not it gained recognition by the operators. Tom Ewen criticized the 'leftist' character of Sloan's remarks about the Red International, noting that his interpretation was being 'freely seized upon by the capitalist press and politician and reformists to the detriment of the miners' struggle.'[5]

On the second day of the strike, Sloan had to leave Estevan on union business. At 1:45 A.M. on 10 September, he and Martin Day boarded the west-bound CPR train for Calgary to attend the sixth national convention of the MWUC. He would be gone for almost two weeks. To ensure that his strategy of union recognition would precede everything else, he apparently took with him the only available copy of the proposed agreement with the operators[6] (see appendix 2).

At the convention, Martin Day made a moving and effective speech describing the situation in Bienfait and the struggle to gain recognition for the union local there. Prompted by this report, the convention voted to donate $600 'for the most immediate and needy cases' among the strikers. In a letter to secretary Harry Hesketh of the Bienfait local, the assembled delegates, claiming to represent six thousand miners from British Columbia to Nova Scotia, sent 'greetings to the Southern Saskatchewan lignite miners, on strike against the misery and starvation forced upon you by your bosses. Comrades, on behalf of the miners represented, the delegates urge you to stand solid demanding union scale of wages and conditions ... your fight is also our fight and your victory will be also our victory. Therefore, we support your fight as our own.' In a similar militant frame of mind, the miners' delegates took pleasure in tweaking the noses of the mine bosses in Canada by contrasting the rotten life of coalminers under capitalism with the security and respect enjoyed by miners under socialism in the Soviet Union. A cabled message to the miners of the Soviet Union greeted their 'great contribution to the Five Year Plan of Socialist Construction' and recognized in their victories 'an inspiration to fight for our own economic freedom from capitalist oppression.'[7]

When the operators' lawyer and chief negotiator, W.W. Lynd, learned that President Sloan had departed the scene, he seized the opportunity to do something which the operators had adamantly refused to do just two days earlier. In the absence of Sloan, he requested a meeting with the strike committee for the purpose of entering into negotiations. The strike committee, inexperienced and mindful of Sloan's instructions, went to the meeting without their detailed negotiating papers and presented no demand other than that the operators should recognize their union. This played into Lynd's hands. Flatly refusing to negotiate on that basis, he was able to tell the press that he had no idea what the miners' grievances were. The union had presented nothing requiring redress. Perhaps there was nothing so bad about conditions in the coalfields after all!

The operators followed up by publicizing the strike committee's sole demand and launching a propaganda campaign to discredit the union, which they said was nothing but a conspiratorial organization affiliated to the Third International, power-hungry and interested only in revolution. To this end, the operators placed a large advertisement in the *Mercury*, 'The Truth about the Strike,' to influence public opinion and bathed themselves in self-congratulatory tones, suggesting that they were acting in the best interest of the community and the public at large by refusing to deal with a 'red' organization.[8] Sloan's strategy had opened a door for the operators and in his absence they had clearly pushed the miners onto the defensive.

Before the union could reassess the situation and repair the damage, the operators kept up the pressure by starting to recruit a few unemployed men and some of the desperately poor farmers, not enough to operate the mines but sufficient to provoke a confrontation with the strikers, which they calculated would force the police into action. If the strikers fell for the provocation, then their union would be destroyed by the state acting 'to protect law and order' and the operators would have a free hand once again. With these thoughts in mind, C.C. Morfit, on behalf of his colleagues in the Southern Saskatchewan Coal Operators' Association, contacted the local head of the criminal investigation branch of the RCMP, Detective Staff-Sergeant Walter Mortimer, on 12 September, four days after the strike began, telling him that several of the mines would be reopening with outside men on Wednesday, 16 September, at 7 A.M.

Although kept 'waiting in the wings' until now, the police had not been idle nor had they neglected to make preparations for an expected confrontation between the operators and the miners. The force carefully briefed its officers on section 501 of the Criminal Code, which provided for fines of one hundred dollars or three months in prison for anyone guilty of acts of violence, threats, intimidation, and 'watching and besetting' to 'compel any other person to abstain from doing anything which he has a lawful right to do.' The force also had three undercover special constables, two stool-pigeons, and a paid witness working for them during the coal miners' strike. Special Constable J. Eberhardt, who could speak Ukrainian, was able to rent a room at the Boruk's

Boarding House, listen to conversations there, and mingle among miners in Bienfait for a few days until wary miners decided that he was not just an ordinary person passing through town.

The identities of the stool-pigeons, one at the M&S mine and the other at Taylorton, are protected in the police files. To judge by his writing skills, one of them must have been a fairly educated person of British background and well known to the miners in Bienfait. Unfortunately for the police, their stool-pigeons were not part of the union leadership nor members of the critical twenty-eight-member strike committee. Thus, they were never exactly sure of the strikers' plans and were fated to react to unfounded rumours. Nevertheless, one of the stool-pigeons knew all the militants by name and supplied lists to the police of those he considered to be radicals and communists as well as those he knew to be more reluctant participants in the strike, possibly willing to disown the union. 'I have noticed that all Jews in Estevan and Bienfait are 100% behind the Communist movement,' he wrote in one report. He attended all the general meetings of the miners, reporting the content of speeches and the gist of overheard private conversations. Apart from anticipating the strikers' moves, the police hoped to catch the militant leaders advocating violent strike tactics, which could become the subject of criminal prosecution and possibly deportation proceedings.[9]

How would the strikes react to the news that the operators were going to open the mines with strike-breakers? After listening to days of excited discussion and planning at the Red and Green halls – their members now joined together in the struggle for the union – one police informer wrote that the miners and their wives were making plans to resist any attempt at strike-breaking and that it appeared 'highly probable that there would be acts of violence and disorder if strike-breakers came in.' Another informer heard something else and advised Detective Sergeant Mortimer that, while the miners were going to hold out, he was satisfied that there would be no violence. Mortimer, in reviewing the situation with Sergeant Mulhall, who was in charge locally, decided that twenty-five police officers would be needed to contain the situation, that is, fifteen additional to what they had. They would be gathered from surrounding towns on Tuesday, 15 September, on the eve of the operators' attempt to reopen three of the mines – Western Dominion Collieries at Taylorton, M&S, and Eastern Collieries.

There began three days of high drama for the strikers and careful stickhandling by Sergeant Mulhall who did not wish his enlarged squad of police officers to be used as agents for the tyrannical and unpopular coal bosses. Mulhall instructed his officers that they were to preserve law and order and 'to be sure they had good reason for doing so before they interfered.' The officers were to be neutral as between strike-breakers and strikers; their only task was to keep the peace and see that no violence or damage to property would occur.[10]

The miners' tactics were to bring one or two hundred people to each of the mines at an appointed time and then fade away, leaving a dozen or so pickets in place. Whenever the police asked these pickets why they remained near the premises of the mine, their reply was always the same, 'We are here to see that nobody damages the mine property for which we might be blamed.'[11] Sergeant Mulhall chose to accept this ingenious response and let them be.

The owner of Eastern Collieries, Herbert Wallace, had no sooner hired two strike-breakers and ordered the striking miners living in shacks on his premises to vacate them than several hundred miners turned up to protest. They stood on the other side of the railway tracks under the watchful eyes of three RCMP constables, while a delegation led by John Billis, Fred Konopaki, William Klymyk, Allen Carroll, Walter Molyneux, and James McLean went in to interview Wallace. Whatever they said convinced Wallace to pay off the two scabs and the pickets quietly moved away. Earlier, Wallace had tried to get the police to eject his tenants but they declined, saying that they would intervene only after he himself had tried and met resistance. If he laid charges, they would act. The police discovered that Wallace had acquired firearms illegally. He was on decidedly shaky ground.[12]

Mine manager A.C. Wilson had hired seven strike-breakers for the M&S mine. Prepared to go to work the next day, they were lodged by Wilson in the mine's boarding house. This was the boarding house run by Elizabeth (Bessie) Sherratt Davies. Hundreds of miners led by Dan Moar, president of the local union, soon began arriving and Moar went in to talk to the strike-breakers. Presently, Bessie Davies decided to show her colours. She emerged in the doorway and called out to the assembled strikers, 'What should I do about the scabs? Should I feed them?' 'No! No!' the crowd roared. She let Wilson know that she felt obliged to follow the advice of her regular customers. Then Dan Moar emerged with four of the strike-breakers, who said that they had not heard about the labour dispute and they would be going home. The strikers gave a great cheer. Unable to start a violent confrontation with the disciplined miners and out-manoeuvred by Bessie Davies, Wilson led the other three scabs away, smarting from the sting of defeat. Looking on at the

"WORKERS OF THE WORLD UNITE"

WORKERS' UNITY

| Vol 1, No. 5 | Official Bi-Monthly Organ — "WORKERS' UNITY LEAGUE OF CANADA" — Canadian Section, R.I.L.U. | Price 5c | October 30, 1931 |

The masthead of the Workers' Unity League paper, *Workers' Unity*, stressing workers' international solidarity.

A conference of the Mine Workers' Union of Canada in 1932. Front from the left: John Stokaluk, secretary; James Sloan, president; H. Morris, treasurer; Harvey Murphy; vice-president. 2nd row left: Sam Scarlett. 3rd row, third from left: Martin Day of Bienfait Local 27.

Joseph Forkin: union organizer.

Harry Hesketh: secretary of Local 27, Mine Workers' Union of Canada, in Bienfait.

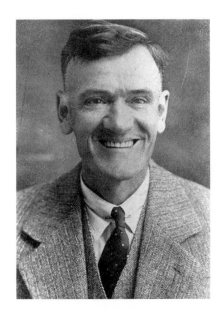

Thomas A. Ewen: national secretary of the Workers' Unity League.

Jim McLean: Estevan miner, elected check-weighman at Crescent Collieries after the strike.

Charles Pavo, farmer, with his children in Birsay, Sask. Pavo was a leader of the Farmers' Unity League, which helped raise relief supplies for the Bienfait miners' strike in 1931. He provided sanctuary for Sam Scarlett.

Sam Scarlett, famous orator of the Workers' Unity League. The police had this picture of Scarlett when they captured him at Pavo's house.

Annie Buller speaking to miners in Bienfait on Sunday, 27 September 1931. Seated on the platform is Dan Moar, president of Local 27 of the Mine Workers' Union of Canada. This photograph was taken by RCMP detective Walter Mortimer and entered as an exhibit in the Estevan trials.

The miners assembling their cavalcade to Estevan on Tuesday, 29 September 1931.

Sergeant William Mulhall. Mulhall was removed from Estevan for showing too much sympathy to the miners.

Inspector F. Schutz. Schutz backed Sergeant Mulhall.

Inspector C. Rivett-Carnac. He led an RCMP force to Estevan in October 1931 and helped prepare the 'evidence' for Annie Buller's trial.

J.T.M. Anderson. Premier of the Conservative government in Saskatchewan in 1931, Anderson journeyed to Bienfait in October to help establish a branch of the Canadian Legion as a counterweight to the Mine Workers' Union of Canada.

Rev. T.C. Douglas. The future socialist premier of Saskatchewan was a Baptist minister in Weyburn, Sask., in 1931. He went to Bienfait during the strike and spoke words of encouragement to the miners, while his church sent a truckload of relief supplies for the miners' families.

The 1925 wedding picture of Alex Boruk and Tekla Scribialo, both of them immigrants from western Ukraine. This was Tekla's second marriage; her first husband, Jacob Boyko, died in the flu epidemic after the First World War and is buried in Taylorton cemetery. The Boruks were first generation members of the Ukrainian Labour-Farmer Temple Association (ULFTA) in Bienfait and took an active part in the affairs of the Red Hall. The Workers' Unity League organizers stayed with them during the 1931 strike.

Boruk's Boarding House and Bakery, left, and their family home. Behind the fence is their garden, well, and outbuildings for livestock and storage.

Stella Boruk. A talented musician and an outgoing person, Stella, seventeen at the time of the strike, was leader of the youth activities around the Red Hall. Later she became a teacher in the Bienfait school.

The wedding picture of Ursula and John Billis, 1913, in Pittsburgh, Pennsylvania. Later they returned to Lithuania and then immigrated to Canada. John dreamed of a socialist future and became one of the most active leaders of the 1931 miners' strike.

Ursula Billis and her daughters Annie and Amelia, preparing to leave Lithuania in 1924 to rejoin her husband in Bienfait.

Bienfait miners. Left to right: Peter Markunas, [?] Danksha, Charles Perles, unknown, Charles Grigalis, Adam Uza, all of whom came from Lithuania. Markunas was shot dead while Grigalis was arrested, tried, and sentenced to jail after the strike.

Peter Gemby heading home after work with his lunch pail. He was blacklisted for ten years after the 1931 strike.

Front-page cartoon appearing in *Workers' Unity* on 1 October 1931, at the time of the Bienfait miners' strike.

William Choma and family. Choma was a member of the strike committee in 1931. Two of his sons, Gene and Wrally, later became executive members of Local 7606 of the UMWA in Bienfait.

Steve Baryluk. Miner, member of the Green Hall, and father of nine children, Baryluk was one of those wounded by police bullets during the miners' parade in Estevan.

Major M.A. McPherson. Attorney General of Saskatchewan in 1931 and guest speaker at the Bienfait legion during the miners' strike.

Matthew and Liza Popowich, people of many and varied talents, mentored the music and drama program of the Red Hall in Bienfait from their base in Winnipeg.

First generation members of the Red Hall of the ULFTA in Bienfait, 1930. 1st row from left: Lena Scribialo, Mrs Markowski, Stella Boruk, Mary Markowski, unknown. 2nd row from left: Mrs Fred Elchyson, Mrs Nick Bachynski, Mrs Steve Antoniuk, Tekla Scribialo Boruk, Mary Bachynski, Mary Konopaki. 3rd row from left: Olga Andruschuk, Jean Moroz, unknown, unknown, Stella Bachynski Gemby. 4th row from left: Harry Andruschuk, Harry Michalowski, unknown, John Bachynski, unknown, unknown. 5th row from left: Mike Scribialo, unknown, unknown, Stefan Wozny, unknown, Fred Konopaki, unknown, John Markowski. 6th row from left: unknown, unknown, Alec Boruk, Alex Konopaki.

The youth group at the ULFTA of Bienfait took an active part in supporting the miners' strike in 1931. Left to right: Victoria Germann, Annie Billis, Mary Elchyson, Stella Katrusik, Stella Bachynski, Mrs Louis Konopaki, Phyllis Bachynski, Mike Boruk, Ann Elchyson, John Konopaki, Stella Boruk, Lawrence Scribialo.

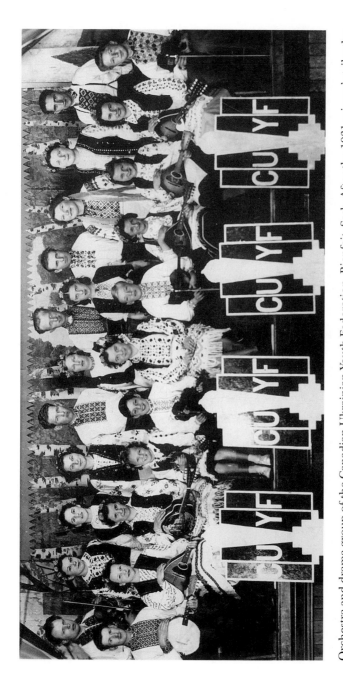

Orchestra and drama group of the Canadian Ukrainian Youth Federation, Bienfait, Sask. After the 1931 miners' strike the youth group continued to grow and, led by Stella Boruk, performed benefit concerts for the press and other causes of the labour movement in the new hall of the ULFTA on Carbon Avenue. 1st row from left: Gordon Carr, Mary Elchyson, Stella Bachynski Gemby, Olga Boruk, Walter Germann, Stella Boruk Elchyson, Eugene Choma, Rose Seper, Rose Hallas, Jessie Elchyson Lutes, Walter Boruk. 2nd row from left: Mike Boruk, Elsie Wozny Tryuda, Polly Mashiuk, Rose Baryluk, Paul Rohatyn, Mary Baryluk, Peter Gemby, Elsie Rohatyn, Tony Bachynski, Mary Harhura, Moskolu, Roman Tryuda.

scene as the strikers departed were three RCMP constables who, as instructed by Sergeant Mulhall, had not noticed anything requiring 'the enforcement of law and order.'

Events at the Taylorton mine were more sustained but no more successful from the operators' point of view. C.C. Morfit, mine director, had recruited twenty-five strike-breakers from outside the community and half a dozen special constables whom he planned to put up at the briquette plant. 'Even if we only load one car of coal a day,' said Sam Holley, the mine's manager, 'we will have broken the strike.'[13] But by the time automobiles containing strike-breakers drove up on Tuesday, 15 September, groups of strikers were already standing around on the road allowance, being watched by several RCMP officers from a distance. Morfit was unable to persuade the cooks there to feed the strike-breakers, so he requested a police escort from Sergeant Mulhall to take the scabs over to his Taylorton mine. There he had no better luck, being greeted by a dozen members of the womens' auxiliary and Elisabeth Sloan Uhrich, who ran that boarding house. She announced that she could not feed the men because the miners owned the well at Taylorton and they refused to supply any water for cooking or washing for the strike-breakers. Morfit did not give up and arranged for some provisions to be brought over from the company store.

Ever anxious to get the police involved, Morfit claimed that there were over a hundred strikers milling around the boarding house all night singing and shouting. But when Mulhall withdrew his force at midnight, he said that there was only one picket and a group of six men sitting at the side of one of the buildings playing a musical instrument and singing. Nothing happened that night. An ominous quiet fell over the coalfields. Since an attempt at starting up the mines was expected in the morning and there were pickets at all of them, Mulhall ordered his force, now swelled to eighteen officers, to be at the mines by 5:30 A.M., according to instructions, and he kept six officers in reserve with himself in case trouble developed somewhere. Heightening the tension was the well-publicized offer of the Canadian Defenders, a strike-breaking organization in Calgary headed by an ex-pugilist, ex-trade unionist, and ex-communist, Lewis Macdonald, alias 'Kid Burns,' to send 500 men to Estevan 'to protect loyal British subjects against the activities of Communists.'[14] Joe Forkin had responded with a telegram to the Lumber Workers' Union in Port Arthur, knowing that the police would intercept a copy: 'Rush five hundred unemployed union men to Bienfait carefully routed. Miners fighting for their lives and families.'[15]

The next morning, Wednesday, 16 September, 'saw the ghostly shapes of cars and lorries, each filled with striking miners, moving towards the Western Dominion Collieries,' wrote a reporter for the *Leader-Post*. When the police patrol arrived in Taylorton as the sun rose, there were already more than one hundred strikers and members of the womens' auxiliary standing about near the boarding house. Morfit again had to arrange for provisions to give breakfast to the men and his special constables, but apart from that there was no movement of strike-breakers towards the mine. Morfit was in no hurry. At nine o'clock, Sergeant C. Richardson, who was in charge of the patrol, noticed more trucks and numerous cars arriving, carrying strikers from other mines in the district. He informed both the strikers and the strike-breakers that the police patrol was neutral and was there only to keep the peace. The leaders on both sides promised that no violence or damage to property would occur. At noon, when the police were patrolling over at the company store, members of the womens' committee went into the boarding house, followed by some of the strikers. Morfit was waiting for this development and called for police assistance. Richardson went in and found the strikers standing at the foot of the stairs and the strike-breakers at the top. It was just after an incident where a strike-breaker had hurled a pick handle at one of the strikers who received a gash on the side of his head. Richardson telephoned Mulhall for reinforcements. In the meantime he directed the strikers to leave the building and order was quickly restored. Richardson made no arrests.

After this incident Morfit took Sergeant Richardson aside.

'Forget that you are a police officer,' said Morfit, 'and tell me, man to man, what would you do?'

'I would discharge the men [strike-breakers],' replied Richardson, looking him in the eye. 'There is no doubt that there will be trouble if you keep them on.'

This was not the answer Morfit wanted. In his frustration he blurted out, 'If this was in the States it would soon be settled. We deal with matters a lot differently. The strikers would be mowed down with machine guns if they carried on the way they do up here.'[16]

Boiling mad, Morfit ordered his payroll clerk to pay off all the strike-breakers and special constables. The battle of Taylorton was over. The jubilant pickets disbursed to the union hall in Bienfait. The operators had been tamed, a signal and historic victory for the union miners, a victory that had been made possible by their unity, by the attorney general's restrictions on the police force, and by the guidance of its local commander. To the astonishment of everyone, the forces of 'law and order' had behaved in a carefully measured fashion, putting people's rights ahead of property rights. Dan Moar, president, and Harry Hesketh, secretary, of Local 27 of the miners' union, Bessie Sherratt and Elizabeth Sloan of the women's auxiliary, Martin Joseph Forkin of the WUL, and Sergeant William Mulhall of the RCMP were local heroes while Sam Scarlett laughingly joked with the constabulary that he would be willing to help them organize themselves into a workers' union.

Sergeant Mulhall personified the unexpected attitude by the Mounties in the first ten days of the Bienfait miners' strike. Who was he?

His profile reveals a twenty-two-year veteran of the force who had fought in the Boer War and in the First World War; a man who was scrupulously honest and determined to enforce the law as he understood it. He had been in trouble with the mayor of Estevan for ensuring that the liquor laws were obeyed. Mayor David Bannatyne, who wanted a free hand even before the coal miners' strike, complained to the RCMP headquarters asking that something be done about this awkward sergeant.[17]

Mulhall apparently was content to be in charge of a small two-person detachment in semi-rural Saskatchewan. His chief pleasure was in marksmanship and he took pride in all the trophies he had won in various competitions across the province.[18] His lack of ambition to rise to higher ranks was perhaps a factor in his closeness to the pulse of the community in which he served and a reason for his remarkable willingness to stand up to pressures from the business and professional elite in Estevan.

He did make contact with the entrepreneurs of Estevan – the manufacturers, mine owners, mine managers and pit bosses, medical doctors – but they declared him to be unsociable, lacking in tact, devoid of the common-sense qualities required of a police officer. They wanted him removed. What particularly annoyed them was that Mulhall visited the mining camps, talked with the miners and, their families and without becoming overly familiar, became intimately aware of their deplorable living and working conditions. He thought that they needed a break and when they organized their union and staged pickets, which the bosses called unlawful assemblies, he declined to take forceful action. When he saw two hundred miners sitting quietly on a hillside near a mine entrance, he would report that everything was peaceful and drive on to the next mine. Sometimes he would speak to the striking men, warning them to keep off company property, and more than once he tried to facilitate meetings between the strikers and the employers, but mostly he told the owners that if they felt aggrieved by the strikers' behaviour they were always free to lay charges.

As a result of his contacts with the mine bosses during the strike, Mulhall became suspicious of their motives and their morality. Especially of C.C. Morfit. Mulhall had early expressed his opinion that Morfit, for his own business reasons, welcomed the prospect of a strike shutting down his briquette plant, which was losing money, so that the blame could be put on the strikers. In reporting to his superiors after the events of the previous days, Mulhall analysed the situation at Taylorton, contrasting his policy with that of Morfit and emphasizing that the coal operator was trying to provoke a crisis which would necessitate police interference:

> It seems that Mr. Moffatt [sic] brought in about two dozen men to act as strike breakers, the main object being to provoke the strikers to some overt act of violence thus creating a situation demanding police interference and promoting a crisis.
>
> My reason for arriving at this conclusion is that it would be impossible to work the mines at Taylorton with the number of men he brought in, particularly as they were inexperienced in the work they were to be employed at. Also as I have already stated no provision was made for boarding these men the cook having refused to cook meals for 'scabs.'
>
> Mr. Moffatt is an American with extreme ideas, who has experience in the Pennsylvania U. S. A. strikes, when riots occurred and the miners were literally 'mowed down' [;] his attitude is that the present situation should be handled by the police in a similar manner.
>
> It has been my endeavour to handle the situation with care and patience and it is to our credit that there has been no violence or destruction of property ... I am satisfied that at no time has there been any authentic reason for police interference, except perhaps at Taylorton on the 16th inst. In which connection I am having Sergt. Richardson who was in charge of the details at that point, render a separate report.[19]

The backlash by members of the elite class in Estevan was swift and vengeful. The Southern Saskatchewan Coal Operators' Association issued a public statement saying that the police had 'failed utterly' to offer protection to the mine owners.[20] The chief medical officer for the coalfields, Dr James Creighton, and Mayor Bannatyne, both of whom had mining investments,[21] were enraged at the lack of forceful police action. Backed by the mayor, Creighton wrote an angry letter to the federal minister of labour (with copies to all and sundry) calling the RCMP in Estevan a 'rabbit' force, 'a disgrace,' and Bannatyne demanded that Mulhall be sent somewhere else.[22] The police leadership in Regina resisted their demands at first, based on their analysis of the local situation. But when the head of the RCMP, General MacBrien, learned of the complaint, he disagreed. 'This seems peculiar,' he wrote. 'If the operators wished to take in strike-breakers they and their property should be given every protection unless there are some reasons for contrary action which is not explained.'[23] His opinion was an ominous indication of what was to come in the next ten days of the strike. The Regina depot gave in and removed Mulhall, although not without finding face-saving ways to affirm their confidence in the sharp-shooting sergeant as a diligent and competent police officer.[24]

The miners and their families, several hundred people in all, gathered at an open-air meeting in Bienfait on Friday afternoon, 18 September, to celebrate their achievement and to bolster their will and courage to carry the struggle on to victory. With Dan Moar, president of the local union, chairing the meeting, Sam Scarlett, the now familiar voice of the WUL, came to the platform first. 'The aim of this strike,' he said, 'is to secure humane working conditions, and it is receiving the widespread support of labour all over Canada.' Amid laughter, Scarlett mocked the press for calling the miners 'Red': 'The mine owners work us until we are white,' he said, 'then we feel blue, and finally the blood starts to run red in our veins and we are "Red."'[25] As he walked back and forth on the little makeshift stage at the corner of Main Street and Souris Avenue, he congratulated the miners for sticking together and advised them to keep together until the owners recognized the union. He warned them about diversionary tactics calculated to confuse the issue. 'This strike will be made a Flag issue before its finished,' he said. 'The good old Union Jack. They will give you flags for breakfast, dinner and supper and a flag for a blanket.'[26] At this very moment the sailors of the battleship HMS *Valiant*, flagship of the British Atlantic fleet, were on strike against drastic wage cuts imposed by the lords of the admiralty, wage cuts that the sailors said were 'the forerunner of tragedy, misery and immorality among the families of the lower deck.' The result was that 'the proudest ships of the navy lay idle and helpless while 12,000 sailors refused to obey orders.'[27] This was the kind of current news with which Scarlett liked to drive home a point. Who could be more British, more patriotic, than the men of the British navy? Even while cheering the king they had taken into their own hands the right to defend their families' livelihood. After explaining the mistreatment and advantages that capital had over working men and miners in particular, Sam ended with a rhetorical flourish: 'I defy the operators to recruit even 24 strike-breakers in the Estevan district at the present time.'

Joe Forkin, introduced as acting secretary of the MWUC in Sloan's absence, spoke of a fight to the finish. 'I have a certified cheque for $600 from our brothers in Calgary for strike relief,' he said, 'and there is more to come. The United Farmers of Canada, Saskatchewan section, has promised foodstuffs if we pay the freight.' He repeated his pledge that 'we will see that no mothers or expectant mothers or children will be hungry.' He referred to the report that Lewis Macdonald of Calgary was coming to Bienfait with five hundred strike-breakers to save Canada from communism. 'If it's a fight they want we will give them fight,' Forkin declared. 'Macdonald is one of the worst scab herders in America and for every man he brings here we will bring five unemployed men from Winnipeg. They will be able to get here. R.B. Bennett has taught the workers how to travel, and how to exist without money.' Forkin reflected on the allegation that the union was 'red,' an allegation that in his view was not something to be denied, conceded, or apologized about. 'The miners,' he said, 'have never asked the operators to recognize Soviet Russia; they have asked them to recognize a miners' union.' We must fight on, he concluded, 'and when the operators recognize the union you will go back to work under conditions of your own choice.'[28]

The other speaker was a newcomer, a Baptist preacher from Weyburn by the name of Thomas C. Douglas. Douglas and his wife, Irma Dempsey, had come to Estevan on the invitation of the Reverend Gordon Tolton, who, as already noted, was a strong supporter of the miners' union. The three Baptists spent the earlier part of the day touring the coalfields and talking to the strikers. Shocked by the things they saw and heard, Tommy Douglas accepted a spur-of-the-moment invitation to speak at the miners' open-air meeting in Bienfait. He greeted them on behalf of the Independent Labour Party of Weyburn. When it was pointed out to him that he was associating with 'reds,' he is reported to have said that it is a mistake to 'give up on a good cause because there are a few communists in it.'[29] There is no record of what he said at the meeting because the twenty-eight-year-old, who would become the doughty premier of Saskatchewan for almost twenty years, was still relatively unknown. But the encouragement he gave to the miners' cause may be inferred from the topic of his next sermon in Calvary Baptist Church in Weyburn: 'Jesus the Revolutionist. Would Jesus revolt against our present system of graft and exploitation? How would Jesus view the coal miners' strike in Estevan? Were he to come to Earth again would we crown him, crucify him, or merely deport him?'[30] Douglas organized a truckload of food for the strikers and their families. The epic struggle of the Bienfait coalminers would become a turning point in Douglas's thinking, leading him to leave the pulpit for the political arena.[31]

The greatest challenge to emerge from the activities of the previous few days was the fact that the Truax-Traer strip mining operation, whose machine drivers were not in the union and not on strike, had resumed full operations. On the Wednesday when Morfit, Wilson, and Wallace had failed to start up their mines, Truax shipped 125 boxcars of coal. On Thursday the company loaded and shipped another 75 rail cars. That evening the worried operators invited leaders of the strike committee to the Estevan town hall for negotiations. They wished to reach a solution in order to save their markets from their voracious competitor. But when the miners' delegation insisted on recognition of their union, the meeting ended five minutes later. C.C. Morfit was adamant. The operators would not recognize the miners' union because 'that union is an emissary of the Third International.' Even the government of Canada, he said, 'refuses to recognize the government of Russia.' This hypocrite, whose American parent company was up to its neck in dealings with the Soviet Union, could see no reason why the Saskatchewan operators should recognize an organization which he derided as 'communistic and Russian in its origin and government.'[32] The coal operators, having made a necessary gesture, went to Regina for another meeting with the provincial cabinet, at which they asked for more police protection to open their mines.

The provincial government listened but was hesitant about the operators' request for the moment and put forward another plan. This was to join with the federal government in appointing a royal commission to investigate conditions in the coalfields. The commission would begin hearings in October and the workers would be urged to return to work pending the results of the inquiry. If it worked, then this course of action would solve the operators' problems. But when the union miners heard about the proposal for a royal commission, they were not enthusiastic. The deplorable conditions were already well known. What they wanted was some instrument to change them. They were afraid that a royal commission hearing would be long and drawn out and that by the time its results were known the operators would have stockpiled enough coal for the season's orders and they would simply close down, leaving the strikers with no recourse.[33] The two governments went ahead anyway and on 19 September Prime Minister Bennett announced the appointment of district court judge Edmund R. Wiley, a Masonic Lodge member and United Church elder in Estevan, to head the commission.

Meanwhile, over the next few days there were more abortive meetings to find a settlement, mediated through the chief conciliation officer of the federal department of labour. Forkin and Scarlett believed that the strike was at a crucial turning point. Fearing that the miners would once more be put on the defensive by W.W. Lynd for seeming to be intransigent, while at the same time being unable to stop the production at the strip mine, they went to the International Hotel in Estevan on 22 September to meet the federal conciliator. They advanced the WUL's negotiating position that union recognition had ceased to be a precondition in the strike settlement. If discussions could take place for an agreement on wages and altered working conditions, the miners would return to work pending the results of the royal commission hearings. The federal conciliator arranged for a meeting with the operators.

But when James Sloan returned from Calgary the next day, he angrily denounced this concession, still insisting that the operators would have to concede union recognition before anything else could happen. The strike committee agreed with Sloan. Their union was a legitimate Canadian union which represented almost 3,000 coal miners in neighbouring Alberta. Why could it not come to Saskatchewan, if the miners here wanted it, without having aspersions cast upon their patriotism? Almost six hundred of them had taken out membership cards. What could be more democratic, more above board, and more 'British' than that? Unfortunately, they did not yet have the weight of the law on their side. That only came in 1944 when the CCF government in Saskatchewan, led by Tommy Douglas, passed a Trade Union Act establishing compulsory union recognition if a majority of workers requested it.[34] It was from the early struggles and sacrifices of the miners in Bienfait and workers elsewhere in Saskatchewan that the impetus for that law came.

For the union, the dye was cast. Since the operators would not meet them as a union, the union miners would have to try to find some way to shut down the stripping operation of Truax-Traer or else lose the strike and, as they thought, have their jobs disappear forever. This daunting challenge occupied the second ten days of the strike, from 18 to 28 September.

Chapter Six

Strikers versus the Strip Mine

To stand on the hillside and look out over the scene of high pressure activity is to realize that the finger of destiny is now pointing directly at Estevan and the Coalfields, and that an era of wide industrial expansion is in full swing.

– *Mercury*, Estevan, 1 May 1930

The whole disturbances and irregularities were started solely through the outside Communistic influences. The foreign element in the mines is uneducated and easily led.

– RCMP Inspector W.J. Moorhead, 24 September 1931

You are taking our bread and butter.

– banner, held by the women's auxiliary, MWUC, Bienfait,
at the strip mine, 24 September 1931

It was just a year since the Canadian Manufacturers' Association had heralded a new era of industrial development for the Estevan-Bienfait era. This optimism was based upon the decision of Truax-Traer Coal, of North Dakota and Illinois, to invest almost a million dollars in starting up a lignite strip mine on the coal-rich prairie two miles east of Estevan. The investment began a technological revolution in the method of coal mining.[1]

Instead of sinking a shaft and working underground to extract the coal and hoist it up to the surface, the new method exposed the vein of coal by stripping away the surface soil. This was accomplished by a giant electric shovel with a bucket capacity of eight cubic yards which heaped the soil on the side in slag piles thirty or more feet in height. Following along behind was a smaller electric digger which scooped up the coal for transportation on a narrow gauge railway to the tipple, where it was screened and graded in much the same way as at other mines. A little train of ten dump cars, each with a capacity of five tons, could be loaded with coal in less than eight minutes, about seven tons to the minute, compared with a miner working underground who would be fortunate to load seven tons in half a day. To cope with this extraordinary labour-saving capacity Truax-Traer built a tipple costing $100,000 which could handle 500 tons of lignite in an hour. This structure, 'representing the last word in engineering attainment,' produced five separate grades of fuel and sent it down to railway cars waiting on six lines of track running beneath the coal hoppers. The heaped-high railway cars then moved along two miles of track, passing over weigh scales, and on to the CPR or CNR yards in Bienfait for shipping.

It was observed that the mining camp laid out by Truax-Traer reflected its faith in the future of the coalfields. It had been designed 'with perma-nency, stability and attractiveness.'[2] It had an office building of brick and hollow tile, finished in the most modern style, providing a large general office 'in which only the latest equipment and accounting systems' were in use, executive offices for plant officials, and, on the second storey, bed-room suites for the accommodation of out-of-town directors. A triplex apartment house, also of modern construction, provided housing for mine officials and the sales force. Plans existed for the employment of seventy-five men after the plant was fully operational. When the miners' strike began in September 1931, however, there were only twenty-three workers at the plant, most of them young men from North Dakota. They found their own room and board in town and were picked up by a com-pany truck each morning. Living and working in such a fashion, these workmen had little contact or interaction with people in the community other than with the company by which they were employed, and when approached by union organizers they expressed no interest in joining.

Heading up this new enterprise as managing director was Eleazer W. Garner, former mayor and a Liberal member of the Legislative Assem-bly representing Estevan until the 1930 general election. Garner already had ten years' experience as a manager in deep-seam mining, and when Messrs Truax and Traer made him an offer, he converted the two sections of land he controlled into a 5 per cent ownership and a vice-presidency of the new enterprise, in this way giving the American capi-talists the necessary resources of coal to gain an initial foothold in the Saskatchewan market.

In a field of industry that was already overcrowded and suffering from chronic over-production, recurring unemployment, and social dislocation for hundreds of miners, how did Eleazer Garner imagine that he could pilot this new enterprise to success and still have any friends in the community? The new technology put in place by his company effectively doubled the productive capacity of the Estevan-Bienfait coalfield in one stroke! Could all this new investment pay dividends if Truax-Traer became just another mine working far below capacity?

Garner had no doubt talked these matters over with Arthur H. Truax, whose North Dakota and Illinois strip-mine operations had managed to come out on top in a similar situation. The Truax-Traer combination had driven the competing deep-seam operations out of the field in North Dakota, taking ownership of their coal leases in the process. And the North Dakota coal deposits, a few miles distant across the U.S. border, were similar to, one might say simply a southerly extension of, the Saskatchewan coalfields. With a superior technology in hand, was it not then just a matter of good management and hustle in the marketplace before the same success would occur in Canada? It was pointed out that, with competitors out of the way in North Dakota and Illinois, coal prices there were rising. One thing Truax probably did not discuss with the Canadian who had such a unforgetable biblical name was his company's connections with the criminal underworld in Chicago. It was these ruthless thugs who had given Truax-Traer a decisive edge in winning and keeping the tenders to supply coal for the furnaces of the municipal offices and schools in the hub of the American mid-west.[3]

Being a sophisticated man, Eleazer Garner likely had a well thought-out plan of action and public relations to launch the firm in Canada. A prime task was to raise the present annual consumption of Bienfait lignite coal from 500,000 tons to the 2,000,0000 tons required to make coal investments profitable. He would start by trying to enlist the owners of existing deep-seam mines in a campaign of education to acquaint the public with the benefits and economies that they could have by switching to lignite in both domestic and industrial applications. He also had an engineering department to design and promote efficient equipment for furnaces using this soft coal. Then he had a sales department employing four keen young men who were sent out to Regina and Winnipeg and all places in-between to gather up orders. Perhaps there were other hidden programs as well. When suggestions were put forward to stabilize the market by establishing a coal-marketing board similar to the boards that existed for eggs and milk, and grain under the Wheat Board, Garner would hear none of it. 'I think this thing will iron itself out,' he said, 'there is plenty of room for all the operating units that are in this field at the present time.'[4] He was all for competition in the market.

It was not as easy to break into the market as Garner had hoped since J.R. Brodie, acting for the major owners, 'the Group,' had the existing market in his pocket, complete with price-fixing and production limits.[5] Garner's salesmen found it tough going. Rival salesmen deprecated their product, saying to potential customers that 'surface-mine coal is inferior stuff, wet and mushy, something that even a gopher could dig out.' It soon became clear that the only recourse for Truax-Traer was to undercut their rivals' prices, selling at a loss if necessary, and thereby creating chaos in the market. Garner publicly and heatedly denied that he was selling at a loss, but confidential records forced out of him and kept secret by the royal commission investigating the miners' strike in 1931 revealed the price-cutting tactics he was employing. In order to stay in the business, J.R. Brodie's group was forced to lower their prices about 25 per cent in the year after Truax-Traer came on the scene, selling their coal for about $1.60 per ton, barely above cost, but they still could not match Garner's salesmen who were disposing of their product for a loss at $1.08 or even less. This was the tactic that Truax-Traer had used to bankrupt its competitors in North Dakota. It was only after the strike in Bienfait began in September, when rivals were out of the picture and his mine was able to continue producing with increased tonnage, that Garner raised prices to realize a profit.

In spite of some adverse environmental implications, the open-strip technology of coal mining was the wave of the future. There was no doubt about that. To try to restrict it by laying special taxes on it, as members of Brodie's group proposed, could not be done, Garner argued, unless it was decided that cheaper coal would not be of benefit to the two million consumers. 'Let me put it another way,' he said. 'Will anybody ask today that we should go back and cut our grain with a sickle? Will anybody put a law on the statute books to the effect that a tractor cannot be sold in the province of Saskatchewan, or a combine?'[6] But along the way to that restructured future of strip mining, did it have to be the miners who must shoulder the burdens and hardships of the transition? So far, that was what the wage cutting in 1931 had done. Supposedly driven by impersonal and invisible market forces, wages had been forced down by as much as 25 per cent in the year since the arrival of Truax-Traer.[7] The miners and their families were not Luddite-style machine smashers, but they gradually became aware that unless they

TABLE 6.1
Truax-Traer Coal Production and Profits
(Six months ending 31 October, 1931)

	Tonnage	Cost per ton	Average price rec'd per ton	Profit or loss	Profit or loss per ton
May	5,950	$3.46	$1.082	−$14,165	−$2.38
June	7,086	2.61	1.016	− 11,383	− 1.60
July	4,469	1.95	0.849	− 4,953	− 1.11
August	5,458	1.27	0.997	− 1,499	− 0.27½
September*	25,105	.78½	1.280	+ 12,434	+ 0.49½
October	40,533	.77	1.345	+ 23,256	+ 0.57⅓

*The strike in the deep-seam mines commenced.
Source: Wylie Commission, 1931, exhibits, folio 5, J.R. Cox, 'Confidential Data Submitted to the Commissioner, regarding the Truax-Traer Coal Company, Limited.'

confronted and exposed the rogue Truax-Traer operations that were playing havoc in the coal industry, their desperate struggle for union protection would be lost.

During the first week of the strike against Brodie's group of mines, the keen young salesmen of Eleazer Garner were out on the road working overtime knocking on doors. Garner was not yet shipping any coal, but he foresaw a golden opportunity to make gains at the expense of his competitors and he was stockpiling coal in 125 railway cars. Worried by the probable hostility of the miners when this news spread, he asked Sergeant Mulhall to allow him to hire six special constables armed with shotguns. Mulhall refused, saying that such a request would certainly 'increase the undercurrent of bad feeling' towards his company. Not seeing anything to substantiate Garner's fears, Mulhall advised him to hire a night watchman, unarmed.[8]

In the second week of the strike, on the same day that 'the Group' tried unsuccessfully to deploy strike-breakers, Garner had enough orders to send out the 125 pre-loaded rail cars. His mine was now working full blast, around the clock night and day. He hired on new workers and soon had sixty-three men on his payroll. In a few days he was making record shipments. But he was also fearful and kept telephoning Mulhall for police protection against miners' demonstrations that did not materialize. Since there were no pickets at this mine, Mulhall mistakenly thought that perhaps it was working with the consent of the mine workers' union.

As the third week of the strike began, with no break in sight, the strike committee decided that something had be done about the strip mine. A plan to approach the manager and the workers was set for Thursday, 24 September. By 7:00 A.M. that morning, several hundred strikers had arrived at the mine and a delegation of four led by Martin Day went to the office seeking an interview with Garner. But Garner was out of town and not expected back until the afternoon. The office secretary telephoned to Estevan for police protection. Other groups of strikers led by Dan Moar and William Klymyk went to the pits where the big shovels were operating, hoping to talk to the foreman and to request permission to speak to the men. While they were doing this, members of the womens' auxiliary unfurled large banners in the pit reading, 'YOU ARE TAKING OUR BREAD AND BUTTER,' and another showing a large shovel digging dollars on the Canadian side of the border and dumping them into the United States. By now, the fourteen RCMP officers stationed on strike duty in Estevan had arrived at the mine and stood on guard with guns and riding crops at the ready. Sergeant Mulhall walked to the pit. There he heard the foreman denying to members of the strike committee that Truax-Traer was filling orders which were usually the business of the deep-seam mines and refusing them permission to talk to his men. The foreman, backed by Mulhall, ordered the strikers off the property. There was some further discussion during which it was agreed that a committee of four would come back to the office at 6:00 P.M. for an interview with Garner. After Mulhall declared loudly that a gathering of this nature might be construed as an unlawful assembly, there was a consultation and show of hands among members of the strike committee followed by an announcement by Dan Moar, president of the union, telling everyone to return to Bienfait. Slowly the crowd drifted off.[9]

That afternoon Moar returned to the Truax-Traer mine accompanied by strikers Edward Knight, John Smythe of the M&S, and Jim McLean of Estevan, as agreed.[10] The delegation had some pointed questions to ask Eleazer Garner. They wanted to know why he was hiring American mechanics to operate his shovels when there were many unemployed Canadians available. Garner calmly replied that he would be quite happy to hire Canadians if he could find anyone capable of operating the shovels but had been unable to do so. The delegation complained that he was working in cooperation with the deep-seam mine owners to fill their orders for them while the strike was on. Garner flatly denied that this was the case. They requested him to appoint a day and an hour when they might come and speak to his employees. Again Garner said that he would be quite willing to do this but he had already questioned his employees in this connection and they had replied that they would not meet the committee. The delegation left empty-handed. Their attempts to contain the threat posed to the success of the strike by the activities of the strip mine were getting nowhere.

From an informant in the union, Mulhall gained the impression that there arose strong currents of dissension within the organization as a result of the failure to shut down the Truax-Traer mine. Some of the younger strikers, influenced by newly arrived Winnipeg agitators Isadore Minster, Orton Wade, and David Rowsen of the Unemployed Workers' Association, and supported by Sam Scarlett, thought that it had been an error not to rush in and have the men of the strip mine off the job before the police came. They were reportedly in favour of organizing an 'advance party' of about thirty men who, should the occasion arise again, would take orders from one man only and would be prepared to fight. No previous notice would be given to these strikers about when they were to gather at a particular place. They would be loaded into trucks and cars and would not know where they were going until they arrived at their destination. This sort of talk alarmed George Wilkinson, president of the Taylorton branch of the union, and some of his friends. Wilkinson said that he thought the strike was going to be conducted in a peaceful manner but was now coming to the conclusion that there was a 'red' element who thought differently. He was reported to have said that, if there was any 'red' connection in the mine workers' union, he would tear up his card and have nothing more to do with it.[11]

The potential split in the union was good news to the RCMP. The commander for the Southern Saskatchewan District, Inspector R.R. Tait, commented that Wilkinson's attitude 'will materially assist us in controlling the situation.' Tait estimated that 50 per cent of the strikers belonging to the union were not in sympathy with the 'red' propaganda being preached by Scarlett and others, but 'they do not go so far as to say they will relinquish their connection with the union.' How long the strike could go on was difficult to estimate because 'the strikers,' said Tait, 'are being supplied with the necessary means of subsistence through the various organizations.'[12]

Special Constable J. Eberhardt and a police stool-pigeon covered two crowded meetings of miners in Bienfait in as many days after the failed attempt to shut down the strip mine. They heard defiant workers condemning the newspapers and the government for not investigating their grievances, saying that 'the government will protect the rich mine owners but so far they failed to protect the poor working man.' A voice from the crowd shouted, 'Blow up the track.' The stool-pigeon summed up the proceedings by saying that 'the whole meeting to my mind is nothing else but a big stab from the communist party to paralyze the whole country with discontent and take the whole country under communist rule.' Neither of them heard of any plan to storm the strip mine.[13] However, Detective Sergeant Mortimer, to whom these men reported, was convinced that such an attack would occur in the next few days and he telephoned Regina for police reinforcements.

In response to Mortimer's call, Inspector F.W. Schutz hurried to Estevan for a second time, arriving after dark the same day. He had with him, crouching on the floor of his automobile, an undercover operative, who was taken to the Truax-Traer mine to be hired on as an 'ordinary' worker. Kucey's task was to identify strikers if they came in to persuade the workers to cease work. Inspector W.J. Moorhead, with eleven armed men, arrived from Regina by automobile at 5:00 A.M. the next morning and went straight to the strip mine so that his presence would be noted. From now on there would be a twenty-four-hour police presence to prevent the big American investment from being closed down.

The members of the Brodie 'Group' continued to be highly incensed at the lack of police protection for themselves. They spent another half-day in the provincial capital arguing their case to the cabinet but apparently got nowhere since the cabinet preferred to await the results of the royal commission hearings. 'The Group' vented its anger in a lengthy telegram to Attorney General M.A. MacPherson which they released to the press. The strike, they said, was 'fostered one hundred per cent by communists' and 'information spread over the country by this communist movement of deplorable working conditions ... is entirely false.' The deep-seam companies, 'financed entirely by British and Canadian capital' and employing five hundred men, had contributed greatly over the years to the growth and prosperity of Estevan/Bienfait and now they were forced to lie idle for lack of police protection against mob rule. In contrast, the newest and largest operation in the field, financed 95 per cent by American capital and employing only fifty men, was running to capacity. 'Our deep seam mines will very rapidly lose their markets ... we are compelled and must resume operations immediately ... It is our right to operate our plants and it is our right to demand the necessary police forces to ensure protection to life, property and the peaceful operation of our industries.'[14]

It was against this continuing pressure from the deep-seam operators and their refusal to recognize the union that the strike leadership sought to concentrate attention. They would have to exert counter-pressure, try to keep their ranks united, and cope with growing hardships now that the company stores had cut off credit and miners were facing the prospect of eviction from their homes. Unfortunately, James Sloan stubbornly kept to his negotiating tactic of recognition of the union before anything else, leaving everyone in the dark about the concrete demands on wages and working conditions and making it impossible to put the operators on the defensive short of their total capitulation.

Somehow, George Oliver, owner of the hardware store on Main Street and an elder of Trinity United Church in Bienfait, heard that a talented thirty-five-year-old woman organizer of the WUL from Ontario was in Winnipeg and would be available to come over to Bienfait for a few days. A good speaker, such a person might be able to inject new spirit into a three-week-old strike that was beginning to languish. Oliver was sympathetic to the miners' cause and he offered to pay her rail fare.[15] This was how Annie Buller, one of the legends of the miners' strike, came to Bienfait.

Another Bienfait merchant, Bill Adler, and his wife, Eva, agreed to have Annie as their house guest and provided her with a room at the back of their general store which was also located on Main Street just north of the Red Hall. Annie spent time touring the coalfields with women active in the strike and then had various conferences with the women's auxiliary, especially over the issue of the distribution of strike relief. The farmers and unions had been generous in sending relief supplies, and miners' families with vegetable gardens and livestock shared with neighbours in need, but still there were cases of severe hardship not being looked after. This was especially true among some of the foreign-born workers. When selecting people to the strike committee and the women's auxiliary, Joe Forkin had tried to give these bodies an all-English complex, catering to the anti-foreign and chauvinistic sentiments that were so widespread in the Estevan district. This was a mistake; a majority of the miners, perhaps 60 per cent, were from continental Europe, and so Forkin's approach excluded some of the best and most active people. When it came to relief distribution, some needy cases were not properly brought to the attention of the committee.[16] Buller spent her first day in Bienfait trying to resolve some of the apparent difficulties, sharing her experiences from other strike situations and building up the sense of solidarity.

On the next day, Sunday, 27 September, there was an open-air meeting. Hundreds turned out, their interest heightened no doubt by the remarkable prospect of a woman addressing a gathering of coalminers. Buller was a great admirer of Sam Scarlett's platform style and followed his example in thinking that a meeting of workers would not be complete without giving some outline of the bigger picture, the current situation, not only in Canada but throughout the world. Unfortunately, there is no record of Buller's speech other than the 'secret' notes made by a stool-pigeon and an RCMP officer. But in view of the role that interpretations of her speech would play in subsequent events, it is worthwhile to notice what these two men wrote down at the time.

The stool-pigeon's report offered considerable detail. 'Anna' Buller had been to Berlin and Soviet Russia but had not seen such bad conditions as in the Estevan district; she dwelt on the miners' grievances and ridiculed Prime Minister Bennett, his starvation budget and all election promises, 'for which she obtained applause.' The present government had not sent police stool-pigeons and agitators to help the miners but to help mine owners and capital. She urged the miners to stay together and fight because their fight was the workers' fight all over Canada. The stool-pigeon concluded by quoting Buller as saying, 'We are going to help you with ammunition in the way of men and food and see that you are well protected, but the only thing I ask you is to, be united, go over the top of Truax mine and make those men quit working.' Detective Staff Sergeant Mortimer, head of the criminal investigation branch in Saskatchewan, wrote only one sentence, to the effect that 'Anna Buller,' a 'well-known woman organizer of Winnipeg,' dealt with all aspects of the situation, 'condemning the Coal Operators for the working conditions of the men and the living conditions of their families' and claiming that the 'working masses of Canada were behind the miners in their fight and would support them.' He took a photograph of her speaking from the platform.[17] Neither the stool-pigeon nor Mortimer made any comment about her remarks being seditious or an incitement to attack the police. Inspector W.J. Moorhead, who saw her from his car window as she was speaking, made no move at that moment to have her arrested because of something she said or did or any effect she was having on the crowd. But later, when the police wanted to pin an accusation of 'incitement to riot' on her, they changed their tune.

Chapter Seven

The Parade

Somebody has a lot to answer for ... It is fairly certain that, had the parade permit been granted, no loss of life would have resulted. This has been the usual experience in the past. Surely a parade is an absurd issue on which to stake life and death.

— *Manitoba Free Press*, 1 October 1931

They broke that union up through all their mounties and machine guns. The shooting put a lot of hatred in people's hearts, something which to this day has never all died out.

— Thomas Hesketh, Bienfait miner, interview by Michelle Rohatyn in 1979

The strike committee decided to hold a parade from the coalfields into Estevan culminating in a meeting at the town hall. It was scheduled for Tuesday, 29 September, two days after the open-air meeting in Bienfait where Annie Buller spoke. Its purpose was to win public support. The parade turned into a massacre: three miners shot dead and more than twenty people wounded by the town police and the RCMP.

The community was astonished. 'Even today we are puzzled that something this savage could happen in our midst,' said the member of the Legislative Assembly for Estevan as he stood at the spot of the massacre addressing a commemorative gathering sixty years later. He decried the greed, stubbornness, and intolerance that 'once led to senseless murder in the name of law and order' and he warned that it could happen again unless we constantly remind ourselves that our society today has no place for yesterday's inequities.[1]

How did it come about? What happened? The answer to this question is coloured by the fact that there were many 'eye-witnesses' to the events. The version that dominated the news at the time and for many years afterwards was that put out by the police and spread by the newspapers across the country. Wishing to deflect responsibility for the tragedy from themselves, they depicted the miners as intent on mayhem and riot in Estevan on that September afternoon.

Informed by Inspector W.J. Moorhead, who headed an RCMP presence of fifty men from Regina, no less a person than the commissioner himself, General J.H. MacBrien, who was in Regina at the time, sent a telegram to authorities in Ottawa reconstructing the events, a reconstruction that was as lurid and exaggerated as it was deceitful. According to this account, five hundred miners marched on the town of Estevan carrying the Red Flag and armed with clubs. MacBrien stated that the chief constable of Estevan met the parade on the outskirts of town and advised the leaders of a proclamation by the mayor prohibiting any parade through the town. Two strikers allegedly attacked the chief, rendering him unconscious. The strikers reportedly completely destroyed the Estevan fire engine sent to spray the crowd, and they caused $60,000 damage to the stores along the street. The rioters, it is claimed, rushed twenty-four RCMP officers who were present, engaging in hand-to-hand combat and opening fire with guns, seriously injuring eight police officers. The police retaliated, resulting in the death of three strikers and some wounded. Ten rioters were arrested and the riot quelled. In case of some reoccurrence, MacBrien had that night dispatched to Estevan by special railway car an additional forty men led by Inspector C. Rivett-Carnac and fully equipped with rifles and machine guns.[2]

Another version is recorded by Chris Higgenbotham, a staff reporter for the *Leader-Post*, who accompanied the procession from Bienfait along the highway to Estevan. 'It started so simply and peacefully,' he wrote. 'One might have imagined the miners and their wives were starting out for a big picnic.' The men stood around in groups in the village laughing and talking. Women and children crowded into the waiting automobiles. On one of the cars was 'the white ensign of the British navy.' Children turned out from the small schoolhouse to wave and the miners returned salutations. The procession drove into Estevan along Fourth Avenue (which was also no. 39 provincial highway) to the new court house and cenotaph where the police had cordoned themselves to block the roadway. Instead of stopping, the lead truck dodged up Souris Avenue. 'The onlookers laughed. The joke was on the police ... We saw the police rush to stop the lorry ... Still no thoughts of trouble.'

Higgenbotham said that 'the storm that was to take a toll of two lives and leave a score of injured broke with startling suddenness.' He saw a lorry dart past the police cordon and make its way at breakneck speed down the main street. A crowd of strikers and their women bore down on the police cordon. A banner bearing a protest against 'Starvation Wages' was trampled under foot as a mob formed around the police. 'In the mêlée that ensued riding crops and batons flashed into action.' The fight developed bitterly. The miners picked up pieces of iron from a nearby dump and showered them at the policemen. The police retreated back to the wall of the town hall with 'the women throwing rocks with precision.' To 'the din and clamour' was added the shriek of a siren as the fire engine arrived on the scene to spray water on the strikers. Higgenbotham then went to look for a telephone to call his editor. When he returned, people were 'scurrying for shelter.' The Mounties had drawn their revolvers and started shooting. One striker fell dead with a bullet through his heart. Mounted policemen lost their hats in the fray and 'the hats were kicked about by the women.' Suddenly, police reinforcements arrived from the Truax-Traer mine; 'they tore down the main thoroughfare at breakneck speed,' led by Inspector W.J. Moorhead. 'I saw rifles leveled,' wrote Higgenbotham, 'and bullets could be heard whizzing through the air.' Another man was shot dead. Arrests were made. The strikers retreated. The battle of Estevan was over. On the streets of Estevan, men and women asked each other, 'What will happen next?'[3]

In a confidential letter to the attorney general of the province, the commander of the Southern Saskatchewan District of the RCMP, Inspector R.R. Tait, confessed that 'it has been a difficult matter to obtain a connected story of what actually took place.'[4] The 'connected story' that the police eventually put together came to light in the mass court trials that unfolded in Estevan six months later.

The miners had their own versions of what happened, depending on where they were in the procession of sixty-three cars and trucks. Opinions differed on various points but a general consensus on the events of the parade might flow something as follows.

The union leaders met on Sunday, 27 September, after Annie Buller spoke, to determine what further initiative they could take as a means of putting pressure on the coal operators to begin negotiations to end their harsh conditions of work. Based on stool-pigeon rumours, the police thought that the strikers were going to shut down the strip mine and they placed a large contingent of men there to forestall an attack.

The strike committee, however, had no intention of attempting a confrontation with an armed force. Moreover, the Strassburg Resolution never contemplated or recommended such a move. Instead, the miners had already booked the Estevan town hall for Tuesday evening, when President James Sloan would reveal for the first time the list of detailed demands formulated by the union. Leading into the meeting, they now planned to have a parade with banners proclaiming their grievances to attract public attention to their cause. Impressed by Buller's speech that afternoon, they decided to take advantage of her presence to have her speak on 'The Truth About the Strike' in the town hall.

The word was spread and on Monday the union committee worked all day with Sloan to put the finishing touches to the union's negotiating document. Martin Day contacted all the picket captains to inform everyone of the plans: cars and trucks bringing participants from Taylorton would congregate at Bienfait around 1:30 P.M. and move from there to the Eastern and Crescent collieries to pick up more men and women en route in time to arrive in Estevan around 3:00 P.M. Meanwhile, at the union hall people busied themselves preparing signs and banners: 'We refuse to starve,' 'Down with the company stores,' 'We want houses, not piano boxes.' John Billis went over to Jake Lishinsky's store to ask if he would drive his truck to take demonstrators into Estevan. The Bienfait merchant, who owned a brand new 1931 Ford truck, agreed, not asking for money.

Determined not to allow the miners to air their grievances in Estevan, Mayor Bannatyne called an emergency meeting of the town council at 10:30 A.M. on Tuesday morning. The council, which was composed entirely of business and professional people, passed a motion proposed by councillors James Parkinson (a mine operator) and W.D. Niblett (a foreman). It stated that 'no public demonstration or parade be allowed in any public place in the Town of Estevan by strikers or operators and that the chief of police and Inspector Moorhead be placed in charge to prevent any such public demonstration or parade.' Another unanimous motion resolved 'that the Town Hall shall not be rented to either operators or strikers for the purpose of holding any public meetings and that all parties be so notified.' In pretending to be impartial as between the workers and employers, the councillors demonstrated once again the truth of Anatole France's ironic aphorism that 'the law in its majestic equality forbids the rich and poor alike from sleeping on park benches.' When the meeting ended at 11:15 A.M., the town clerk set about informing the parties concerned by telephone, telegram, and letters. The chief of police, McCutcheon, requested Inspector Moorhead of the RCMP to help him 'prohibit such parade or meeting in the Town Hall; and the carrying of banners.'[5] Banners, apparently, were dangerous things and the mayor ordered the Reverend Gordon Tolton, of Stirling Baptist Church, to remove signs supporting the miners' cause from the lawn of his church.

The telegram to James Sloan read: THE COUNCIL HAVE RESOLVED UNANIMOUSLY THAT NO PARADE BE ALLOWED IN THE TOWN OF ESTEVAN NOR MEETING IN THE TOWN HALL. WRITING. A.B. STUART, TOWN CLERK. In this message Stuart neglected to mention that Inspector Moorhead and the police would be on hand to enforce the resolution. Belatedly, hours after the tragic events of Tuesday had passed, and with an eye to establishing culpability, Stuart posted a letter to Sloan to confirm the telegram, this time including the previously omitted notice of the council's instructions to the police.[6] This letter arrived a day later, on Wednesday morning.

By the time Sloan received the Tuesday telegram and had gathered Dan Moar, local president, and other available members of the strike committee for consultation, it was already past noon and miners and their wives from the scattered mining camps were assembling at Bienfait under the direction of Martin Day. It was too late to cancel everything. 'After some discussion,' Dan Moar recalled, 'it was the opinion of the committee at Bienfait, that while the Town Council might prohibit a walking parade, the resolution would not apply to a motor-car procession.' The committee believed that the automobiles could safely travel on Highway 39, which ran through the centre of Estevan, because the town did not have legal jurisdiction over provincial highways. The participants would be instructed not to get out of their vehicles. The procession would pass through the town with banners flying and then back again for an open-air rally without running afoul of the town council's edict. The miners had no knowledge of the town council's instructions to the police, and if they had known, said Moar afterwards, 'the miners would never have attempted to hold either parade or motor-car procession in Estevan.'[7]

With a light piece of wooden lathe in hand, Martin Day lined up the procession. Leading off with a huge Union Jack was Lishinsky's new truck, driven by Jake and carrying about twenty-five people including John Billis, his son-in-law Peter Markunas, Steve Baryluk, Peter Gemby, and probably some members of the women's auxiliary. Passengers in the lead car included Joe Forkin; then came William Cunnah driving a

Buick coupe with union president Dan Moar, secretary Harry Hesketh, and Sam Scarlett as passengers, followed by a vehicle with Katherine Carroll, Stella Boruk, Mary Scribialo, Anne Sernick, and Jean Mc-Cosky,[8] members of the women's auxiliary. Martin Day was in a car in the middle of the sixty-three-vehicle procession.

The reason for providing all this detail on the organization of the procession is that one of the widely believed lies spread about the union leaders and the WUL organizers was that they knowingly sent the miners and their families into a police ambush and that they themselves were absent. This was not the case. All the local leaders of the union and two of the national leaders of the WUL were at or near the front of the cavalcade as it headed into Estevan. Whether Buller was in the procession or not is a matter of controversy to be settled later. Of the important mine union leaders, only Sloan was absent. He stayed in Bienfait, reportedly working out the fine print of the negotiating document that he was going to release to the press at the public meeting later in the day. He may have had another reason that only he and the police were aware of, namely, he was under suspended sentence for 'incitement to riot' for an incident in the Alberta coalfields and liable to forfeit of a $2,000 bond if he failed to 'keep the peace.'[9] Buller was under a similar restraint for her part in leading an unemployed demonstration of the WUL in Hamilton, Ontario, two years earlier and she was still required to report to a probation officer in Toronto once every month.

With Martin Day running up and down the line issuing instructions, the motorcade set off slowly westward, stopping at Crescent Collieries to pick up additional participants. When it reached the outskirts of Estevan at First Street, the Union Jack flying high from Lishinsky's truck and banners waving from cars, there was no police chief or anyone else there to warn about not proceeding farther. Inspector Moorhead was waiting expectantly with twenty men two miles south of the highway at the Truax-Traer strip mine. The first indication Jake Lishinsky had that something was amiss was when he arrived at Souris Avenue (Tenth Street) in the heart of downtown and saw a line of Mounties who had cordoned themselves across the roadway in front the new courthouse and the war memorial cenotaph. He swung right along Souris without stopping, the cars following him, and then right again around the block to come back to the highway. Should he turn left and head back to Bienfait or turn right and try again to lead the motorcade down the highway through Estevan? It was a fateful decision made in a few split seconds, possibly in conversation with John Billis or whoever was sitting in the cab of the truck with him. Lishinsky turned right. Followed by two or three of the lead cars, he easily drove through the police cordon which was by now much thinned out since many officers had run down Souris Avenue to prevent the procession from bypassing them on other east-west streets to the north of the highway. Lishinsky and the others parked their vehicles on the highway by Goodman's store near Twelfth Street and, contrary to plans, everybody jumped onto the sidewalk and began walking back to Tenth Street to see what was happening. The whole way was lined with curious spectators from the town, shopkeepers, trades-men, farmers, unemployed, merchants, lawyers, town councillors, the mayor; A.C. Wilson and the other mine operators were also there.

By now the motor-car procession had ground to a halt, caught in a cul-de-sac made by the police inadvertently or otherwise. It was at this point that reporter Chris Higgenbotham saw the police swinging their riding crops and batons, whacking people through open car windows, telling them to get moving. The cars that had followed Lishinsky's lead around the block found their passage stopped by the rear cars of the procession that clogged the highway. It was impossible to move any-where. C.C. Morfit was about to gain his wish for gunfire.

Martin Day came running up, the lathe still in his hand. When the blustering, red-faced town police chief, McCutcheon, confronted him, Day tipped the chief's hat off onto the ground with the lathe. Realizing what he had done, he dropped the stick immediately, but the incident gave the Mounties an opening to make an arrest. As Day was dragged off, some of the miners tried to save him and the mêlée was on. A few more arrests were made. Then, as pre-arranged by the police, the fire truck roared up, attached its hose to the hydrant on Souris Avenue, and began to spray the crowd. One of the miners, Nick Nargan, found an axe on the back porch of a neighbouring house and was in the act of chopping the fire hose when Chief McCutcheon shot him through the heart with his revolver. For the next ten minutes there was mayhem. The people were enraged at this act of murder. By all accounts, apart from fisticuffs and hand-to-hand fighting with the police at close quar-ters, some people began to pick up stones and bits of metal from a scrap heap to hurl at them. Fearing that some of the demonstrators would get in behind them, the twenty-four Mounties, many of them cut and bruised by now, backed up towards the town hall at Eleventh Street. Here they drew their revolvers and began firing. It was at this moment that Inspector Moorhead arrived with reinforcements armed with rifles. They levelled their guns and started shooting. Julian Gryshko fell dead.

Dozens were wounded. People scattered. As the police gave chase, firing on the run, members of the women's auxiliary stood their ground protecting their men. Elizabeth Sherratt Davies opened her coat and shouted out defiantly, 'Here, shoot me first!'[10] Tekla and Stella Boruk and Ellen Pryznyk, age seventeen, were arrested and taken to the town jail to join about ten men already in police custody.[11]

Some of the injured miners fled in cars back to Bienfait, fearful of being arrested. Others, more seriously wounded, were carried by their comrades to Dr Creighton's hospital, only to be cursed at and told that patients must pay a week's deposit in advance to be admitted to the hospital. Angry and desperate, strike committee member Jim McLean lost no time in getting a car to take the two most seriously wounded miners to Weyburn General Hospital, which was fifty miles distant. The two were Peter Markunas, twenty-eight, with a gunshot wound in the abdomen, and Steve Baryluk, fifty-three, father of nine children, shot in the hip. It was too late for Markunas. He died two days later after an emergency operation, while Baryluk underwent a long convalescence before he could resume work. For their part, the RCMP, who ascertained that McLean had 'guaranteed all expenses' to Dr J. McGillivray of Weyburn, tried unsuccessfully to locate and arrest him 'as a ringleader' during his mission of mercy.[12]

Among those returning to Bienfait after the police charge were the WUL organizers Joe Forkin and Sam Scarlett. They went immediately to Boruk's Boarding House where, together with Sloan and Buller, they decided on a plan of action to defend the strikers and save the union. The main thing was to get some new organizers in quickly and to publicize what happened in Estevan in order to raise defence funds. If they stayed in Bienfait, they would soon become the object of police interference and a liability for the defence efforts; if they left, they would be subject to criticism that they had run away. They decided to take that risk and leave immediately to get help. Miners with cars were ready to assist their departure. Sloan and Scarlett headed west while Forkin and Buller travelled east through Brandon to Winnipeg. Next morning the RCMP issued warrants to detachments across the prairies for the arrest of the four leaders, who were 'wanted,' they said, 'in connection with rioting at Estevan, Sask.'[13] A massive campaign of repression and police terror to destroy the miners' union and to put the deep seam mines back into production had begun.

Chapter Eight

Sticking with the Union

Red propaganda is busy ... Unless it is hit, and hit hard, right now, there will be troublous times.

                     – *Mercury*, 1 October 1931

It appears to me that the moment a man submits himself to be appointed on a Committee or some position in a Union, and he has nerve enough to approach the Owners on behalf of the workers, he is immediately branded a Red. I have not yet interviewed the Owner or Manager of a mine in regard to the red element, that has not given me the names of all of the men on the Pit Committee and the names of some official of the Union.

          – Detective Sergeant J.G. Metcalfe, RCMP, Estevan, 3 December 1931

I defy these operators to say that I am anything but an honest Englishman ... but the way I have been used it is enough to make me a Red.

          – Harry Hesketh, secretary-treasurer, Local 27, MWUC, Bienfait, 31 October 1934

We were blacklisted. Why? They called us Bolsheviks, we backed up the labour class. We belonged to labour organizations.

          – Alex Konopaki, Bienfait, miner, b. 1901, in 1979 interview by Michelle Rohatyn

The day following 'the parade' ninety fully armed mounted police,[1] led by inspectors Moorhead and Rivett-Carnet, descended on Bienfait, a village of five hundred souls, to carry out calculated acts of intimidation. They placed machine guns in strategic places – at the Saskatchewan Wheat Pool Elevator pointing across the street to Boruk's Bakery and Boarding House, on the verandah of the King Edward Hotel, on Main

Street opposite the Red Hall of the Ukrainian Labour Temple – giving an impression that chaos and revolution were imminent. All day long, posses went on the rampage, searching homes in the village and in the mining camps looking for wounded miners, making further arrests, and generally spreading an atmosphere of terror. Boruk's place was surrounded and Moorhead himself barged through the rooms looking for Sloan, Forkin, Scarlett, and Buller, only to discover that they had left the previous evening. Constant day and night armed patrols were maintained for two weeks throughout the area.[2]

The next day, the new organizers of the WUL arrived in Bienfait. They came quietly so as not to arouse the attention of the police. Sloan had arranged to send two men from Alberta – John Stokaluk, national secretary of the MWUC, and James Bryson, a leader of the Unemployed Workers' Association in Lethbridge, while Forkin and Buller had contacted the Canadian Labor Defense League (CLDL) in Winnipeg. The CLDL sent John Weir, a member of the Ukrainian Labour-Farmer Temple Association and, like Sam Carr, a recent graduate of the Lenin School. Weir brought with him the news that Annie Buller would be addressing a mass rally in Market Square in Winnipeg the following Sunday, 4 October. The CLDL also sent a Winnipeg defence lawyer, Soloman Greenberg, and later sent two other lawyers from Regina, W.H. Heffernan and Frank J.G. Cunningham. These three lawyers were to appear at the hearings of those who had been arrested.

The first task was to arrange a funeral for the three miners who had been shot down in Estevan, a funeral that would comfort their relatives and do honour to the cause for which they had laid down their young lives. It would be a public occasion and their coffins were placed in the Red Hall where people could openly come to pay their respects. And they came by the hundreds. Since the body of Peter Markunas had to be returned from Weyburn, the funeral was not scheduled until Sunday, 4 October. In a remarkable defiance of the continuing police intimidation, the miners' union declared a six-day period of mourning in the coalfields, firmly rebuffing pressure from the operators for immediate negotiations to reopen the mines.

On the day of the funeral, a large crowd gathered on Main Street in front of the Red Hall. Observers recalled the scene.[3] At 3:45 P.M., miners, their wives, and children – fifteen hundred by police estimate – took their places in the funeral procession. The women were first, several of them carrying babies in their arms. The men stood four abreast. Some of them held banners invoking honour to the dead: 'They fought for bread; they got bullets instead,' 'Honour to martyrs for the workers' cause,' 'Murdered by the bosses hired police thugs.' 'A solemn stillness descended upon the village, broken only by the shuffling of feet and the hushed voices of those in charge as they organized the cortege.'

Then, out of the meeting hall, eighteen members of the union, all ex-service men, bore upon their shoulders three simple caskets. Strewn on the tops were beautiful wreaths of flowers, many of them prepared by the wives of the strikers. An advance guard of union men, all of them veterans of the First World War, took its position at the head of the procession and the impressive gathering moved slowly away up Main Street, west on Railway Avenue, past Boruk's Boarding House and the Saskatchewan Wheat Pool elevator, and on to the concession road and the cemetery, half a mile north of the village. In the slanting rays of the late afternoon sunshine, the pallbearers laid the three caskets beside one large grave, while a group of women sang the chant-like measures of a Ukrainian funeral hymn. Then A. Brock (actually John Weir), an official of the CLDL of Winnipeg, stepped forward and in a low voice read the burial text from the *Handbook of the Western Federation of Miners*:

Fellow Workers – today we are gathered here for the purpose of paying a last tribute of respect to our departed brothers, who but a short time since were with us, sharing our joys and sorrows, but have now passed on into the great beyond from whence none return.

We do not understand life, how then can we understand death: but we do believe that death is only the entrance to a fuller and better life. Our presence here today and our tokens of respect would be mere symbols if we did not believe that out of the great infinity beyond the comprehension of mankind, the soul of our departed brothers are looking down on us today, conscious of our reverence.

Our departed brothers shared the ambitions and hopes that are common to most of us: the right collectively to work and live in peace, getting that portion of this world's rewards that would keep them and those they loved in comfort and decency, and at the end that their brother workmen would tenderly place them to rest in the graves of their fathers.

They have, therefore, left us a duty to see that we make every endeavour to realize for their loved ones and all others who must pass this way, the rewards for which they hoped.

And so we lay on the grave of our departed brothers these evergreens as a token of our respect and esteem, believing that this world is a better place because of them having been here. Amen.[4]

Someone read a translation of the prayer in Ukrainian, followed by the singing of another Ukrainian hymn. Then, from the huge crowd, swelled the familiar strains of 'Nearer My God to Thee,' interjected spontaneously by the English-speakers. As the coffins were lowered into the grave, a reporter noticed the young wives of Gryshko and Markunas almost overcome with grief and men weeping unashamedly. 'Impressively simple and sincere, the ceremony was concluded.' That evening a further memorial gathering took place at the union hall with a mandolin orchestra from Moose Jaw in attendance.

Concurrent with the memorial meetings in Bienfait, a large rally gathered in Winnipeg's Market Square to hear Annie Buller speak on 'Murder in Estevan!' Thousands of people wanted to know the truth of what happened. The tension was high in the crowd since everyone knew that police were waiting to pounce on her. She rose to the challenge, roundly condemning the coal operators, the Estevan police, and the RCMP for their treatment of the miners and appealing to the crowd to help arrested strikers. She spoke of the murdered men: 'They were good union men, loyal workers, who faced death every day when they went underground – men with callouses on their hands who had given the best years of their lives to building up the industry – men who loved their families – men who did not own shares and did not exploit their fellow men – men who died for the union – eternal glory to them!'[5]

The crowd was greatly affected, protecting Buller from arrest by keeping tightly packed around the platform and contributing hundreds of dollars to the miners' defence fund. The RCMP had tried but failed to seize her before the rally. As a result, they put half a dozen detectives in the square to effect her capture immediately afterwards. But as she stepped off the platform she exchanged her trademark hat, which sported a small white feather, for another woman's hat and put her glasses in her pocket. The police arrested the wrong person. They mistakenly detained several other women 'of the same size, build and general appearance.' Buller walked away free, proceeding on to Toronto to continue with her organizing work and to report to her probation officer. It took the red-faced Mounties two months to figure out where she was. When Steve Baryluk's family, who had been members of the Green Hall in Bienfait, heard of this episode years later, they were quite astonished. 'We thought she had run away from Bienfait a coward,' they exclaimed. 'And here she was, a woman ahead of her time!'[6]

The coal operators and other members of the local business elite were thoroughly alarmed by the show of sympathy and community support for the union and for the strikers which the massive turnout for the martyrs' funeral represented. They determined to reverse this situation. By a campaign of deceitful propaganda and careful organizational measures – some open and some secret – they would try to break up the union and end the strike on their terms. But the union had made a deep impression among the miners, and although weakened by defections, it held together under its committed leaders, Moar, Hesketh, and Harris, continuing as an instrument to protect the workers and as a means to wage the class struggle.

The first event after the six days of mourning was the opening of the royal commission in the Estevan courthouse on Monday, 5 October. It was a reassuring development for the miners, giving them a place to air their demands publicly, and they planned to cooperate fully with the investigation.

The commissioner, District Court Judge E.R. Wylie, a long-time resident of Estevan and elder in the local United Church, was a sympathetic and fair-minded individual, as was the local agent of the attorney general, W.J. Perkins, a Roman Catholic and member of the Estevan Conservative Association, who was legal counsel for the commission. The miners began by putting forward two key witnesses, John Howell Harris and Harry Hesketh, secretary of Local 27, both from Brodie's Bienfait mine. The judge was so impressed by Harris's command of the subject and detailed presentation on what was wrong in the industry that he accepted him as 'Technical Advisor on behalf of the Miners' for the duration of the five-week sitting. In that capacity Harris heard everything that transpired and could cross-examine W.W. Lynd, counsel for the operators, when he made statements that were out of line. After the first day, when the workers had put their grievances on the record and before the operators had a chance to respond, Judge Wylie adjourned the hearings to allow for negotiations to reach an agreement to end the strike. For the miners it was a good beginning. They exposed the operators for their greed, their contempt for the Mines Act, their lawlessness.

The operators hoped for an immediate return to work pending the results of the royal commission but the strike committee insisted that there be initial concessions on wages and working conditions. In the face of this impasse, the provincial government stepped in, sending deputy minister of labour Thomas Molloy to mediate, backed by the continued heavy police presence.

After a four-hour session on 6 October, at the Estevan town hall, Molloy announced an eight-point truce pending findings of the royal commission. In the temporary agreement, management agreed to recognize union pit committees in each mine; miners could appoint their own check-weighman as provided in the Saskatchewan Mines Act; the companies agreed to pay for removal of all water in the mines; they agreed to an eight-hour day for contract miners from portal to portal, nine hours for company men; they promised no victimization of or discrimination against men because of the strike; and questions of coal-car weights would be negotiated between the operators and the pit committees. The truce also provided for another negotiation to reach a permanent agreement on wages within ten days, which would be retroactive to the date of the truce. The temporary truce agreement appeared to represent a considerable victory for the miners.

C.C. Morfit, president of the Southern Saskatchewan Coal Operators' Association, and Dan Moar, designated as 'president of the miners' executive' rather than as President of Local 27 of the MWUC, shook hands. The operators had got their way about not recognizing the union, but Moar and the union bargaining committee insisted that the agreement would have to be submitted to a meeting of the union miners for ratification before work could resume.[7]

That evening, in the middle of the night and on the complaint of village overseer A.H. Graham and mine manager H.M. Freeman, RCMP Inspector Moorhead sent nine constables to raid Boruk's Boarding House. There they roused seven men out of their beds, suspecting them of being out-of-town agitators who might try to persuade the miners not to accept the truce agreement, charged them with vagrancy, and held them without bail in the Estevan jail for four days before releasing them. The next morning, using the same trumped-up charge, they repeated the performance, arresting a WUL organizer, James Bryson, at the union hall while he was making a speech. These were patently illegal acts by the police, intended to frighten the miners. Standing truth on its head, lawbreaker Moorhead, having had sleeping men arrested in their beds and charged with vagrancy, congratulated himself, saying his orders 'had a salutary effect on would-be lawbreakers.'[8]

John Weir was also in Boruk's Boarding House at the time of the police raids and had a narrow escape. 'They took Orton Wade out of the room across from mine,' Weir recalled, 'but they missed me. A local miner quickly told me to cover myself up in the bed while he put on the light and flung open the door, standing in it. At that time they were only taking outside people; they had a spy with them to point out who was local and who was a stranger. I moved over to Wade's bed. Later that night there was another raid. This time they looked in the bed I had been in – but didn't bother about Wade's. Such was the atmosphere of terror after the murders.'9

Two days later, on 8 October, with three hundred miners gathering in Bienfait to vote on the negotiated truce agreement, Inspector Moorhead led forty armed police to Bienfait from Estevan on the pretext of preventing 'the Communist element' from holding a meeting to influence the vote on the proposed return to work. Halting the patrol at the edge of town, 'in readiness for any eventuality,' Moorhead strolled into the village and spoke to groups of strikers on the street to the effect that he was not here for trouble, but that if it arose he would not run away from it. Urged on by A.H. Graham, Moorhead entered the union hall where the miners were gathered. While the startled miners looked on, he mounted the stage to 'reassure' them that they had 'nothing whatever to fear from the police' who would 'safeguard life and property at all costs.'10

After this intrusion and thinly disguised threat, the meeting ignored the advice of the WUL and accepted the operators' discriminatory demand that only those who had been actually on the payroll at the start of the strike would have the right to vote, thus excluding about three hundred union members who had not yet been rehired for the busy season.

The vote to resume work passed 130 in favour, 41 against.11 The thirty-day strike ended. The next morning, when the miners returned to work after 5 A.M., they found Inspector Moorhead and his men at the mine entrances, waiting there until the mine bosses reported that all employees were at work. For many of the miners, disappointed at not having gained recognition for their union and driven back to work by hunger, it felt like a slave camp.

Moorhead said that he noticed 'the sullen and restless' attitude of what he called the 'foreign-born miners.' He pretended that British-born miners were not involved in agitation even though it was as plain as the buttons on his uniform that the whole executive of Local 27 and many members of the strike committee were from the British Isles. Absent from Moorhead's way of thinking was any recognition of the tradition of agitation and protest long established as one of the foundations of British institutions. The Bienfait agitators, he claimed, 'consisted largely of Foreigners as very few English-speaking people took part.' He strongly recommended 'discriminate deportation of the radical foreign element.' 'In my opinion,' he said, 'until this method is put into effect there is sure to be continual trouble, possibly of a more serious nature.'12

As Sam Scarlett had predicted, the coal operators and their friends intensified their effort to make the miners' struggle against starvation wages a 'flag issue,' feeding the miners the Union Jack for breakfast, lunch, and supper. Patriotic jingoism, the local United Church minister, the Reverend C.B. Lawson, had warned in a similar vein, becomes the cheap rallying cry of stuffed-shirt militarists and scheming politicians. He wanted to redefine patriotism as 'love of countrymen, rather than love of country.'[13] But the operators and the Tory government paid no attention to this kind of sentiment. They began a determined drive to smash the miners union before the scheduled negotiations for a permanent contract could take place.

This effort started at 'a largely attended meeting' of the British Empire Service League in Estevan on the very day the miners voted to return to work. The opinion of the meeting was that ex-service men were key to controlling the situation and that a branch of the legion should be established rapidly in Bienfait as a 'rallying point for the loyal elements of the district.' Supplied with financial assistance by Dr James Creighton and others, within four days village overseer A.H. Graham had organized a banquet at the King Edward Hotel attended by a hundred and fifty members of the legion, drawn mostly from branches in nearby towns but including sixteen charter members recruited in Bienfait and Taylorton. The guest of honour was none other than the Conservative premier of Saskatchewan, J.T.M. Anderson, who urged the men to stay away from revolutionary movements that were subversive to British institutions.[14]

The strike committee had a meeting that same evening and the legionnaires requested them to come over in a body to the hotel to discuss the question of 'unions.' The committee sent a delegation led by Dan Moar, their president, which reported to the legion meeting that they were quite satisfied with the MWUC and required no other union. After the delegation withdrew, the veterans, perhaps as a joke, elected Dan Moar president of the newly formed unit of the legion in his absence. When Moar was made aware of this 'honour,' he promptly and emphatically declined it.[15] The legion group, pledging itself to 'loyalty, law and order,' then proceeded to choose C.W. Locke, the school principal, as president, and Joseph Bembridge, acting manager at the Bienfait mine, as vice-president.

In hailing the new legion branch, the *Mercury* called for 'patriotism' and the 'war spirit of 1914' to revive the moral stamina of the people that was being 'rapidly sapped by stealthy agents of Red revolution.'

'Canada,' said Donald Dunbar, the editor, 'faces a crisis more terrible than that of 1914 and turns with confidence to the manhood of eighteen years ago to stand on guard again today ... God Save the King!'[16] The Bienfait legion signed up forty-nine veterans in 1931, almost entirely from the Anglo-Saxon side of the village.[17]

The 'shooting put a lot of hatred in peoples' hearts,' recalled retired miner Thomas Hesketh, who was the son of Harry Hesketh. 'That was when the legion started – where they come from I don't know – it was big money that was behind it all. They started up the legion in Bienfait and told them that if any more trouble starts they're going to issue them with rifles – you'd think you were over in Russia or some place, the way they were here. So that forced all the guys to go back to work in the mines.'[18] Steve Elchyson, another retired miner, agreed about the origin and results of the legion in the village: 'The mine foremen were alarmed that army veterans had participated in the miner's union so they formed a legion branch under their leadership. It created a rift in the community.'[19]

To carry on its activities, the legion rented the hall that was next door to Boruk's Boarding House and Bakery. This was the Hawkinson Hall belonging to the National Mines and located at the corner of Railway Avenue and Main Street. With the help of mine managers H.N. Freeman and Robert Hassard, the legion began to sponsor film shows, dances, carnivals, and other social activities as well as fund-raising drives for charitable causes, all calculated to compete with the attractions of the union hall and to wrest the initiative in community affairs away from the miners.

One of the charitable projects adopted by the legion was to raise money to add two rooms to the house of a newly widowed miner's wife who had been left with five small children to raise. In this way, legion members could make out that they were doing something constructive in the community while the union was just causing trouble. It was a simplistic claim. Whereas the union's demand for social justice through standard schedules of wages and hours of work appealed to a sense of fairness, acts of private charity appealed to a sense of pity. There was perhaps room for both in the community but to counterpose private charity to social justice created confusion in peoples' minds, weakening the union to the benefit of the operators.

As the time to negotiate a permanent agreement between the operators and the miners approached, two important and different-minded individuals arrived in Bienfait, each hoping to influence matters their way. One was the attorney general of Saskatchewan, M.A. MacPherson, and the other was Tom Ewen, national secretary of the WUL.

The attorney general spoke to meetings sponsored by the Bienfait legion branch, lashing into the moral character of the union organizers and decrying their political affiliations. He called them self-appointed leaders who manipulated the miners and their families into a confrontation with the police and tried to save their own skins by running away into the woods. Their only purpose, he said, was to create strife and prevent the miners from accepting any settlement. He urged the miners to have a 'regular' union and avoid any sort of union whose principles 'seemed to favor mass action of a revolutionary character rather than an amicable settlement of the troubles.' MacPherson claimed to have proof that the MWUC was a 'Red' organization 'directly affiliated' with the Communist Party of Canada.[20]

MacPherson's crusade in Bienfait to destroy the mine workers' union caused a number of defections but did not succeed in affecting the leading core of Local 27 grouped around President Dan Moar and Secretary Harry Hesketh. Most of this core were certainly not communists but they had talked over the problem of the union being called 'communist' with James Sloan and John Stokaluk, who had assured them that the union was not affiliated with the Communist Party. 'Only a small percentage of the membership of the union were ever members of the Communist Party,' said Stokaluk, 'but any actions taken by the workers to better their conditions are always interpreted as communism.'[21] Sloan explained that the Communist Party took in members one by one, after checking into their background and suitability. The union, on the other hand, took in all working-class miners, regardless of their creed, nationality, politics, religion, or organizational affiliations.[22] An analogy often made was with the Chamber of Commerce. Joining the Chamber of Commerce was not the same as joining the Conservative Party. The chamber might have Conservative Party members in it and might even be led by Conservatives, but it would also have members of other parties or non-party members. The Chamber of Commerce was not 'directly affiliated' to any political party; it was the same with the MWUC. If the bosses could have this kind of organization, why couldn't the miners? These explanations sounded reasonable and satisfied the majority of the workers for the time being. They considered MacPherson to be nothing more than one of those 'scheming politicians' that the Reverend C.B. Lawson had referred to.

Some time later, Dan Moar buckled under the pressure of his fellow legionnaires. He placed a notice in the *Mercury* saying that his connection with the red element had not been for his own good or the good of the coalfields. He was now ready and anxious to regain his former place among his own people and 'to defend the Union Jack and all that it stands for and am ready to serve my country now, as I did in 1914.'[23] That statement, reflecting the psychological atmosphere of the times, came two years later, in 1933. For now, he was sticking with the union.

When Tom Ewen, national secretary of the WUL, arrived in Bienfait in mid-October, it was a moment of high drama. In the aftermath of the tragedy enacted on the streets of Estevan, the executive of the miners' union was about to begin the second round of negotiations with the operators for a permanent contract. The union organized several mass meetings for Ewen to speak to and for him to hear the opinions of rank-and-file miners and members of the women's auxiliary.

A blacksmith by trade with a strong Glasgow accent, Ewen, aged forty-two, was currently out of jail on bail and awaiting trial in Toronto, one of the eight communists arrested by the government of Ontario and charged under section 98 of the Criminal Code for being members of an 'unlawful organization.' Ewen's police dossier, updated in April 1931 prior to his audience with Prime Minister Bennett in Ottawa, describes him as 'well and quietly dressed,' a man with a jaunty gait, 'always in a hurry,' 'moderate beer drinker,' 'a very convincing speaker and has a pleasant personality.'[24] He was, in truth, one of the outstanding Marxist leaders thrown up by the class struggles of workers and farmers in Canada. For the past several weeks, he had been on a speaking tour of western Canada under the auspices of the CLDL, creating public awareness about the grossly undemocratic nature of section 98 and raising money for the legal defence.[25]

When he arrived in the coalfields, Ewen was already feeling unhappy about what he considered the 'stupendous errors' committed by the WUL organizers during the course of the strike. This feeling only intensified as he listened to the questions and complaints voiced at open meetings in Taylorton and Bienfait. He already knew about Sloan's strategy of putting union 'recognition' ahead of all other demands, which he said was 'the rock upon which certain victory was battered into partial defeat in Estevan.' Now he learned about the 'twin brother to this class stupidity,' the atmosphere of 'secret conspiracy that predominated the activities of the Strike Committee and their relationship with the miners throughout the strike.' This included, he said, the preparations for the parade to Estevan. He was devastated when a miner's wife in the mass meeting at Taylorton stood up and put the question this way: 'Is it the policy of the Workers' Unity League to trap us or lead us into a fight with the police? I am not afraid to fight them anytime, since I know there is nothing else for us, but I would like our leaders to give us an opportunity to leave our babies at home. I can fight and did fight with mine in my arms, but I can do it much better when alone.'[26]

For Ewen, this was but one expression of the policy of isolation that had been practised by the strike committee. He learned that whatever demands were drafted by the committee, the completed document was 'entirely unknown to the miners.' That the pursuance of such tactics did not completely wreck the faith of the miners in their union, he said, was a marvel: 'It opened to door for petty grievances and gossip. It paved the way for the disruptive work carried on by a handful of legionaries and business men, with whom Premier Anderson ... aligned himself. It built up an atmosphere of discontent and internal dissension even within the Strike Committee itself. And to cap it all, the District Committee of the WUL [in Winnipeg] ... issued an open letter to the miners following the temporary settlement, which in essence declared that [treacherous elements in] the Strike Committee had sold out the miners and practically lost the strike.'[27]

This open letter, pinned up on telephone poles all around the mining camps, was issued exactly forty days after the strike began. Until now, Ewen observed, 'not a single leaflet, bulletin or working class newspaper, carrying a description or analysis of the strike was issued to the miners.' 'Even with this last drop of bitterness poured into a cup that was already overflowing,' he wrote, in a frank and wide-ranging article for the *Worker* (which was reprinted in the *Ukrainian Labour News* for non-English speakers), 'the miners stood solid by their union.' He criticized Stokaluk and Weir, who had made some changes in the draft negotiation document before getting it printed and distributed and had done so without the knowledge of the committee, thus putting them at a disadvantage before their own members and with the bosses and their lawyer W.W. Lynd. He called them the 'WUL muddlers':

When we remember the veil of conspiracy with which the Strike Committee was shrouded, under instructions from leading members of the WUL – whom the Strike Committee in its inexperienced way trusted implicitly; when we remember that this [open letter] is the first document given out at any time to the miners; when we remember the efforts of the legion that flourished on the existence of isolation between Strike Committee and the rank and file; and lastly when we remember, that for all these examples of criminal neglect of the most elementary principles of revolutionary trade unionism, the District leaders of the WUL is wholly and solely to blame, then all that remains is a profound admiration for the bulk of the Estevan miners who are still prepared to fight for their union in the face of overwhelming odds. To talk of strategy and tactics in strike struggles and at the same time to forget the human beings involved is not only foolish but criminal.[28]

It was harsh language, possibly too critical considering the extreme pressures under which the organizers were working. More surprising is that Ewen published his passionate criticisms so openly in the press as a way to have the WUL hear from its friendly critics and learn from its mistakes.

Whatever might be the case about errors, Ewen believed it ought never be said that the miners did not fight. 'On the contrary,' he wrote, 'their fighting spirit and courage compares with the greatest in the history of trade unionism on the continent. This courage and loyalty to their Union is even more vivid,' he said, 'when the bankrupt tactics and strategy of the WUL leadership comes under the searchlight of criticism.'[29]

Ewen spent several days in Bienfait working with the union, going over the negotiating document, and dealing with grievances about the distribution of relief supplies. When he left to continue his speaking tour, he felt that relationships between the rank and file and the executive had materially improved and that clarity of policy had been introduced which would keep the union together and allow for successful negotiations with the operators.

When the operators and the miners' executive commenced their negotiations a few days later, Attorney General MacPherson interposed himself with each group. He cajoled the operators and issued a dire warning to the miners. He told the operators that they should make concessions and accept the fact that the workers had a right to have some kind of union represent them; to the miners he said that if they did not give up their 'Red' union and accept what the operators would agree to, then the deep-seam mines would close down permanently and the jobs would be gone for ever.

The miners did not panic. They presented a detailed wage demand and drew up a list of twenty-seven points for changes in working conditions. The operators again rejected union recognition but agreed to have pit committees elected in each mine. These pit committees were composed of some of the staunchest men, including John Billis, William Choma, and Allen Carroll in the Eastern mine; the Konopakis and William Sherratt in the National Mines; Martin Day, Dan Moar, and Alex Peattie in Crescent Collieries; John Harris, Harry Hesketh, William Klymyk, Steve Antoniuk, and John Bachynski in the Bienfait mine; and Fred Booth, Joe Rohatyn, and others in the M&S mine; and John Pryznyk and George Wilkinson at Western Dominion Collieries. The operators offered a 10 per cent raise, accepted fifteen of the points on working conditions, and promised not to discriminate against workers for taking part in the strike.

The union called a mass meeting of miners to vote on the proposed contract, chaired by the national vice-president, Maurice Ludwig, who had come specially from Calgary for this purpose. However, the newly organized legionnaires, who were also card-carrying union members, voiced strong objections both to Ludwig's presence and to the idea that all the union members, including those currently unemployed, should have a chance to vote on the proposed contract. They managed to disrupt the meeting, which disintegrated without having a vote taken.[30]

During this time, Detective Sergeant Mortimer, who was still much in evidence around Bienfait, again confronted WUL organizer James Bryson, searched him, and, finding only ten cents in his pocket, telephoned this information to Inspector Moorhead, who ordered his immediate arrest on a charge of vagrancy. Bryson was taken before Mayor Bannatyne, who was acting as a justice of the peace, sentenced to thirty days for vagrancy, and railroaded to jail in Regina all within one afternoon.[31]

In these ways the operators got their wish that the vote take place in the pits and be limited to currently employed miners. Even then, at each pit, when they went to vote, the miners had to walk past Inspector Moorhead's men, armed with rifles.[32] To prevent a possible challenge to the verdict, the ballot boxes were gathered up and taken to A.H. Graham 'as a neutral person,' to be counted in the presence of a union delegate. The announced result was 221 in favour, 82 opposed.[33]

No sooner had the agreement to end the strike been accepted by the miners than the operators began to violate its provisions, especially in respect to discrimination against the strikers. Local 27 held mass meetings and reacted swiftly. Defiantly signing himself as 'secretary-treasurer of Local 27,' Harry Hesketh sent letters to the managers listing the union men who had to be rehired and objecting to the employment of outside men. Unless new employees joined the union, Hesketh added, the union men in the pits 'will refuse to serve them with cars.'[34] Non-recognition by the operators had not caused the union to go away.

C.C. Morfit was incensed. He wrote the attorney general about this 'intimidation' and he came to the police with Hesketh's lists of men to be rehired. In Morfit's Western Dominion mine, these men, Peter Gemby, Mike Boruk, Michael Rohatyn, Dan Petryk, Wasyl Stefiuk, and five others, were living rent-free in shacks in Taylorton Hollow. Morfit, the American, described them as 'unmarried foreigners' on relief whom he claimed were 'out and out communists' with no intention of becoming naturalized citizens. He thought that investigation would also prove that 'money made by these men in the past has been transferred to their families in the Old Country, nearly all of whom are Ukrainians.' (The money made by Morfit's mine, of course, was transferred to the stockholders in Britain and bondholders in New York.) Morfit called for 'firm action' to stamp out 'the "Red" movement' in the coalfields which the men in Taylorton Hollow supported.[35]

Detective Sergeant J.G. Metcalfe, in charge of the criminal investigation branch in Weyburn, made the rounds of the mining camps but could find little to substantiate Morfit's charges. He interviewed the alleged communists, checked at the post office to see what letters and publications they were receiving, and submitted personal history files on all of them. But his conclusion was that the managers were 'out to break the back of the Union.' 'It appears to me,' he told his commanding officer, 'that the moment a man submits himself to be appointed on a Committee or some position in a Union, and has nerve enough to approach the Owners on behalf of the workers, he is immediately branded a Red.' Metcalfe had yet to interview an owner or manager of a mine in regard to the red element who had not given him the names of all of the men on the pit committee and the names of some official of the union. 'I might state,' Metcalfe said, 'that there is a Communist Movement amongst the miners, but in my opinion they are not all on the Pit Committees, and with the assistance of [blanked-out name of undercover agent] I will endeavour to have all Communists reported upon in due course.'[36] Following his investigations, Metcalfe placed his hopes in the emergence of a new union organized by miners 'without any Red Affiliations.'

Of most immediate interest to the government was the chance to arrange for the deportation of as many as possible of the union men who had taken a prominent part in the strike. With such men being blacklisted from employment, more and more faced starvation unless they applied for food relief. This provided the necessary opening since any person with less than five years' domicile in Canada who asked for relief was liable to deportation proceedings.

Graham, the supposedly neutral village overseer, was more than willing to participate in this process since he was one of the ones busy helping to create a replacement union that would not issue union cards to the leaders of the 'Reds.' A month after the end of strike he wrote to the attorney general offering on a 'strictly confidential' basis to identify leaders 'dangerous to the Community' whom he would like to see deported or sent away to camps or farms. 'By getting rid of these men,' he wrote, 'the followers of the "Reds" will most likely take a lesson, and settle down as more peaceable citizens.' He believed that it would 'foster the spirit of loyalty' and have a great influence on 'our young people' who in the next decade would be able to use their influence 'in dominating the Community.' His initial list to the attorney general of those who had applied for relief and who he said 'do not wish to be Canadian' included the names of Harry Michalowski, Louis Stelmaschuk, John Fedoryshyn, and Steve Wozny, all active members of the Ukrainian Labour Temple.[37]

Some of the miners most active in the strike had already been arrested and booked for trials in the regular court system. By the end of 1931, the focus of the union's attention had shifted to the mass trials of eighteen people, scheduled to be held in the Estevan courthouse in the spring assizes of 1932.

Chapter Nine

The Trials

It seems impossible to get in on anything ... I was at the boarding house last night ... I am still talking 'Red' and lots for the Union also against the police and operators, but no one except me seem interested.

– stool-pigeon, Taylorton mining camp, report to RCMP, 27 October 1931

There is not sufficient evidence available to warrant bringing Forkin and Mrs. Buller to trial.

– A. McCutcheon, chief of police, Estevan, 25 November 1931

There began in Estevan the trial of the miners and their leaders. Class hatred dominated that trial. It was the first mass trial of workers in the history of Estevan and of the province. The court was crowded every day. The accused gave a good account of themselves.

– Annie Buller, *National Affairs Monthly*, May 1949

'At all times in court conduct yourself calmly and deliberately ... You are not speaking for yourself alone, but as a representative of your class.' The speaker was the Reverend Alfred E. Smith, of Brandon, Manitoba, who came to Estevan for three weeks at the time of the court trials to help the arrested miners organize their defence. He knew that most of them, and the friends who came to speak for them, would never have been near a courthouse before; they would find the court language unfamiliar and they would feel small, ill at ease with the pomp and ceremony and the complicated proceedings.

Smith was a preacher who, like Tommy Douglas, believed that Jesus was a revolutionary in his day, concerned to bring glad tidings to the poor. The challenge for a Christian preacher, therefore, was less about saving souls for the afterlife and more about helping to create a more Christ-like world for the living. Following the Winnipeg General Strike of 1919, in which he played some part, Smith grew restive with his church responsibilities, preferring to engage in activities more directly associated with the struggles of working people for a better life. As he said in his autobiography, he 'moved from the Methodist pulpit to the Marxist platform.' He joined the Brandon Labour Party and, with the support of radicals like the Forkin family, was elected to the Manitoba legislature in 1920 representing that city.

With the great increase in the number of people arrested for their activity in the labour movement in the 1920s, Smith began devoting his energies to assisting them. For this purpose, he helped to found the CLDL to assist workers to conduct self-defence in the courts. His position on self-defence went beyond the desire to avoid, where possible, spending workers' money on lawyers' fees; he also thought that self-defence played an important role in exposing the nature of capitalist justice and bringing out 'the class implications of the trial before the working class at large.' 'We were not looking for justice in the courts of capitalism in 1931,' he said. 'Our task was to expose the lack of it.'

Smith advised those who would be taking the witness-stand in Estevan on court procedure: 'If you do not wish to be sworn on the Bible,' he said, 'the law permits you to say instead "I affirm," raising your right hand.' Smith told them not to be bulldozed by the court into answering 'Yes' or 'No.' 'If you feel that a question cannot be answered "Yes" or "No," say, "I can't answer that question that way and I refuse to do so, because an answer that way may be construed as untruthful and would prejudice me in my right to present a full defence to the charge."' The defendants should not be intimidated by the anti-working class testimony of police and stool-pigeons. Since they had been arrested at a strike demonstration, they and their witnesses should tell the court about the purposes of the demonstration, of the rotten conditions that had brought on the strike and the strikers' demands. 'Do not try to crawl out of the charges against you by lies and dodges. You will only involve yourself in a net of conflicting statements. By the strength of your cause, make capitalism the defendant, and yourself the prosecutor.'[1] This is the way he prepared sixty-eight witnesses for the defence.

With the police laying charges of vagrancy, unlawful assembly, and riot against more than thirty working men and women, the provincial government, its attorney general, and its courts began the largest mass trial in the history of Saskatchewan. The cases of twenty-one of the accused who went to trial, and their appeals, involved 190 witnesses, 202 jurors called to serve in the courtroom, and 2,702 pages to record the evidence and proceedings.[2]

The workers had to raise the amazing sum of $100,000 in bail to allow those arrested the freedom to prepare for their hearings and to fight the government's assault on their rights. They also had to hire lawyers. A.E. Smith had come to Estevan with a pocketful of money to pay a lawyer, but it was not enough. 'I stood at the telegraph office in the Estevan station one night and sent out appeals to some twenty points,' Smith recalled. The situation was very difficult but loyal friends responded to his urgent cry and in the next three days over $1,200 was received. He retained W.H. Heffernan of Regina to head the defence and paid him $2,650. Later, Heffernan sued for another $400. 'That case is still pending somewhere,' Smith mused twenty years later.[3]

What had been a straightforward contest between owners and workers now became a trial of strength between representatives of the working class and the state over whether or not an effective union could take root in the coalfields. In the months between the time when the accused were booked for trial at preliminary hearings in October and the trials at the Court of King's Bench in March 1932, the crown attorneys and the police located witnesses and prepared the prosecution's case to prove incitement to riot, rioting, and unlawful assembly. But, in spite of the strenuous efforts of detectives J.G. Metcalfe and Walter Mortimer, it soon became clear that it would be difficult to find credible civilian witnesses; virtually none of the miners came forward to testify against their fellow accused.

This was especially embarrassing for the government in the highly publicized cases of the communist leaders Sloan, Forkin, Scarlett, and Buller. The police had decided that these four 'were responsible for inciting the riot,'[4] and the higher authorities were anxious to have them suitably punished. Sloan, however, had to be released at the preliminary hearing because there was no evidence that he had incited anyone or had been anywhere near Estevan on the day of the police riot. Although some police witnesses were willing to implicate Forkin, the crown counsel, W.J. Perkins, knew that Forkin had been standing beside him on the sidewalk in Estevan smoking a cigarette during the course of the mêlée. Perkins recommended that the charge against Forkin, 'the generalissimo of the strikers,' not be proceeded with. That left Sam Scarlett and Annie Buller.

In the evening after the police riot, Scarlett quit Bienfait in the company of Sloan and they had gone to the Coteau Hills where Finnish farmers of communist sympathies were numerous. Sloan found shelter with George Bowes at Elbow on the South Saskatchewan River while Scarlett stayed at the farm of Charles Pavo across the river at Birsay.[5] Pavo was an active member of the Farmers' Unity League and a trusted colleague of Scarlett's, and therefore his farm was a place where Scarlett could safely await developments. About two weeks later, Mrs James Sloan went to the post office in Lethbridge and sent a postal money order made out to Charles Pavo in Birsay. The postmaster recognized her and, aware of the warrant out for Sloan, notified the police of this piece of mail. It was an illegal action by the postmaster but the RCMP staked out the post office in Birsay, and when Pavo came to pick up his mail the local postmaster identified him and the police followed Pavo home expecting to find Sloan. Instead, they were able to arrest Scarlett (as well as Pavo) and bring 'the fugitive' back to Estevan in a great blare of publicity. The fact that Scarlett had been 'in hiding' for two weeks fuelled a presumption of some kind of guilt in the public mind.

Scarlett felt no sense of guilt and went on the offensive. From his jail cell, while awaiting the preliminary hearing, he issued a statement to the press in which he vigorously criticized Saskatchewan premier J.T.M. Anderson and the suggestion that the miners sever their connection with the MWUC and join another trade union organization. 'Dr. Anderson,' he said, 'was conspicuous by his absence while the strike situation was developing. The kind of union he suggests to the miners in place of their affiliation with the Mine Workers' Union is like a meal ticket found on the sidewalk with all the nourishment punched out of it.'[6]

During Scarlett's absence, detectives Metcalfe and Mortimer were busy trying to line up witnesses to tag him with engaging in activities calculated 'to disturb the peace tumultuously' on the streets of Estevan. After numerous visits to the mining camps, all they could find was one miner who confirmed that Scarlett had been a passenger in one of the lead cars in the procession into Estevan.

Several people interviewed in Estevan had more to say. The proprietor of the Princess Café stated that Scarlett had been in his restaurant drinking a cup of coffee at the height of the street fighting. The proprietor recognized him and said, 'You are one of their leaders – why don't you go down and stop them as they are being shot down?' To which Scarlett reportedly replied, 'They have their own leaders who will look after them.' This was not quite the picture the government prosecutors needed.

Another witness came forward. This was Thomas McLean, Jr, younger brother of James McLean, who was already under arrest as one of the union's most active members. The younger McLean, who strongly objected to unions, was a convicted felon of dubious reputation and well known to the police. He apparently bumped into Scarlett in the vicinity of the courthouse during the disturbances and reported Scarlett as saying, 'I wish I had a gun – I would be right in there with them shooting too.' This evidence was more promising than that of the café owner but it was immediately modified by an Estevan solicitor, N.J. Lockhart, who told Detective Mortimer that he was present and heard Tom McLean say, 'Hello Sam, what are you doing up here?' And Scarlett, who was alone, not agitating anyone, and heading east away from the centre of town, replied, 'It was no use to go up against a man with a gun unless you had one yourself.'[7] Needless to say, the crown prosecutors did not introduce Lockhart's statement at trial.

The crown was so desperate about the weakness of its case against Scarlett that it turned to A.C. Wilson, manager of the M&S mine. The day before the Court of King's Bench began its sitting, on 29 February 1932, Detective Metcalfe was sent to interview 'Outlaw' Wilson in Taylorton. Metcalfe came back with a signed statement in which Wilson said he was prepared to testify that he saw Scarlett standing on Fourth Avenue behind the police line waving his arms to stop Lishinsky's truck. When it stopped, Scarlett blew a whistle and waved his arms, beckoning the twenty-five or thirty men to get off the truck and advance towards the police lines. 'Nearly all of them had clubs,' said Wilson, 'and they acted just like Indians.' Scarlett disappeared down the sidewalk and Wilson did not see him again.[8] The implication of this last remark was that Scarlett had deserted the miners, leaving them to their fate.

When Wilson repeated his story in court, defence lawyer Wilfred Heffernan called him 'an unmitigated liar' who had been brought in as a pinch-hitter to ensure a crown victory, and A.E. Smith described him as 'wearing a cynical grin' as he stood in the box framing his 'evidence.' These men claimed an undeniable frame-up by the coal operators, but the jury, composed almost entirely of farmers, believed Wilson and found Scarlett guilty of acting to 'disturb the peace tumultuously' as charged. 'Happy' Wilson could savour his revenge on the WUL.

The crown had called eighteen witness; Scarlett called none, opting instead for a short, simple trial. When the judge asked him if he had anything to say, a jam packed courtroom watched with keen anticipation as Scarlett rose to his feet: 'Your Lordship,' he began, 'I must thank you for the opportunity extended to me ... to address you and the court and I take the opportunity of extending my warm handclasp to the coal miners of the Estevan fields and to all of my friends who have stood by me loyally at this time. I bear no rancour or ill-feeling to those that couldn't see life as I saw it. I think that is all; I await your sentence.' That an orator of such renown chose to speak so briefly and with such simple dignity came as a shock, something of a disappointment even, but left a strong impression on the mining community.

Scarlett's sentence was one year in jail plus a $100-fine or six months' additional imprisonment. There was to be no hard labour in consideration of his poor health.

By this time eighteen miners had been tried by the court in groups of four or six at a time. The judge in these cases was the formidable John Fletcher Leopold Embury, a big, loud-spoken former general in the Canadian army, a graduate of the University of Toronto, and now affiliated to the Conservative Party, the free masons, and the Anglican Church. Judge Embury missed no opportunity to direct the proceedings along the desired course. But, in spite of his efforts, the crown was successful in convincing juries to convict only twelve out of eighteen persons brought to trial in his court. Part of the problem may have been in having to employ Thomas McLean, Jr, so frequently owing to the lack of other civilian witnesses. McLean was 'supposed to be feeding the police [RCMP] information,' recalled constable W.D. 'Mickey' MacKay, a veteran of the town police, 'but they never knew whether he was telling the truth or not.'[9]

The crown, therefore, relied heavily on the testimony of police officers. And the prosecutors worked hard to prepare them for this task. On one occasion five constables went to the Regina jail where sixteen prisoners were paraded before them, one at a time, in the visitors' room, for the purposes of identification and listing their misdeeds. Then, three days before the trials, prosecutor W.J. Perkins journeyed to Regina to meet with the police officers scheduled to testify in order 'to connect up the evidence.'[10]

One of the constables especially proficient at identifying 'rioters' was Horace W. Taylor, who, though barely six months in the RCMP, had served in Scotland Yard for nine years before emigrating to Canada. Although Taylor arrived on the scene in Estevan only at the last minute, having been with Inspector Moorhead's troop guarding the Truax-Traer strip mine, he volunteered to swear evidence against the strikers in eight of the court cases. This unusual enthusiasm did not pass unnoticed. That he was a young policeman eager to get ahead and willing to

John Roberts, photographer at Whitby's store in Estevan, took five pictures on Fourth Street at the height of the mêlée on 29 September 1931. As he snapped the pictures, he said, 'there were guns being fired' and 'stones being thrown.' These are his first and third pictures, which show that the crowd was already dispersed. At the trials, the defence entered the photos as exhibits, hoping to convince the jury that the RCMP overreacted in opening fire with their guns.

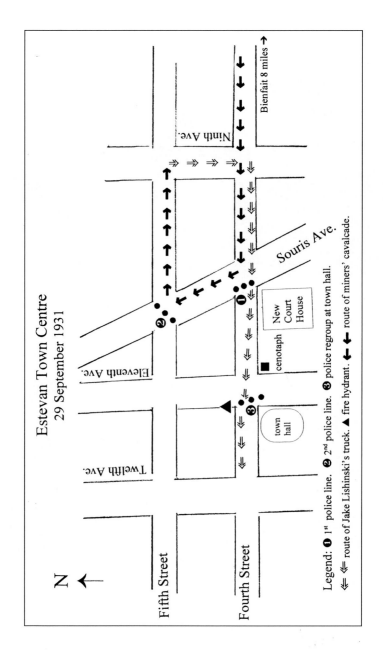

Estevan Town Centre
29 September 1931

N

Fifth Street

Fourth Street

Twelfth Ave.

Eleventh Ave.

Ninth Ave.

Souris Ave.

Bienfait 8 miles →

town
hall

cenotaph

New
Court
House

Legend: ❶ 1ˢᵗ police line. ❷ 2ⁿᵈ police line. ❸ police regroup at town hall.
⇚ route of Jake Lishinski's truck. ▲ fire hydrant. ↤ route of miners' cavalcade.

Map of Estevan town centre.

The three slain miners: Peter Markunas, Nick Nargan, and Julian Gryshko.

Main Street, Bienfait, looking north. Miners and their families gather in front of the Red Hall (3rd building from left) on the days before the funeral of the three slain miners.

The funeral procession for Peter Markunas, Nick Nargan, and Julian Gryshko forms up four abreast on Main Street, Bienfait, on the way to the village cemetery. The police estimated that there were 1,500 mourners.

The headstone of the martyrs' tomb read 'Lest We Forget. Murdered in Estevan, Sep. 29 1931 by RCMP' and had a red star at the top. The monument was soon defaced and the words 'RCMP' were removed by order of the village council.

In 1939, when the Bienfait miners formed a new local union No. 7606, they placed a marker at the foot of the grave, 'District Miners No. 7606.'

Annie Buller. The trial of Annie Buller is remembered as the most famous criminal case ever heard in Estevan judicial district.

Katherine Carroll. A high school student at the time, Carroll appeared in court on behalf of Annie Buller. She testified that a police witness had approached her on the street in Estevan asking if she were Mrs Buller.

William and Eva Adler. The Adlers were host to Annie Buller during her stay in Bienfait and testified that she had been working in her room at the time of the miners' parade, not rioting in Estevan.

The household belongings of strike leader Martin Day piled up on the prairie at Crescent Collieries. Although the jury declined to convict Day of any crime during the strike, the coal company evicted his wife and children on 1 April 1932 and the federal government deported the whole family out of the country.

When the miners' union was reborn in 1939, the ensuing strike for recognition by Local 7606 was long – two months – and bitter. The picketers built sod houses of the early settler type to keep warm.

The government sent 150 Mounted Police to Bienfait during the 1939 strike.

Amelia Budris, widow of Peter Markunas, unveiling a plaque honouring the 'Labour Heroes' presented by the Saskatchewan Federation of Labour (SFL) in May 1997. In the background, right of cameraman, are Stella and Peter Gemby. Far right with microphone is Barbara Byers, president of the SFL.

Labour Heroes

This plaque marks the final resting place of three brave trade union activists who lost their lives during the Estevan Coal Strike of 1931.

On September 7 of that year, all of the more than 600 coal miners employed at the twenty-two underground mines in the Souris coal fields went out on strike.

The miners, members of the Mine Workers Union of Canada, were protesting unsafe working conditions, starvation wages, squalid housing and the monopoly of company stores.

While taking part in a strikers' parade through the streets of Estevan on September 29, 1931, Julian Gryshko, Peter Markunas and Nick Nargan were shot by police and killed.

A week later the mine owners agreed to settle the dispute and make improvements in working conditions and rates of pay.

On the 65th anniversary of the Estevan Coal Strike, the delegates at a Saskatchewan Federation of Labour convention unanimously voted to place this marker as a tribute to the fighting spirit of the 1931 strikers, and the courage of the three miners who gave their lives to better the lot of other workers.

This plaque was unveiled May 10, 1997 by Amelia Budris, widow of Peter Markunas.

Present at the ceremony were veterans of the 1931 strike, including miners who were blacklisted for ten years following the Estevan Coal Strike.

The plaque.

'Coal Miners' Corner' in Estevan. A cairn in the form of a coal cart was established by the Estevan Labour Committee in 1981 at the site of the 1931 shootings.

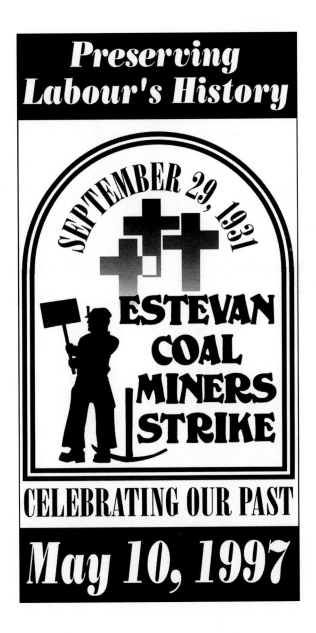

Cover of the program and T-shirt sponsored by the SFL and the Estevan Labour Committee to remember labour's history.

Illustrating the new open-pit method of extracting coal in the Bienfait coalfields after the Second World War.

The historic CPR station. Preserved and moved to a village park, it is now the Bienfait Railway and Mine Museum and holds extensive exhibits of mining methods and equipment and photographs of the 1931 miners' strike.

offer perjured testimony was suggested by Constable W.D. 'Mickey' MacKay. Some of the Mounties, MacKay said later, were able 'to identify a lot of people they never saw before ... I always thought they were stretching a little bit.'[11]

As a result of the flimsy evidence available, when A.E. Smith entered appeals for two of those sentenced by Judge Embury to the harshest punishment – two years less a day with hard labour for Isadore Minster of Winnipeg and eight months at hard labour for James McLean of Estevan – the government let them go without a further hearing after just three months in jail.

There was another questionable aspect of the trials. Agents of the attorney general tried to find out the political sympathies of farmers on the jury list. They especially wanted to know of any potential jurors who might be members of the United Farmers of Canada, Saskatchewan section. They approached Dr James Brown, a rural doctor who had been in the district and who knew everyone for miles around. Dr Brown went over the jury list for them, carefully pointing out those who were, in his words, 'good reliable men that would do justice' and others who 'were not reliable jurymen and were very radical.'[12]

This attempt at jury rigging was also not all that successful. Although the crown challenged forty-six jurors, for some unexplained reason three of the 'radicals' on Dr Brown's list became members of the jury in the case of *Rex vs. Martin Day et al.* As might be expected, this jury could not agree on a verdict. Day was put on trial a second time and again the jury disagreed. Unwilling to let the man chiefly responsible for organizing the parade go free, the crown scheduled yet another trial for Martin Day in the autumn of 1932. But this trial never took place. Instead, W.L. Hamilton, the owner of Crescent Mines, evicted Day, his wife, and their three small children from their rented house, pushing them onto relief, and the government quietly deported them out of the country. For A.E. Smith and his followers in Bienfait, the treatment of Martin Day was a prime example of the lack of justice in the court system of capitalism in the Great Depression.[13]

The most dramatic sequel to the striker-police mêlée was the arrest and arraignment of Annie Buller on charges of incitement to riot, unlawful assembly, and rioting. According to local historians, her trial and that of Sam Scarlett were the most famous criminal cases ever heard in the Estevan court.[14] The courtroom was always jammed to the limit of its seating capacity and the upstairs corridor, according to the *Mercury*, was filled with women waiting patiently to have first call on seats.

People came to the Estevan trials of Buller for different reasons. They had three chances to get a glimpse of her – at her preliminary hearing in December 1931, at her trial in the Court of King's Bench in March 1932, and during the Court of Appeal a year later. For some, it was a tale of the wild west: a fugitive from the law is finally captured in a faraway place; no less a person than the head of the RCMP's criminal investigation branch, accompanied by a matron, is sent two days and two nights by train to take control of the prisoner and then travels back two days and two nights in a first-class carriage to bring this dangerous person from Ontario to the scene of her crimes; here she will be brought before His Majesty's courts to face the judgment of her peers and likely be sentenced to a long term in jail with hard labour. This was the drift of many a dinner-time conversation and promised a spectacle not to be missed.

For others, the main point of attraction was the fact that a woman, a mother, and a wife, a union organizer operating in a man's world, was being brought to task by men – all-male juries, male judges, male prosecuting attorneys, and male newspaper editors. Could she stand up to this barrage or would she be psychologically destroyed, flattened like a pancake?

Another reason for seeking entrance to the courtroom was Buller's reputation as a public speaker, already known to hundreds of people who had listened to her at the corner of Main and Souris in Bienfait. That audience had enjoyed her fiery remarks, akin to sedition sometimes but always falling well short of calling people to pick up sticks and stones to fight the police; as they listened to her they had imagined that she was about to drop off the platform into the waiting hands of the law, only to save herself by a clever turn of phrase. This was the kind of daring oratory they hoped to hear more of, especially when directed at the coal operators and their friends in high places.

Finally, there were the members of the women's auxiliary of the mine workers' union who came to bring their supporting testimony and to offer their moral encouragement to a brave and talented woman who had so recently befriended them in their struggles for a better life.

Two months after the fighting on the streets of Estevan, the town's chief of police and the attorney general's agent, W.J. Perkins, arrived at the conclusion that there was 'not sufficient evidence available' to warrant bringing Buller to trial. Their views were reluctantly communicated to the provincial government and, perhaps equally important, to the RCMP commissioner, General J.H. MacBrien, in Ottawa.[15] It may be assumed that this news caused extreme irritation in the mind of the latter gentleman, whose opinions about dangerous 'Reds' on the loose already verged on paranoia.

MacBrien had in his hands detailed descriptions of Buller, also known as Mrs Harry Guralnick. The facts were as follows: born: in Montreal; age: thirty-six; height: 5'10"; weight: 140 pounds; build: medium; hair: dark brown; eyes: brown, wears heavy dark rimmed spectacles; religion: loyalty to the working class. Other particulars – 'Is a very powerful speaker; very well liked. Dangerous agitator. Resides at Toronto. Is a member of Political Committee of Communist Party.'[16] MacBrien's force had just recently succeeded in putting eight members of the political committee of that organization behind bars for five years. Why should this alleged member escape a similar fate? What would people think of the RCMP if she did?

It will be recalled that earlier the RCMP had been derided as a 'rabbit force,' accused of being 'too friendly' with the striking miners, soft on the MWUC, and blind to the activities of the WUL in the Estevan district. That had been a great embarrassment, partially redeemed when inspectors Moorhead and Rivett-Carnac had led a mighty armed unit into the coalfields. Now it was imperative that the forces of 'law and order' avoid further embarrassment. If Buller and Scarlett could not be convicted, then the four principal leaders would appear innocent of any wrongdoing and the police left to shoulder the blame for the woundings and killings. Such an outcome was unacceptable, unthinkable!

By one means or another, the attorney general's agent and the RCMP proceeded to fabricate a case against Buller as they had for Scarlett. But in Buller's case, the fabrications were, if anything, more blatant.

The government strategy was to try to convict their quarry on two counts: inciting the workers to riot during her Sunday afternoon speech in Bienfait, and then of playing a leading role in directing the fighting that broke out on the street in Estevan two days later.

The first objective was advanced by means of a forgery created by Inspector Charles Rivett-Carnac, one of the most senior officers of the RCMP. Inspector Rivett-Carnac carefully studied the secret reports submitted by police agents covering Buller's Bienfait speech. He set to work to compile a new, shortened text. And in that text he inserted a passage that could surely nail Buller. The sentence he added read: 'Then she continued referring to the Police, those yellow hireling of Bennet, [sic] why you can go through them like that (snapping her fingers in the air) they are nothing.'[17] These forged words found their way into the trial testimony, placed there by two policemen who perjured themselves, saying that they heard the accused utter them in Bienfait. In his charge to the jury, Judge Hector Macdonald did not neglect to direct the jury's attention to that part of the 'evidence.'[18]

Proving that Buller was on the street in Estevan urging the strikers to fight the police was a much more ambitious and daunting task. Of course, there was Thomas McLean, Jr. The police paid him five dollars[19] and he signed a statement saying that he would be willing to come to court and swear that he saw Buller on the south side of Fourth Street waving her hands to the men and women and hollering to them to come along, all the while shouting and booing the police. In spite of warnings from his father, Thomas McLean, Sr, that 'some of you will be up for perjury' for talk about seeing Buller at the parade,[20] the younger McLean, and his friends Thomas Cronk and George Mathieson, delivered that message at the trial.[21]

The prosecution also had Constable Horace Taylor, who was happy to add another arrow to his quiver of sightings. Arriving on the scene after most people had scattered and run for cover because of police bullets flying around, he would say that he had seen Buller standing on the other side of Fourth Street, opposite the cenotaph, calling to a crowd of women 'to give the police what they are asking for.'[22]

During the long train ride from Toronto to Regina, Sergeant Metcalfe, had spent considerable time in conversation with Buller, trying to elicit information that would help in obtaining evidence about her part in the parade and the events in Estevan. He found her to be a 'very well educated and exceeding clever' person but confessed that he was unable to discover any information of value.[23] She appeared quite confident that the charge against her would be dismissed.

But on the last day Buller made an unfortunate slip. In talking with Metcalfe, she mentioned that she would be placing a call to Mrs Eva Adler, her host during her short stay in Bienfait in September. This chance remark gave Metcalfe the clue he had been searching for as to whom Buller might invite to witness on her behalf.

The next morning, as soon as the train arrived in Regina, he telephoned to Sergeant John Molyneux, in charge of the Estevan RCMP detachment (now that the 'soft-hearted' Mulhall had been transferred out), and instructed him to proceed to Bienfait immediately and obtain a signed statement from Mrs Adler as to whether Buller was with her on the day of the riot.

Eva Adler was a high-strung sort of person. On the day of the parade,

Annie had been in her kitchen all afternoon, back of the grocery store, preparing her talk for the evening meeting and typing a report for a trade union conference in Winnipeg where she would be speaking the following weekend. When news of the shooting in Estevan reached Bienfait, Mrs Adler became exceedingly worried that the police would soon arrive, looking for Annie, and that she and her husband would somehow be implicated in the troubles that were sure to follow. Mrs Adler begged Annie to leave, which she did immediately, going around the corner to the Boruks' place.

Now, two months later, when a uniformed Mountie turned up at the store asking to speak with her, wanting to know if she knew Annie Buller, all Mrs Adler's nervous worries came flooding back. She told Sergeant Molyneux that she had done nothing wrong, she did not want to have anything to do with any court cases, she did not wish to be a witness. He reassured her, told her not to worry. Then, taking a page out of his notepad, he wrote:

Bienfait
Dec 17th 1931
Mrs Eva Adler states I remember the day of the Parade at Estevan Sept 29th 1931. I never seen Mrs Anna Buller on that day. I know her personally she might have been in the store but I did not see her.[24]

Putting it before her, Molyneux indicated that if she signed this little scrap of paper she would not have to come to court, there would be no trouble. After a hurried glance, and not thinking of the implications for Annie, she signed her name and Molyneux added his signature as witness. It was a major coup for the prosecution and they made full use of it in the court case.

But if Buller was not in Adler's apartment, where was she that afternoon? The prosecution still needed a believable witness to say that she was part of the parade and in Estevan. Heavily censored police records show that numerous futile efforts were made to find such a witness in the coalfields.[25] One group of Mounties went to the home of Mary Harris[26] in the Bienfait mining camp and asked her to sign a statement that she had seen Buller taking a lead in the parade. Mary Harris was a feisty character. 'I did not see Mrs Buller in the parade and I am not signing any papers,' she declared. When she was told that she would be cut off relief, she shot back, 'You can shoot me, but I am not signing any statements.'[27]

After news got around that the police were trying to push people into signing statements against Buller, the miners and their wives rallied around her and the government was unable to get a single witness from Bienfait to testify against her. Eight men and eight women from the village came to court for her defence, including Mr and Mrs Adler. Eva Adler, still nervous and asking if she could sit down, told the court how she had signed the scrap of paper to protect herself from trouble; but the contents of the paper were contrary to the facts of the matter: Annie Buller was in the Adlers' apartment all afternoon on the day of the parade, typing her report. Mr Adler and William Klymyk, a miner who bought some tobacco at the store during the time the mêlée was still in progress in Estevan and saw Buller there, both confirmed Mrs Adler's testimony.

The jury in the case, which had to consider what had been said by the judge and thirty-five witnesses over a four-day trial, was out for only three hours. It came back with a verdict of guilty of incitement to riot (but not of rioting) and recommended leniency. In view of this recommendation, the defence counsel immediately jumped up to request a suspended sentence. But Judge Hector Macdonald had other ideas. A native of Cape Breton, Nova Scotia, whom A.E. Smith described as giving the appearance of an 'escetic religionist,' the judge had shown a strong dislike of the prisoner and all she stood for throughout the trial. There would be no leniency.

After calling Buller to stand up to receive the sentence of the court, he first asked her if she had anything to say. In a firm clear voice that rang through the silent courtroom, she replied:

Your Lordship, I appreciate the opportunity you grant me. I am prepared to receive your verdict and I want to state further that when I received the invitation from the miners to come and assist them in connection with their relief I felt it my duty to assist these miners. My speech on the Sunday afternoon before the disturbance was of no character to incite the crowd to riot. My intention was ... to make a speech of an educational character. As such it has since been commented upon by a number of miners. I am not of the destructive type. I aim to educate my class. Throughout my short life I have endeavoured to be ... loyal to that class I belong to ... my activities were all directed to the welfare of the men and women that toil. In some small way I have made an effort to assist those who are thwarting those who are exploiting the workers and farmers of this country.[28]

Without allowing a moment for the prisoner's words to sink into the minds of listeners, the judge started reading out in sharp staccato tones a little homily he had written on a piece of paper in justification of the verdict.

'The verdict of the jury was, in my opinion warranted on the evidence and as I have said, in my opinion you are more guilty than any of those who used physical violence.' 'You have the fatal gift of eloquence ... which you have used, or rather abused, to stir up the feelings of the workers against their employers and as between class and class.' He remarked that, if it were not for such interference of professional agitators, many of the difficulties between employer and employee which so often result in suspicion and hatred and misery and distress would be amicably settled if not prevented. 'Before you arrived on the scene,' he said, 'the relations between the strikers and the police were peaceable and friendly ... but hard on you coming there ensued a riot resulting in bloodshed and death.' As to the jury's recommendation of leniency, the judge surmised that that was out of feelings of gallantry towards her sex. He could find no other basis for it. In these days when women assumed and claimed an equality of opportunity with men, he thought that they should be prepared to accept an equality of responsibility. The sentence of the court, he said, 'is that you be imprisoned in the common gaol at Battleford for one year with hard labour, and forfeit and pay a fine of $500.00 and in default of payment thereof, a further term of imprisonment for six months.'[29]

As everyone watched, Buller stepped down from the elevated prisoner's dock in the centre of the courtroom and shook hands with her counsel and with the grey-haired A.E. Smith. To the press she said, 'I never felt better in my life.' Under escort from the police, she left on the evening train to begin serving her jail sentence.[30]

But the saga of Annie Buller in Estevan was not yet over. The judge from Cape Breton, itself a place of epic coal-mining strikes, had shown so much animus and bias in his conduct of the Saskatchewan coalfields trial that A.E. Smith and his legal advisers had little difficulty in drawing up a bill of particulars to appeal the verdict.[31] After three and a half months in jail, Buller was free again and back on the union trail.

In the second trial, beginning in March 1933, the evidence was much the same but this time the court was presided over by Judge Embury, a man who shared the opinions of Judge Macdonald and had the added mannerisms of a military commander. In his charge to the jury, Embury did his best to inflame their passions, all the while, like Brer Rabbit pleading not to be thrown into the briar patch, he implored the twelve men to pay no attention to his opinions. *They* were to be sole judges of the evidence. Instructing them to be free of the spirit of revenge or prejudice against the accused and to give her the benefit of any doubt, Embury prejudged for the jury the 'scandalous riot in the streets of Estevan' which had such 'dire results.' 'She ran away,' he said, and 'was in the company with people who scandalously, iniquitously and wickedly deceived these poor foreign people in Bienfait.' It was one of the 'most cowardly and scoundrelly' acts he had ever heard of in his experience as a judge. Was 'her conduct in running away ... more consistent with innocence or with guilt?' That was a question he thought they should ask themselves.[32]

While supporting prosecution witnesses, Embury derided those for the defence. Of Katherine Carroll, a Bienfait high school student, who had been standing near the cenotaph with a friend when Sergeant Molyneux approached her asking if she were Annie Buller, the judge was particularly cutting. Miss Carroll, he said, in coming to the aid of the accused with her claim of mistaken identity, was 'looking for a certain amount of glory.' Embury, naturally, did not consider that he was prejudicing the minds of the jury. Nor did three other judges who later reviewed his conduct of the proceedings in the trial.[33]

For the miners and their families, however, the novel and exciting aspect of the Court of Appeal was that Buller carried out her own defence without a lawyer. Having Patrick Forkin, the younger brother of Joseph Forkin, by her side as her secretary in the courtroom, she conducted the cross-examinations of the prosecution witnesses, led her own witnesses to give their evidence, and made a memorable concluding speech to the jury. She did all this in a manner that won the grudging admiration of the judge. She was a woman of high ability, he said, 'who had conducted her defence in a very creditable manner indeed.'[34]

'Mr. Perkins outlined the charge to you,' Buller began, in her summing up, 'but he also interpreted for you a speech that I had made on Sunday, 27 September, 1931, emphasizing, of course, that my speech was of an inflammatory character, and hence two days later a "riot" took place.' She continued:

The blame must be laid at somebody's door, – and why not at mine? Mr. Perkins did not tell you why there was a strike; nor did he tell you that it was the conditions under which the miners worked and lived that forced them to organize a union and strike for human conditions. This, of course, would be portraying the struggle of the miners, and, of course, it is not Mr. Perkins' job to do that. He is representing the Crown. I am representing the workers. I am not standing before you, Gentlemen of the Jury, as one who is trying to get out of a tight corner. I consider that my efforts to assist the miners and their wives were worthwhile.

She pointed out that the strike in the mining field was not caused by the leaders of the miners; it was caused by the bad conditions in which the men lived and worked. It was caused by the violation of the Mines Act by the operators and by the low wages and short weights. Out of that strike developed this 'riot' in which three miners lost their lives. The coal operators did not intend to take the blame for that 'riot'; neither did the town council nor the RCMP nor the government of Saskatchewan. So someone had to be found to saddle the blame upon; that 'someone,' all are agreed, must be the miners' leaders. And so the press is brought into play to put the leaders of the strike in a wrong light in the public mind. 'Let me say, Gentlemen of the Jury, that leaders are not leaders because they so style themselves. No, they are leaders because of their deeds and actions.'

She reviewed and rebutted the crown's case in a careful, serious manner, her arguments including a rejection of the racially biased suggestion by the prosecutor that Mrs Alder had come to give evidence on her behalf because she was of the same Jewish origin as herself. 'As far as workers are concerned there is one nationality, one race – the race of workers,' said Buller. Eva Adler had come to the court not out of racial clannishness but to tell the truth as she knew it.

Buller analysed the contribution of her own witnesses, most of them miners, their wives, and their daughters. These witnesses, she said, had shown how the union was resisted by the operators to the limit. This had been the case for thirty years. They also had shown that the Mines Act in the province of Saskatchewan had been continuously violated and that the gentlemen responsible were not now in jail but walking the streets as free men. No, the mine owners do not go to jail. But these same individuals now come forward and blame agitators for the 'riot' that grew out of the strike against this violation of the Mines Act and other rotten conditions.

She argued her thesis by analogy. Issac Newton was famous for his discovery of the law of gravity. He did not make the law of gravity – he discovered it. And that is what men and women do when they go out to organize labour. They ascertain and discover the conditions under which the workers are living and working; and on the basis of those conditions, demands are formulated for betterment. On those demands the workers stand together. The conditions in the mines and company towns caused the strike. The organizers of the union did not make those conditions. The mine owners did. 'And this charge that I am being tried on,' she said, 'must be looked at from that viewpoint. It is a trial of the workers by the bosses. It is the working class that is on trial here. And as such this trial will merit a page in the history of the labour movement of this country.'

'Gentlemen of the Jury,' she concluded,

> I am not apologizing for any of my actions. I cannot be justly convicted on this charge because I was not in Estevan at the time of the 'riot,' and my speech on the Sunday previous was not a speech inciting riot.
>
> When I face you here I face you with my head erect. I face you as a worker with ideals and convictions. Those ideals and convictions are linked with the tide of human progress. You cannot stop that tide of progress any more than you can stop the tide of the sea with a pitchfork. Regardless of what arguments or what legal points Mr. Sampson may raise, I am not guilty of this charge. But Mr. Sampson is the Crown Prosecutor, and it is his job to get a conviction. I have said before, and I say again, that it is not Annie Buller who is on trial here. It is the great class of producers that stands in the prisoners' dock, and no one realizes more than I that the forces against us are very great. But, Gentlemen of the Jury, regardless of the outcome of this trial, I am going to remain loyal to my class, the working class, the builders of the future.

The jury still found her guilty and Annie Buller, union organizer, returned to the Battleford jail to serve out her sentence. But her words continued to reverberate. To provide inspiration to others who might find themselves in the prisoner's dock, A.E. Smith included the transcript of Buller's speech to the jury in a new edition of a little five-cent instructional handbook distributed across Canada by the CLDL entitled *Workers' Self-Defense in the Courts.*

Chapter Ten

Spreading of Seeds

Without a minimum of hope we cannot so much as start the struggle.
— Paulo Freire, *Pedagogy of Hope* (1994)

The Saskatchewan miners' strike of 1931, its unexpected rise and its savage repression, profoundly affected the thinking of a whole generation of Canadians. From Vancouver to Glace Bay, they remembered 'the wave of shock, indignation and anger that swept across the country' when they heard the news of the murder of the three Bienfait miners.[1] This was the generation that grew up during the Great Depression, went off to fight a war in Europe, and returned to join trade unions and cooperatives and to engage in successful struggles to achieve the benefits of a universal social wage.[2] For members of that generation, news of the strike was one of the deciding events that drew them into political life and the labour movement and made them conscious of the need for working people to build their organizations and their political parties.

Unionized or otherwise, workers and farmers are the producers of the material wealth in the economy. This is the bedrock of their strength. But to win a just share of the benefits from their vital place in society is another matter. It depends upon tapping into the wellsprings of working-class consciousness and requires the emergence of a capable, dedicated leadership which has the confidence to negotiate gains from the owners of capital and is experienced enough to ward off blows from the capitalist state. Long-run success depends on having ideas about how society can be restructured so that the needs of the many replace the greed of a few as the yardstick by which progress is measured. In so many words, this was the core Marxist theory of the Workers' Unity

League and it was that value system, matched by deeds, which made it so attractive to tens of thousands of Canadian working men and women during the Great Depression of the 1930s.

As noted earlier, the RCMP grossly exaggerated when they entitled their file on the miners' strike 'Sam Scarlett, communist agitator.' In fact, the miners' unrest erupted from the previous thirty-year history of their struggles and discontents. But there is no doubt that it was the WUL organizers and their supporters in Bienfait who produced a catalytic effect in 1931, an effect that continued to reverberate until trade-union rights became firmly established in the lignite coalfields of southern Saskatchewan.

When the WUL arrived on the scene, its ideas and methods of operation alarmed the mine owners and displeased the government. It had large ideas. It was definitely trying to shift the boundaries between management rights and worker rights, between property rights and peoples' needs. One way or another, all strike struggles are about the right to control the terms and conditions of labour but these matters can be negotiated in different ways. Management called for a 'cooperative' and 'responsible' attitude on the part of its employees, preferring that there be no union of any kind but if necessary they would recognize one whose leaders were, by tacit understanding, safely under their control. Governments and the conservative unions tended to favour conciliation and mediation boards where both sides stated their case and a third party made non-binding, unenforceable recommendations; militant or radical unions like those affiliated with the WUL preferred direct negotiation with the bosses supported by social pressure and the election of shop or pit committees to enforce the results of agreements. In taking this stance, the WUL defined itself as a revolutionary trade union centre. This frightened some people, but was it an appropriate self-description?

Many WUL organizers went to jail or were deported on the grounds that they advocated or threatened 'force and violence' to overthrow the existing social and political order. In reality, the league was prepared to engage in civil disobedience if necessary, but not in armed insurrection. It had no arms, and in that sense it was non-revolutionary. In Canada, at least, all power did not come from the barrel of a gun; some of it came from the tradition of parliamentary struggle.

But two characteristics of the league suggest themselves as of a revolutionary nature, allowing it to claim that honour or suffer such rebuke. The first was that it tried to raise political issues in the context of economic struggles. Whereas conservative unions prided themselves, and were praised by the capitalist owners, for keeping to 'strictly union questions' by accepted methods, WUL organizers tried by various means – such as parades, public meetings, petitions, mass picketing – to involve the wider community – other unions, farmers' organizations, the unemployed, housewives, schoolchildren, professional people – for strike support and to increase political and social consciousness. This concept of union activity became widely practised in Canada after the Second World War and is now known as 'social' rather than 'revolutionary' unionism. The fruit of 'social unionism,' it may be noted, was the substantial Canadian social safety net put into law by various political parties between 1941 (unemployment insurance) and the 1960s (medicare).

The second revolutionary characteristic of the WUL was that it offered the results of the Russian revolution as an alternative to capitalism, as a form of society that it believed worked well and operated to the benefit of the working class. The league's affiliation to the Red International of Labour Unions, which brought together like-minded unions, was of the greatest psychological importance, especially to the league's leading members and organizers. That alliance gave them the feeling of being part of a world-wide concern, of being in a liberation movement of great power and attraction which, in moments of doubt or distress, provided assurance that they, too, were on a solid path to a better future. This sense of international solidarity and attachment to a functioning socialist society helps to explain the extraordinary confidence with which a sizeable group of Canadian working-class men and women could meet and challenge their social superiors, whether on the platform, in the hallways of parliament, around a bargaining table, on the picket line – or in court.

It was this confidence and energy that so irritated Prime Minister Bennett and his friends and led them to apply section 98 of the Criminal Code against the Communist Party in 1931. Hurriedly passed by parliament at the time of the Winnipeg General Strike in 1919 but never used until 1931, section 98 was aptly described by McGill University law professor F.R. Scott as a part of the Criminal Code, which, 'for permanent restriction of rights of association, freedom of discussion, printing and distribution of literature, and for severity of punishment, is unequaled in the history of Canada and probably of any British country for centuries past.'[3] The leaders of the liberal-democratic state which was Canada were neither liberal nor democratic when the interests of their state were significantly challenged by the left in 1919 and again in the 1930s.

Inevitably, the international affiliation of the WUL gave the employers an excuse to cry about 'patriotism' and 'undesirable foreigners' in the multi-ethnic mining community. Such charges naturally raised tensions in Bienfait. Even schoolchildren were drawn into arguments over the definition of patriotism. 'My family belonged to the Red Hall alright,' said Tony Bachynski, 'but I fought kids in the school yard when they called me a "Red" because they said that meant that I wasn't a real Canadian!'[4]

From its experience in the miners' strike and for other reasons, the league dropped its affiliation with the Red International of Labour Unions at its second national convention.[5] This happened without any great fanfare and a fraternal relationship was put in its place. While the change did not reduce the 'red-baiting' to any extent, the majority of league members felt more comfortable; it was an easier relationship to defend and it still allowed the important practical, emotional, and moral aspects of international connections to find expression in the activities of the league and its affiliated unions. The WUL, barely a year old when it entered the lignite field of Saskatchewan, shed an affiliation it had previously considered to be a matter of principle.[6]

The gains that the Bienfait miners made as a result of the thirty-day strike were substantial[7] but they could not be maintained without union recognition. It was as James Sloan had predicted. Within a short time the operators violated almost every point in the agreements they had signed with the separate pit committees. The unrecognized union Local 27 made a stand at the Crescent mine when owner W.L. Hamilton had the union check-weighman, James McLean, removed from the premises with the help of two policemen. McLean had been hired by the miners in that mine according to their understanding of the provisions of the Saskatchewan Mines Act, and he was discovering the old practices of short weights by the company. Martin Day and Alex Peattie, leaders of the pit committee, protested McLean's illegal expulsion, and when the owner ignored them the mine was struck in February 1932. Hamilton, through his lawyer W.W. Lynd, had the pit committee arrested for violating the federal Industrial Disputes Investigation Act; the union replied by having Hamilton arrested for breaking the provincial Mines Act. Strike votes were taken in the other mines and the workers at the Bienfait and Eastern mines walked off the job in sympathy with the Crescent mine workers. However the local judge found in favour of Hamilton on a legal technicality and the workers were forced to go back to work under the old conditions.[8]

From now on, the operators brazenly enforced a blacklist against the workers who had challenged their management practices. Scores of miners lost their jobs and their housing and were unable to regain employment in the deep-seam mines of the 'Group' for ten years – not until labour shortages arose during the Second World War.

'Looking back, it's hard to realize that people pulled through in those hard times,' said Peter Gemby, one of the blacklisted men.[9] Some of the families moved away to Alberta in search of work in the larger coalfields in that province. Others opened up 'gopher hole' mines to dig coal for the local market and in the summer they grew gardens and caught fish for their meals. 'I remember apples and salt fish coming from eastern Canada to help the starving people,' said Steve Elchyson.[10] 'People acted out of friendship and fellow feeling for each other,' recalled William Baryluk, son of one of the wounded miners. 'We never had any money!' A farmer friend ploughed a strip of land for the Baryluks to plant potatoes and the kids walked several miles to do the seeding, hoeing, and harvesting. 'We got 30 bushels in our cellar!'[11] One group of miners led by Alex Konopaki and Dan Bozak started the North-West Coal company, with deep-seam and later strip mining, which provided work for up to forty of the blacklisted men. They needed some capital to run a spur railway line down to the mine site, recalled George Wozny, and 'they invited my widowed mother, who had collected $1,500 from an insurance policy, to invest some of her cash. That was a lot of money in those days! She accepted and became a partner.'[12] These were some of the ways in which the miners coped with hard times after the strike.

The miners received a moral victory of sorts when Judge Edmund Wylie released his royal commission report on the mining dispute.[13] Although Wylie considered the strike illegal and denied the miners the right to have their union, his report made a number of findings and recommendations for amending the Saskatchewan Mines Act with respect to health and safety, living conditions, and hours and methods of payment which vindicated the miners and gave them grounds to appear before a committee of the Legislative Assembly. A strong delegation from Local 27, led by Harry Hesketh, Martin Day, John Harris, Fred Booth, and Allan Carroll, travelled to Regina in April 1932 to argue for these amendments to the Mines Act, but their efforts were largely nullified by the appearance before the committee of J.R. Brodie, C.C. Morfit, Robert Hassard, and William L. Hamilton of the coal operators association, who said that the changes would be too costly for the industry to support.[14]

After this, Local 27 continued a more-or-less shadowy existence in

Bienfait for several years, its affairs being conducted by Harry Hesketh, the secretary-treasurer. Hesketh and his close colleagues did a number of things to keep alive the memory of the 1931 strike and to maintain the union even after some of its most active members and leaders had resigned, been jailed or deported,[15] or otherwise driven out of the area. In the summer of 1932 they invited Joseph Forkin to return to Bienfait and Taylorton to speak at well-attended meetings;[16] James McLean organized an open air May Day rally in Estevan in 1933;[17] and Hesketh himself appeared before yet another royal commission on behalf of Local 27 in 1934.

Perhaps the most significant act was the daring design which Hesketh and John Elchyson made for the martyrs' tombstone in Bienfait cemetery: a five-pointed red star, the names and ages of the three men, and 'Lest We Forget. Murdered in Estevan Sep. 29 1931 By RCMP.' This tombstone, which stands on the northwest corner of the little cemetery, is etched in the memory of all who live in Bienfait and is a magnet to those who visit the village while travelling across the prairie. It is an untranquil image linked by words to those other young people who gave their lives for Canada and who lie in Flanders Fields; and it is a reminder of the 'greed ... and intolerance that once led to senseless murder in the name of law and order.'[18] It is also a landmark signal, a cue, a prompter to pay attention. No sooner had John Steinbau, the shoemaker, cut the letters out of rubber and cemented and smoothed them over into the headstone than the village council passed a by-law establishing a cemetery board with the power to remove any inscription of which it disapproved. The letters 'RCMP' were ordered chiselled out. Mysteriously, they reappeared. Removed again, they were restored. This proxy battle of the class struggle continued for half a century, so strongly did people hold to their opinions about the strike of '31.[19]

A thumbnail sketch of what transpired in the Saskatchewan coalfields after the struggle of 1931 includes the fact that a successful reorganization of the miners' union occurred in 1938–9. By then the WUL had passed into history, its place taken by the Congress of Industrial Organizations (CIO), which arrived from south of the border. The CIO, aided by the new labour laws of Franklin Roosevelt's Depression-era presidency, had begun successful organizing drives in companies making automobiles, steel, electrical, chemical, textiles, rubber, and forestry products as well as in mining, maritime transport, and other industries. The WUL welcomed the development of industrial unionism and decided to merge with this powerful new current as it spread into Canada. The league urged its affiliated unions to join the CIO unions in Canada and many of their organizers became leaders or paid officials of the new unions. This was the case with the United Mine Workers of America (CIO) after the locals of the Mine Workers Union of Canada re-entered that union. John Stokaluk, former secretary of the Canadian union, who was a powerful and convincing speaker, 'a dangerous man' according to his RCMP dossier,[20] returned to Bienfait once again, this time on behalf of the CIO.

The result of Stokaluk's initiative was the formation of Local 7606 of the United Mine Workers of America, in which Vincent Clark, a miner, former schoolteacher, farmer, returned soldier and elder of Trinity United Church in Bienfait, became the first secretary.[21] It is noteworthy that the new local union affirmed its link to the earlier struggles by placing a simple stone marker at the foot of the grave of the three martyrs of 1931: 'District Miners No. 7606.'

When recommendations of a government conciliation board favourable to Local 7606 were rejected by the operators, Stokaluk, Pat Conroy, vice-president of District 18 of the United Mine Workers, and Vincent Clark led the miners out on a strike which lasted two months in the autumn of 1939.

'John Stokaluk stood up before the miners,' recalled retired miner Norvine Uhrich, 'and said Mr Brodie needs to be taught a lesson. We will show him!' But Brodie and A.C. Wilson organized a company union, the Saskatchewan Coal Miners Union, which did all it could to undermine the strike. As a result, when the government sent in 150 members of the RCMP to keep the roads open for the strike breakers, 'the lesson' had to be postponed until after the Second World War.[22]

By that time, the government of T.C. Douglas and the CCF had been elected in Saskatchewan. 'After the CCF was elected in 1944 things started to change for us,' said miner Tony Bachynski. 'The mine operators suddenly became more thoughtful of us the workers.' Premier Douglas threatened to assume control of the mines, according to Bachynski: 'He called all the operators to Regina and told them that if they didn't bargain with the workers and recognize their union he would take over the mines and have the provincial government run them, allowing profits to the owners.'[23] In a vote supervised by the Wartime Labour Relations Board in 1945, Local 7606 won recognition as the bargaining unit for M&S Coal, and then, in 1948, it conducted an eleven-week strike for better hours and wages and to gain a welfare fund for the workers. Local 7606 was never able to organize the Western

Dominion mines of J.R. Brodie, but the workers there gained whatever benefits the strikers achieved elsewhere.

When Charles Doerr, the eldest son of Bienfait's original postmaster, Valentine Doerr, started as manager at Western Dominion's Boundary Dam mine in 1957, he decided to allow a real union in – but at all costs not Local 7606, with its militant tradition. Doerr, according to his brother Donald, persuaded the Canadian Labour Congress (CLC) to grant the existing company union, the Saskatchewan Coal Miners Union, a charter as a direct affiliate; it became Local 331 of the CLC.[24] After the Manalta Corporation of Alberta acquired all of Brodie's interests, in 1965, the union's name was changed to the Saskatchewan Strip Miners Union, Locals 1573 and 1623 of the CLC.

Two decades later, these locals became part of the United Steelworkers of America (CIO), Local 9279. In this way the historical divisions and controversies among the Bienfait miners were perpetuated. It was not until 1998, when the Luscar Corporation swallowed up the Mannix Corporation in a merger takeover and wanted one bargaining unit, that the miners voted two to one in favour of having Local 7606 represent them.[25] A restructuring of industry by capital ultimately brought into being a united miners' organization, something that labour had been unable or unwilling to achieve by itself. It had been a long road – sixty-seven years – since the Mine Workers Union of Canada first organized the Bienfait miners into a single, district-wide union (see appendix 3).

Out of the ashes of that first militant union has arisen a special tradition that guards the better and more secure standard of living of the working people in Bienfait and Estevan. This tradition emerges in sometimes little noticed, unexpected, and perhaps forgotten places. May Day, for example. Among the dozen paid statutory holidays guaranteed by the union contract of Local 7606 is one for the first day of May – the original day of international working-class solidarity, a day of inspiration for socialist ideas around the world. This is a rare feature in North American union contracts, but one that may serve to keep the owning class on notice about the latent power of the producing class. 'We call it Gemby Day!' said Tony Bachynski, named after Peter Gemby, the legendary unionist and participant in the unrest of '31 who continues to reside in Bienfait as of this writing.

Then there is the CPR station. Peter Gemby was elected to the village council and, while working with other councillors to help Bienfait keep up with the times, he also strove to preserve its history. After Bienfait was hollowed out by economic restructuring, when strip mining replaced

deep-seam mining in the 1950s and when the railway companies abandoned their yards in favour of loading 'unit trains' directly at the mines,
Gemby and his friends launched a campaign to save the historic CPR
station. They succeeded in having it moved to the village park where it
functions as the Railway and Miners' Museum.

It is ironic and perhaps typical of other Saskatchewan prairie towns
that, as the lives of people improved through the availability of modern
consumer products – refrigeration, clean-running water, telephones,
television, video recorders, personal computers, and especially the automobile – their village centre deteriorated and their collective cultural
life became less varied and vibrant.

Many of the stores on Main Street in Bienfait fell vacant, subject
to sale for tax arrears, part of a depressing trend that troubled many
residents. The once proud King Edward Hotel became the Coal Dust
Saloon, keeping afloat by renting rooms to transient construction workers in the oil and gas fields; Boruk's Boarding House and Bakery burned
down after Alex and Tekla Boruk moved away to Ontario in the 1940s
and the legion hall occupies that land; new immigrants from China
keep up Sandy Wang's modest Chinese restaurant; at the tiny village
office, people come to pay their taxes, take out dog licences, or buy lot-
tery tickets; across the street sits the handsome brick office building of
the Rural Municipality No. 4, and down at the corner of Main and
Souris, Paul Carroll runs a service station with a busy convenience store.
There's not much else. The once thriving shops and groceries of the
Adlers, Cuddingtons, Lischinsky, Lishinsky, Lang, Carr, Oliver, Wilson,
and others which used to line the street bowed out long ago to the automobile and to the popular preference for driving eight miles to the
shops of Estevan – there to spend their money in the co-op supermar-
ket, the liquor store, the hardware chains, the clothing outlets, and the
restaurants.

The former cultural liveliness of the community also diminished.
'The people wasn't making as much money as they do now,' said Peter
Gemby, aged sixty-nine (in 1976), 'but they *lived* happier.' They would
go to one another's homes on the weekends and 'just sit around and
play cards and sing and gramophone playing ... but now no such a thing
is happening.' And the dances, concerts, and plays at the two Ukrainian
halls are no more. 'The older generation were barking at each other,'
said Gemby, but now 'there's nothing doing in both organizations.'[26]
The Green Hall of the Ukrainian nationalists became an Orthodox
church for a time while the Red Hall, a fine new structure built by the

Ukrainian Labour-Farmer Temple Association on Carbon Avenue opposite Trinity United Church, in 1936, was turned over to Local 7606 as a
union hall and later became the village library. The legion hall, with its
beer parlour, became the centre of secular culture for adults.

When Heather Robertson wrote about Bienfait in her book *Grass
Roots*, in 1973, she described it as 'a tough, bleak little town,' 'one big
shanty town' that had been 'bleached and desiccated like the skeleton
of a buffalo picked clean by the birds.' The 'birds' were the strip-mining
companies that had thrown up spillpiles, or slagheaps of brown and
barren earth, which surrounded Bienfait and set it into an immense
moonscape. She observed that 'packs of mangy dogs roam the town
scavenging in the garbage and snapping at passing cars.' The chief rec-
reation of the community was said to be bootlegging and gambling.
'Bienfait is ashamed of its reputation,' she wrote. 'Nobody wants to talk
about the three murdered men in the graveyard ... There is no honour
for the martyrs in Bienfait.' The book is a strange mix of fact and fiction,
written with an engaging flourish and the repetition of amusing or
boastful anecdotes but often short on reliable research. Summing up,
Robertson decided that 'Bienfait is a plain town ... no movie theater, no
park, no bowling alley, no library, no swimming pool, no band,' in
short, a dying prairie town held together by inertia.

But Bienfait has refused to die. In fact, young couples who work for
the Saskatchewan Power Corporation in Estevan are moving there to
live. They think it a good place to bring up their children, and besides,
real estate prices are more affordable than in somewhat more fashion-
able Estevan. The homes of the retired miners are usually small but they
are often surrounded by pleasant gardens and inside they have a warm
and friendly atmosphere; some have refurbished their houses and have
sunrooms or decks facing the southern sky, in sight of the spillpiles that
have begun to sprout trees and shrubs, piles that they call the 'hills of
South Saskatchewan' at the foot of which – in the deep pools of spring-
fed water – some go fishing. The mangy dog problem seems to have
been solved. There is no movie theatre but there is a new school, a park,
a library, a band, a swimming pool, a curling and skating arena, and a
student summer-works program for town improvement. A '55 & Over'
club meets in the former Red Hall on Carbon Avenue and in the spring-
time there are soccer and baseball leagues; parents sign their children
up for figure skating and hockey in winter.

People are still reluctant to speak of past history, having retreated into
silence for so long about what really happened during the unrest of '31.

But this has begun to change. A turning point occurred in May 1997, when the Saskatchewan Federation of Labour and the Estevan Labour Committee conducted an official ceremony honouring the three martyrs, Nick Nargan, Julian Gryshko, and Peter Markunas. The participants in this ceremony completed the ill-fated motorcade of 1931 by returning to the coalfields from Estevan in a solemn automobile procession, escorted this time by the RCMP at their own request.

The procession stretched for over a mile across the prairie. It ended in a sudden windstorm that whipped up the prairie soil from the nearby fields, darkening the sky and enveloping the Bienfait graveyard. Amelia Billis Budris, widow of Peter Markunas, who has lived in the village all her life, stepped forward with great dignity to unveil a memorial plaque on the martyrs' tomb. In the presence of a crowd of veteran miners, family members, local mayors and members of the provincial and federal parliaments, a miners' choir, and other supporters, the Canadian labour movement paid tribute to 'the fighting spirit of the 1931 strikers, and the courage of the three miners who gave their lives to better the lot of other workers.'[27]

Larry Ward, member of the Legislative Assembly for Estevan, spoke to the gathered assembly, observing that 'even today, we are puzzled that something this savage could happen in our midst.' But 'it did happen,' and 'today we are here for a simple, but very profound reason ... it could happen again unless we constantly remind ourselves that the society we have built for ourselves since 1931 has no place for yesterday's inequities. The dirty thirties taught us that. The plaque we are unveiling is testament to that lesson.'[28] Jean-Claude Parrot, executive vice-president of the Canadian Labour Congress, added his thoughts: 'They fought for us, these three young men, and were murdered by the RCMP. And still today police forces are used to end strikes to protect the profits of employers. We have to make our children and grandchildren as proud of us today as we are proud of our forebears of 1931.'[29]

In the fullness of time, the rumours and gossip, the usual account of the communist organizers as a group of violence-prone criminal conspirators, is being redressed. Historians and the labour movement in Saskatchewan are coming to view the lead given by the Workers' Unity League, and the activities of the group of Bienfait miners inspired by Marxist ideas, in a more objective fashion: it was the president of the coal operators, not the union leaders, who advocated violence; it was the government's police who practised conspiracy and used firearms. And it was the workers, and Sam Scarlett, Annie Buller, and their comrades-in-

arms, who went to jail or exile or were placed on a blacklist for exercis-
ing their democratic rights.

Peter Gemby, ninety-four, a miner and original member of the Red
Hall in Bienfait who had participated in the 1931 procession and had
been blacklisted for ten years, told the crowd in Estevan in 1997 that he
had been waiting patiently for this day. 'In the long run, history is on the
side of the people,' he said. 'I hope the young people here will feel
encouraged by what can be achieved when the union makes you strong.'

Appendix 1: The Changing Organization of Capital in the Bienfait/Estevan Coalfields, 1891–1998

(Major Operations)

Souris Valley Coal Co., in Roche Percée, owned by Robert J. Hassard, from 1891 to 1905, was the first commercial-scale coal mine. Hassard sold it to the Taylor family of Winnipeg who renamed it Western Dominion Collieries. The Taylors established a new campsite, Taylorton, in 1919.

Western Dominion Collieries, owned by Taylor family from 1905 until 1927 when British capitalists invested for a major share. In 1939 J. R. Brodie's **Great West Coal Co.,** of Brandon, Manitoba, gained control. Brodie immediately amalgamated Western Dominion Collieries with Truax-Traer Coal Co., and Bienfait Mines Ltd., to form **Western Dominion Coal Mines Ltd.** Brodie's **Souris Coal Distributors** acted as selling agency for most of the mines after 1924. **Manalta Corporation** of Calgary bought out Brodie in 1965 and renamed the company **Battle River Coal Co., Ltd.**

The Briquette Plant, started by government investment in 1921, it was an unsuccessful attempt to convert lignite coal into fuel briquettes. The plant was transferred to Western Dominion Collieries in 1927, but without much better luck. John H. MacDonald of Winnipeg bought the plant from the receivers in 1937 and was successful in creating barbeque briquettes. In 1968 Luscar Ltd bought the operation and it became the Char Division of Manitoba & Saskatchewan Coal Co.

Prairie Coal Ltd: Utility Mine, a large open pit strip-mine located at Boundary Dam, south of Estevan, and **Costello Mine,** at Roche Percée, owned by Manalta Corporation from 1970s until 1998 when Luscar Ltd., of Edmonton gained control of Manalta Corporation.

Shand Coal Co, owned and operated by J. G. Peterson from about 1915 to 1930.

Old Mac Coal Co, extensive strip mine at Roche Percée, acquired by J. R. Brodie and then by Manalta in the 1960s.

North-West Coal Co., 1932 - 1965, owned by Alex Konopaki and Dan Bozak of Bienfait. The owners and employees of this mine were men who had been blacklisted by the major mine owners after the 1931 miners' strike. Bought out by Manalta in 1965

Manitoba & Saskatchewan Coal Co, started by the Hudson's Bay Company in 1905, bought by Winnipeg capitalists in 1907 and operated at a campsite called Coalfields near Bienfait until 1965 when it was purchased by **Luscar Ltd.,** of Edmonton. It continued under that name until 1988 when it was renamed **Estevan Coal Corporation.** It opened a large strip mine at Boundary Dam.

Bienfait Mines Ltd., was started by the Canadian Pacific Railway in 1906 and leased to Maurice Hawkinson. It was known as **Hawkinson's Mine** and then as **Bienfait Commercial Coal Co.,** Ownership of this mine, which operated until 1940, changed several times. W. L. Hamilton and R. J. Hassard bought it in 1915. Hassard sold his share to J. R. Brodie in 1926; Hamilton sold his part to A. C. Wilson who sold out to R. J. Brodie.

Crescent Collieries Coal Co., three miles west of Bienfait, owned by W. L. Hamilton and J. R. Brodie, from 1918 to 1940s.

Eastern Collieries Ltd., owned by Herbert Wallace, and operated from 1920 to late 1940s.

National Mines Ltd., owned by Hon. H. H. Stevens and other West Coast investors who took over some of Hawkinson's leases, around 1929.

Truax-Traer Coal Co., of North Dakota and Chicago, purchased the **Big Lump Coal Co.,** from Eleazer W. Garner, former mayor of Estevan, and started a large strip-mining operation in 1930 with Garner as manager. J. R. Brodie took control in 1939. See Western Dominion Coal Mines Ltd.

Manalta Corporation of Calgary, and **Luscar Ltd.,** of Edmonton, controlled the Bienfait coalfields after 1965. In 1997 they both became public companies trading shares on the stock exchanges. Barely a year later, in November 1998, their rivalry ended when **Luscar Ltd.,** took over Manalta's assets to become the sole producer of coal in the Bienfait-Estevan field. With operations in B.C., Alberta and Saskatchewan, **Luscar Ltd.,** became the sixth largest coal producer in North America, employing over 3,000 people

PROPOSED CONTRACT

Between Operators And Miners of the Estevan District

1. Recognition of the Mine Workers Union of Canada and Pit Committees.

2. Establishment of the eight hour day from bank to bank.

3. Right for the contract miners to appoint their checkweighman.

4. Material to be delivered to the face, or where required by the miners.

5. Powder and supplies to be sold to miners at cost price.

6. No discrimination or intimidation of employees who purchase their goods in private stores.

7. Coal to be sold to miners at cost price.

8. Miners should receive their pay every second Saturday.

9. Bunkhouses to be eliminated.

10. The charge for room and board in the company boarding houses shall not exceed one dollar per day.

11. Contract miners shall have the right to choose their own partners.

12. 75 cents extra wages per day for both contract and day workers working in wet places.

13. Equal turn of cars for all men.

14. Free tools for the men and no charge for sharpening them.

15. A charge of 25c for light or bulb and continuous 24-hour service.

16. House rent to be charged one dollar per room, and proper repairing to be kept up by the company.

17. All companies to install wash houses; the men shall be charged 50c a month for use of the same.

18. Company to supply fresh drinking water.

19. Where the miner has to remove bone clay or blackjack from any portion of the seam. same to be paid on the basis of 10c per inch per lineal yard.

20. The company to remove all machine slack or cuttings, or where the miner loads same to be paid on a mine run basis, on the regular tonnage rates.

21. All rubbish, rock and other material and waste to be handled and unloaded by the company.

22. All water to be removed by the company, on all roads, and at the working face, and same places to be kept as dry as possible.

23. The company to be responsible for all cars lost or damaged in the mine.

24. Where any part of the mine has caved in the workmen not to be held responsible for loss of tools or any other material.

25. All wrecked cars of coal to be paid for by the average weight of same type of cars for the day.

26. Company to supply all chalk to miners free of charge.

27. In any room more than 20 feet wide, over-shoveling to be paid at 50c per lineal yard.

Contract Rates

Electric Undercutting and Shearing Machines

Sullivan 7 foot under-cut, per ton..........$	.11
Jeffary 9 foot under-cut, per ton..........	.06
Jeffery Shearing Machine, per cut..........	.80
Sullivan Bottom Cutter, 9 foot cut, per ton..........	.12
an Gardiner Under-cutter, per ton	.15
Shearer & Under-cutter.	.06
er & Under	
Mini	
ng	

Contract Miners Rates

Pick Mining narrow work 8 ft. wide, loaded by shovel, ton..	1.25
Loaded by fork, single..........	1.50
Loaded by fork, double fork..........	1.75
Yardage in entries, per lineal yard..........	1.00
In entries where bottom is taken out (seam) loaded by shovel, per ton..........	1.60
Loaded by fork, per ton..........	1.85
Yardage in entries, coal is 3 ft. 6 in. & under, per lineal yard....	.75
In entries where coal is 3 ft. 6 in. & under, extra charge, ton..	.25

PICK MINING — **Rooms**

Rooms from 12 to 20 feet wide, loaded by shovel, per ton......	.80
Loaded by fork, per ton	.90
Loaded by double fork, per ton..........	1.15
In rooms where coal is under 3 ft. 6 in. in height, loaded by shovel, per ton..........	1.05
Loaded by fork, per ton..........	1.15
Loaded by double fork, per ton..........	1.10
Yardage, narrow work 8 ft. wide, under-cut, per lineal foot loaded by shovel..........	1.65
If sheared..........	1.50

Contract Mining

Undercut in entries 8 ft. wide, loaded by shovel, per ton......	.85
Loaded by fork, per ton..........	.95
Loaded by shovel and sheared, per ton..........	.70
Loaded by fork and sheared, per ton..........	.80
Where only sheared in entries, per ton	1.00
In entries where undercut & sheared and also shot down, ton	.40
Opening up room necks extra per cut	2.00

Contract Mining IN ROOMS UNDERCUT

Rooms from 12 to 20 ft wide, undercut, loaded by shovel, ton	.65
Loaded by fork, per ton..........	.75
Rooms 12 to 20 ft. wide, undercut and sheared, loaded by shovel, per ton..........	.60
Loaded by fork, per ton..........	70
Rooms 12 to 20 ft. wide, undercut and sheared and shot down loaded by shovel, per ton..........	40

All coal to be weighed and paid on a mine run basis of 2,000 lbs to the ton.

Handling of Cars

The company to handle all cars to and from the working face.

Timbering

Three piece set consisting of a boom and two props, each set	.75
Where boom is needled into the rib side, and prop set under the other end, per set..........	.75
Where prop and cap piece required, and ordered to be set up each..........	.15

Tracklaying

The company to lay and lift all track at the working face, as required by the contract miners.

Brushing

Lifting bottom in entries, price per lineal foot..........	.50
Lifting bottom in room necks and cross-cuts, price per lineal ft.	.75
Lifting bottom in rooms, price per lineal foot..........	.25

Scale of Wages

(Per 8-hour Day from Bank to Bank)

INSIDE WAGES

Miner..........$	4.00
Timberman	4.00
Shot Lighter	4.00
Tracklayer	4.00
Electric Motor Driver..........	4.00
Driver, one horse..........	3.75
Driver, 2 horses (or 25¢ extra for each horse)..........	4.00
Cager	4.00
Steam Incline Haulageman..........	4.00
Pumpman..........	4.00
Tracklayer's Helper..........	3.75
Timbermen Helpers..........	3.75
Cager's Helper..........	3.75
Rope Rider	3.75
Track Cleaners..........	3.75
All Other Unclassified Labor	3.75
Boys under 18 years, 1st year..........	2.50
2nd year..........	3.00

Outside Day Wages

Engineers, per month .... $	150.00
Firemen, per month..........	100.00
Carpenters..........	4.50
Blacksmiths..........	4.50
Machinists	4.50
Electrician	4.50
Box Carloader Engineer	4.00
Car Repairer	4.00
Blacksmith's Helper	4.00
Machinist Helper..........	4.00
Tipple Dumper..........	4.00
Teamster	4.00
Box Car Shoveller..........	4.00
Wash Houseman	3.50
All classified labor	3.50

Appendix 3: Brief History of Union Organization in the Bienfait/Estevan Coalfields, Sask. 1907–1998

(Mainly from Glen Makahonuk in *Saskatchewan History*, Spring 1978)

1907: United Mine Workers of America, District 18, organized Local 2672 in the Roche Percée area.

1908: UMWA District 18, organized Local 2682 in Estevan and Local 2648 in Taylorton. After a short strike and some gains, the UMWA was frustrated by the companies and withdrew from the field in 1909

1915-1917: Sporadic strikes in the coal pits during wartime made some wage gains, but did not result in union organizations being formed.

1920: One Big Union sent in an organizer who was kidnapped and run out of town by vigilantes.

1931: Workers' Unity League/Mine Workers' Union of Canada sent organizers from Winnipeg and Calgary. They signed up 600 miners and formed Local 27 however the operators refused to negotiate with a 'Red' union. After a 30-day strike the miners gained a number of temporary concessions but went back to work without union recognition.

1938: United Mine Workers of America, District 18 (CIO): sent John Stokaluk to Bienfait and within a week the majority of miners were signed up into Local 7606 of the UMWA. Vincent Clark, a miner and United Church elder, was elected president. After a conciliation board report favourable to the union was ignored, the UMWA conducted a two-month strike in 1939.

1939: Mineworkers Central Union of Estevan & District: this was still the UMWA but for the duration of the Second World War the UMWA technically withdrew from the field in return for a signed agreement with the operators of all mines except Western Dominion Coal Mines.

1945: United Mine Workers of America, Local 7606: re-entered the field and in a vote conducted by the Wartime Labour Relations Board, won recognition as the bargaining unit for the Manitoba & Saskatchewan Coal Co., and other mines except those controlled by J. R. Brody. The Mineworkers Central Union was dissolved. Local 7606 conducted an 11-week strike in 1948.

1998: United Mine Workers of America, Local 7606. After Luscar Corporation became the sole operator in the coalfields a vote among the unionized workers settled on Local 7606 to represent all the miners in the field.

1932 Saskatchewan Mine Workers Association: this was a local, independent union fostered by an official of the provincial Department of Labour to counter the influence of the Mine Workers' Union of Canada. It was largely a paper organization.

1938: Saskatchewan Coal Miners Union, a company union, formed the previous year, was granted a closed shop with a dues checkoff in J. R. Brody's Western Dominion Coal Mines and the Bienfait Mine No. 2 owned by A. C. Wilson . This union affiliated with the Canadian Federation of Labour.

1957: Saskatchewan Coal Miners Union becomes a direct charter, **Local 331** of the **Canadian Labour Congress** with a closed shop and dues check-off at Western Dominion Coal Mines, where Charles Doerr is the manager.

1958-1990: Saskatchewan Strip Miners Union, Local 1573, replaces Local 331 and becomes a CLC direct charter local at the mines of J. R. Brody, now owned by Manalta corporation.
1964-1989: Roche Percée Miners Union, Local 1623, becomes a CLC direct charter local with recognition by Manalta corporation.

1990-1998: United Steelworkers of America, Local 9279 replaces the CLC direct charter locals in the Manalta mines.

Notes

Introduction

1 Province of Saskatchewan, Trade Union Act, 1944, section 2.1.
2 'Collective Agreement between Luscar Ltd., Boundary Dam Mine and Bienfait Mine and the United Mine Workers of America, Local 7606, effective July 1, 1999 to June 30, 2003,' courtesy of Garnet Dishaw, Saskatchewan Federation of Labour, Regina.
3 *The Black Diamond Reunion '88* (Bienfait Public Library), 10.
4 Ibid., Ida Smart Nygaard, 26.
5 Lorna Hassard Friess, 'The Unionizing of the Estevan Coal Miners' (1976), 1, *R-E1921*, Saskatchewan Archives Board [SAB].
6 Larry Warwaruk, *Red Finns on the Coteau*, 4.

Chapter 1. The Bienfait Coalfields

1 *Records of the Royal Commission on the Estevan-Bienfait Mining Dispute* (Saskatchewan Archives Board [SAB], 1931), vol. 2. Referred to hereafter as *Wylie Commission*.
2 Ibid., vol. 12, Exhibit O–33, A.C. Wilson to T.G. Thomson, Inspector of Boilers and Industry, province of Saskatchewan, 25 Feb. 1930.
3 According to legend, the name Bienfait came from the pronouncement of the words of a railway-construction crew foreman to his French-Canadian workers: 'well done.' However, Bill Barry, in *People Places: The Dictionary of Saskatchewan Place Names*, 39, says Canadian Pacific Railway files reveal that Bienfait was named by the railway for Antoine-Charles Bienfait, a member of an Amsterdam banking firm that introduced CPR shares to European money markets.
4 Interview with Peter Gemby, May 1995, in Bienfait.

5 *Census of Canada, 1931*, 91.
6 According to the *Revised Statutes of Saskatchewan, 1930*, chapter 105, section 51, the 'overseer' is the chief executive officer of the village, the elected chairperson of the village council, who has special responsibilities to be vigilant that the provincial laws governing the village are 'duly executed' and is expected to recommend 'such measures as may tend to the betterment of the finances, health, security, cleanliness, comfort, ornamentation and prosperity of the village.'
7 *Mercury*, 20 April 1933, 8.
8 Ibid., 16 March 1933, 8.
9 Mervyn Enmark to Michelle Rohatyn (1979), *Sounds and Stories*, tape *R–A1964*, SAB.
10 Interview with the author, Estevan, May 1998.
11 Joe Pryznyk to Michelle Rohatyn, *R–A1957*, SAB.
12 Hilda Carlson, 'Taylorton,' in *The Black Diamond Reunion '88* (Bienfait Public Library).
13 See S.H. Whitaker et al., *Coal Resources of Southern Saskatchewan*, Saskatchewan Research Council Report 20 (1978). According to mining engineers, there remains more coal in these shallow seams than will be needed in the next 100 years; after that there are fourteen deep seams down 250 feet or more below the surface. The Estevan Coal Corporation estimates that Saskatchewan has 7½ per cent of Canada's reserves of coal. 'Estevan Coal Corporation,' a prospectus of 1988, P.O. Box 908, Estevan, Sask.
14 P.L. Broughton, 'History of Coal Mining in Southern Saskatchewan,' in *Coal Resources of Southern Saskatchewan*, Appendix 1. J.H. Richards and K.I. Fung, *Atlas of Saskatchewan*, 'Mining in Saskatchewan.' J. Raffles Cox, mining engineer, *Wylie Commission*, vol. 12, exhibit C27, 12.
15 *Mineral Statistics Yearbook*, 1995, Department of Energy and Mines, Saskatchewan, Miscellaneous Report 96–3; Richards and Fung, *Atlas of Saskatchewan*, 'Mining in Saskatchewan.'
16 Robert J. Lee, mining inspector for the federal government, *Wylie Commission*, vol. 11, 6–8.
17 Testimony of Dan Moar and Frank Newsome, mine manager, *Wylie Commission*, vol. 10, 27, 120–2, 136.
18 This section follows the discussion on mechanization in 'Taylorton, 1955' (Bienfait Public Library), 15–19.
19 *Wylie Commission*, vol. 7, 10–20, 24–5; combustion and mining engineer Robert L. Sutherland testified that, as a result of mechanization, tonnage produced per man per day increased between 1921 and 1929 by 14.8 per cent in British Columbia, 19.5 per cent in Alberta, and 15.3 per cent in Saskatchewan, ibid., vol. 11, 298.

20 Interview with Donald Doerr, engineer with Luscar, in Estevan, May 1998.
21 Andrew King, *Estevan: The Power Centre*, 22–9.
22 On Brodie, see *Who's Who in Canada*, 1936–37, 734; 'Opening of the J.R.
    Brodie Science Centre, 7 May 72,' McKee Archives, Brandon University,
    Brandon, Manitoba; *Wylie Commission*, vol. 2, 2–71; *Mercury*, 8 Oct. 1931;
    Henderson's Winnipeg City Directory (1931), 1816 and 1817; R.J. Dun, *The Mer-
    cantile Agency Reference Book*, July 1931; King, *Estevan: The Power Centre*; on
    Hassard, see *Mercury*, 26 Nov. 1931.
23 Although Saskatchewan's lignite coal was close to the natural market terri-
    tory of Saskatchewan and Manitoba, its annual coal output of 580,000 tons in
    1931 supplied only 6.3 per cent of the Saskatchewan and Manitoba market
    and only 15 per cent of coal used in Saskatchewan government institutions.
    There was room for considerable improvement in market share. Mining
    engineers in the province calculated that, if a market could be found for
    960,000 tons of Saskatchewan coal on the basis of 1929 conditions, the indus-
    try would change from crisis to health: such a volume would reduce over-
    head costs of production from 39.4 per cent to 23.9 per cent; it would allow
    for an increased wage scale of 28 per cent and provide reasonable earnings
    on capital, *Wylie Commission*, 'Commissioner's Report,' vol. 12, 133. Saskatch-
    ewan coal production reached a plateau of 952,000 tons in 1937 but the price
    was still 30 cents per ton below the 1929 level. See *Mineral Statistics Yearbook*,
    1995, Saskatchewan Department of Mines, Miscellaneous Report 96–3, 126.
24 Interview with Jim Davies in Bienfait, May 1998.
25 *Wylie Commission*, vol. 7, testimony of A.C. Wilson, 52.
26 *Wylie Commission*, f.2, exhibits introduced by the 'Operators,' exhibit O27;
    ibid., testimony of A.C. Wilson, vol. 7, 19–25.
27 A.C. Wilson to T.G. Thomson, inspector of boilers and industry for
    Saskatchewan, 25 Feb. 1930, ibid., vol. 12, exhibit O–33.
28 The number of men and horses in the mines are from the testimony of Rob-
    ert J. Lee, mining inspector for the federal government, to the *Wylie Commis-
    sion*, vol. 11, 1–12.
29 For information on Truax-Traer, see Ovid Demaris, *Captive City*, 220ff.; *Wylie
    Commission*, vol. 11; *Turgeon Commission*, vol. 1; Tom Ewen, 'Summary Report
    of Estevan Strike,' Communist Party of Canada Papers, National Archives of
    Canada [NAC], MG28,IV.4, interim box 5, file 51–25.
30 Rev. George Dorey, Superintendent of Missions, southern Saskatchewan, in
    'Report of Visit of Messrs Oliver, Cochrane, Endicott, and Wilson to the
    Dried-out Area of Southern Saskatchewan,' United Church of Canada
    Archives, General Council, Executive and Subcommittee Correspondence,
    1931 (July), UCC, GC, series Ib, box 2, file 21.
31 Ibid., 12.

32 Ibid.; Gordon Barnhart, 'E.H. Oliver: A Study of Protestant Progressivism in Saskatchewan 1909–1935,' MA thesis, University of Regina (1977), 208–11.
33 Tom Ewen, 'Summary Report of Estevan Strike,' CPC Papers, NAC; J. Raffles Cox, 'Confidential Report ... with special reference to the cost and rate situation,' Exhibit C27, *Wylie Commission*; Arthur Nelson to Thomas Molloy, deputy minister of labour, Saskatchewan, 17 Aug. 1931, 'Estevan Coal Strike 1931,' Deputy Minister's Files, Department of Labour, SAB. According to the *Dominion of Canada Census*, 1931, 44–5, Saskatchewan coal miners earned on average $14 per week during the weeks when they were employed, compared to $23 for Alberta miners.
34 Glen Makahonuk, 'Trade Unions in the Saskatchewan Coal Industry, 1907–1945' and 'The Saskatchewan Coal Strikes of 1932.'
35 Thomas Molloy, witness at the *Wylie Commission*, vol. 10, 1–14.

Chapter 2. John Billis and Family

1 This chapter is based on my interview with Anne and Amelia Billis in May 1995.

Chapter 3. Boruk's Boarding House

1 House of Commons *Debates*, 29 July 1931, 4278; Toronto *Mail and Empire*, 10 Nov. 1932.
2 In the Canadian espionage trials of 1946, Sam Carr was sentenced to jail again, this time for conspiracy to obtain a false passport; the offence effectively ended his career as a leader of the Communist Party.
3 Personal conversations with Sam Carr in 1945 and later; interviews with Olga Boruk Wozny in Stoney Creek, Ontario, 24 October and 3 December 1997; interview with Steve Elchyson in Regina in May 1997.
4 Interviews with Olga Boruk Wozny, 1997.
5 James H. Cuddington, 'History of Bienfait, Sask.' (typescript 1978), R–E148, 6, SAB.
6 King's Bench case #52 of 1924, *Kaik vs. Boraska*, SAB; Interview with Steve Elchyson in Regina, 11 May 1997.
7 'Labour Temple at Bienfait, Saskatchewan,' in the *Almanac of the Ukrainian Labour-Farmer Temple Association 1918–1929* [in Ukrainian language] 177–8. Translation by Peter Krawchuk.
8 According to the *Dominion of Canada Census*, 1931, 440–1, there were 134 people of Ukrainian descent in Bienfait, which represented 23 per cent of the village population. Villagers of British origin accounted for 43 per cent of the total.

9 Interview with Steve Elchyson in Regina, 11 May 1997; interviews with Olga Boruk Wozny in 1997.

10 'Mr Popovich of Winnipeg,' by T.B.R., Winnipeg *Free Press*, 25 Nov. 1924.

11 Royal Canadian Mounted Police, Manitoba District, 'Personal History File, Matthew Popowich,' 15 Oct. 1931, file 175/P96, vol. 4162, RG146.

12 Peter Krawchuk, ed., *Our Stage: The Amateur Performing Arts of the Ukrainian Settlers in Canada*, 102–3.

13 Tom McEwen, *The Forge Glows Red*, 183–5; 'Tory Government Rejects W.U.L. Bill,' *Worker*, 18 April 1931. (Note: Tom McEwen went by his father's family name, Ewen, until the 1940s; after that he changed to his mother's family name, McEwen.) A copy of the petition and Ewen's presentation to the prime minister are in the CSIS/RCMP file on the 'WUL – Canada,' vol. 2871–72, RG146, #92-A-00088 (1993), NAC. See Bennett's speech in House of Commons *Debates*, 29 July 1931, 4278.

14 J. Arch Getty and Oleg V. Naumov, *The Road to Terror: Stalin and the Self-destruction of the Bolsheviks, 1932–1939* (New Haven, Conn.: Yale University Press 1999), 41–2.

15 Andrea Graziosi, *The Great Soviet Peasant War: Bolsheviks and Peasants 1917–1933* (Cambridge, Mass.: Harvard University Press 1996), 58.

16 Getty and Naumov, *The Road to Terror*, 45.

17 See 'Moscow Unmasked,' and 'Interesting Items from Current Press,' in *The Friend of Missions: A Journal of Old Time Religion and Sound Missionary Work* (London), vol. 25, no. 9 (September 1932), in *H.W. Dobson Papers*, United Church of Canada Archives, B–12, file 7; 'Russia exports while its habitants starve,' *Mercury*, 24 Sept. 1931; 'Typhus slays thousands in Soviet camps,' ibid., 19 Feb. 1931.

18 The Estevan town hall auditorium was packed to capacity in October 1931 to hear an up-beat illustrated lecture by George Williams, past-president of the United Farmers of Canada, Saskatchewan section, on 'Russia, Land of the Soviet' (*Mercury*, 22 Oct. 1931). See also William's pamphlet *The Land of the Soviets* (United Farmers of Canada, Saskatoon, 1931), SAB; Earlier, Rev. Charles J. Smith, pastor of Stirling Baptist Church in Estevan, had addressed the Rotary Club in tones of guarded optimism on his recent trip to Soviet Russia (*Mercury*, 27 March 1930).

19 Getty and Naumov, *The Road to Terror*, 43.

20 *Worker*, 23 May, 13 June 1931.

21 Interviews with Peter Gemby and Stella Bachynski in Bienfait, May 1995, 1997, and 1998. In 1931 the legion branch in Bienfait objected to the singing of 'unpatriotic songs' in public halls and, in response to its protest, the village council threatened that 'all proceedings of an unpatriotic nature must

be discontinued' or the council would revoke the licence of the Ukrainian Labour Temple. Minutes of Council Meeting, 8 December 1931, Beinfait village archives. When interviewed by Larry Johnson and Ron Adams in 1976, Gemby for some reason expressed considerable defensiveness, even denial, about the existence of communist leadership in the Ukrainian Labour Temple. See tape 1020 of R–A325, SAB.

22 Sam Carr to Tom Ewen, 29 July 1931, from Winnipeg, and 'Programme and Policy of W.U.L. in Canadian Mining Industry,' 12 June 1931, file 175/6847, #92–A–00088, part 1, Workers' Unity League – Canada, vol. 2871–72, RG146, NAC.

23 'The Strassburg Resolution on Strike Strategy and Tactics,' in *Workers' Unity*, no. 6, (August 1931), 5. See also Jane Degras, *The Communist International*, vol. 3 (London: F. Cass 1971), 64. The official language of the Comintern was German, hence the use of the German spelling for Strasbourg.

Chapter 4. August: Gaining Momentum

1 Charles Marriott (Winnipeg) to Tom Ewen (Toronto), 7 Aug. 1931, Estevan Strike File, Deputy Minister's Office, Department of Labour, Saskatchewan, SAB.

2 The narrative in this chapter relies mainly on the *Western Miner*, 8 Sept. 1931; the testimony of Dan Moar, president of the Bienfait local of the Mine Workers' Union of Canada to the *Wylie Commission*, vol. 11, 167ff.; testimony of John Loughran, ibid., 242ff.; testimony of Bernie Winn, ibid., 261ff.; testimony of W.W. Lynd, ibid., 267ff., SAB.

3 *Mercury*, 24 Sept. 1931. See also RCMP 'Personal History File on Martin Joseph Forkin,' file 175P/2772 in vol. 4671–72, RG146, NAC; Errol Black, 'Brandon's "Revolutionary Forkins,"' *Prairie Forum*, vol. 20, no. 2 (fall 1995): 231–54. Interview with Mrs Taime Davis, Forkin's sister-in-law, in Toronto, May 1997.

4 RCMP 'Personal History File on Sam Scarlett,' 175/P2456 in vol. 4901, RG146, NAC. Biographical information about Scarlett is relatively scarce but see Tom McEwen, *The Forge Glows Red*, 58–61; T.C. Sims, 'Sam Scarlett a dauntless fighter for the working class,' *Monthly Review* (official organ of the Communist Party of Canada) vol. 1, no. 5, 10 Aug. 1940, 45–8; Donald H. Avery, 'British-born "Radicals" in North America, 1900–1941: The Case of Sam Scarlett,' *Canadian Ethnic Studies*, vol. 10, no. 2 (1978): 65–85. I learned further details in interviews with Peter and Stella Gemby in Bienfait, May 1997, and with Taime Davis in Toronto, May 1997.

5 'Coal Miners will demand better wages,' *Leader-Post*, Regina, Friday, 28 Aug. 1931.

6 Sometimes the local is referred to as Local 24.

7 For a detailed, scholarly report, see Glen Makahonuk, 'The Working and Living Conditions of the Saskatchewan Deep Seam Coal Miners, 1930–1939.'

8 *Wylie Commission*, vol. 4, Ken John testimony; exhibit C–68, Cox Report, 8.

9 *Census of Canada, 1931*, Table 45, 96–7; *Wylie Commission*, vol. 12, exhibit O-18.

10 J. Raffles Cox, testimony, *Wylie Commission*, vol. 12, 1–57. The evidence of the Wylie Commission suggested that, if Saskatchewan coal operators could find a wider market and the mines worked closer to their capacity, then the contract miners would benefit. Their wage packets, paid according to tonnage output, would have overtaken those of the company daymen who were paid by hourly rates or fixed salaries.

11 From June 1930 to June 1931, 410 people, according to table 31, were employed in coal mining in Saskatchewan. They reported earning on average $14.71 per week worked (table 19), for average annual earnings of $477 (table 15). (Dominion Bureau of Statistics, *Census of Canada*, 1931, 266, 44, 30.)

12 Saskatchewan Coal Mines: Average Employment and Earnings, 1930 and 1931

Year	Wage earners	Days worked	Total wages	Daily wage	Annual wage
1930	529	205	$449,669	$4.15	$850.75
1931	538	196	$404,432	$3.83	$750.68

Source: Dominion Bureau of Statistics, *Coal Statistics of Canada*, 1929–1932, table 100.

13 *Wylie Commission*, vol. 12, exhibit C–36 and O–24.

14 Ibid., vol. 12, exhibit O–6 from Bienfait mine; O–10 from Eastern Collieries; O–18 from M&S mines; O–87 from Crescent Collieries.

15 H. Gordon Tolton to A.J. Macaulay, president of the United Farmers of Canada, 'Report of investigations into the conditions of the Bienfait miners,' 25 Sept. 1931, printed in *Canadian Miner*, 30 Jan. 1932, 3.

16 *Wylie Commission*, vol. 2, J.R. Brodie testimony; vol. 12, exhibit Operator–17, 'Statement of tonnage shipped from M&S Coal Co.'

17 Ibid., vol. 3, testimony of Wilfrid Hogg.

18 Interview, at Bienfait, May 1998, name withheld by request.

19 Interview with Donald Doerr, in Estevan, May 1998.

20 Testimony of Frank Newsome, mine manager, *Wylie Commission*, vol. 10, 120–2.

21 Ibid., vol. 1, testimony of John Harris.

22 Sgt. W. Mulhall, 9 Sept. 1931, RG146, vol. 817, H.V. 7 [i.e, Historical Value #7] vol. 1, 25–6, NAC [hereafter cited as RCMP Estevan file].

23 Interview with Jim Davies in Bienfait, May 1998.

24 Interview with Donald Doerr in Estevan, May 1998. Mr Doerr is Elizabeth Sherratt Davies's nephew.

25 Interview with Tony Bachynski in Bienfait, May 1998. Mr Bachynski is the son of John Bachynski, secretary of the Ukrainian Labour Temple in Bienfait in 1931.

26 Interview at Bienfait, May 1998, name withheld by request.

27 *Wylie Commission*, vol. 7, testimony of A.C. Wilson, 45–9.

28 Ibid., vol. 7, testimony of A.C. Wilson, 8, 51–3.

29 Ibid., vol. 12, f.3, exhibit M–8, 'Notice re Mrs. Molyneux'; f.2, exhibit O–90, 'Notice to Pedlars'; vol. 6, testimony of Edward Edwardson.

30 Ibid., vol. 6, testimony of Mrs Francis Gray, 237–8.

31 Ibid., vol. 7, testimony of A.C. Wilson, 57–9.

32 Larry Johnston and Ron Adams, *The Estevan Strike and Riot, 1931*, interview with Peter Gemby in 1973, R–A325, SAB.

33 *Wylie Commission*, f.1, exhibit C–26, 'Report of Thomas Douglas (Sanitary Officer).'

34 Ibid., vol. 3, testimony of Anne Baryluk, 77–9.

35 Ibid., vol. 6, testimony of William Stalene, 219ff.; William Powlowitch, 358–61; Fred Booth, 111.

36 Ibid., vol. 6, testimony of Steve Lazur and John Salamanchuk. The mayor also suspected that the local RCMP sergeant was reporting names of purchasers to the American border patrol. D. Bannatyne to Sergt. Metcalfe, RCMP, Weyburn, Sask, 'Personal & Confidential,' 9 June 1931, RCMP Estevan file, vol. 1, 1.

37 *Wylie Commission*, f.2, exhibit C–31, 'Notice re Door to Ladder'; vol. 6 testimonies of Sam Davies, Fred Booth, John Lochlin [Loughran], Pete Boruk, and others; vol. 12, exhibit O–33, A.C. Wilson letter to T.G. Thomson, 25 Feb. 1930; three of the large mines in the Bienfait field had zig-zag ladder manways similar to the one at the M&S mine, while the others had slope manways for walking in or out of the mines. See ibid., vol. 11 testimony of Robert J. Lee, mining inspector, 5–12.

38 Ibid., vol. 6, testimonies of Mike Kresko, Joe Slenka, William Stalene, and Charles Hewka; vol. 7, testimony of A.C. Wilson, 9.

39 *Mercury*, 27 Aug. 1931.

40 *Leader-Post*, 1 Sept. 1931, 'Merkley will study ...'

41 Sgt. Wm. Mulhall, I/C Estevan detachment, RCMP, to Det-Sgt. J.G. Metcalfe, I/C Weyburn subdistrict, 5 Sept. 1931, RCMP Estevan file, vol. 1, 3–6.

42 *Mercury*, 3 Sept. 1931. The provincial government did not have a large economic stake in coal since royalties at the time were only five cents a ton. Total royalties levied on Saskatchewan coal operators in 1929 were $29,000

(representing seven-tenths of 1 per cent of their invested capital) but much of this was paid to the CPR and other freehold landowners. *Wylie Commission*, vol. 11, 305, testimony of Robert L. Sutherland, mining engineer.

43 *Wylie Commission*, vol. 11, 267ff., 257.

44 Copy of letter of G.A. Richardson to J.F. Andersen, president of National Mines, Regina, 15 Sept. 1931, RCMP Estevan file, vol. 1, 44.

45 'Re: Estevan Coal Strike,' 9 Sept. 1931, Estevan Strike File, Deputy Minister's Office, Department of Labour, Saskatchewan, SAB, enclosed in Sergt. W. Mulhall report, 5 Sept. 1931, RCMP Estevan file, vol. 1, 3–4.

46 Department of Labour, RG27, T2759, vol. 348, #70, NAC.

47 Sergt. W. Mulhall report, 5 Sept. 1931 RCMP Estevan file, vol. 1. 4–5.

48 Det. Sgt. W. Mortimer, head of the RCMP's criminal investigation branch in Regina, report of 21 Sept. 1931, RCMP Estevan file, vol. 1, 100–5.

49 Sergt. W. Mulhall's reports of 5 and 7 Sept. 1931 RCMP Estevan file, vol. 1, 3–5, 9–10.

50 *Mercury*, 10 Sept. 1931.

51 See biography of Charles Smart in *Black Diamond Reunion '88* (Bienfait Public Library) for reference to maintenance men on the job during the strike.

Chapter 5. September: On Strike

1 *Mercury*, 10 Sept. 1931; *Leader-Post*, 8 Sept. 1931; Inspector R.R. Tait, commanding officer, Southern Saskatchewan District, RCMP, Regina, to commissioner, RCMP headquarters, Ottawa, 8 Sept. 1931, RCMP Estevan file, vol. 1, 15; ibid., vol. 2, 121 [MWUC leaflet]; ibid., Sergt. J. Molyneux, Radville detachment, report, vol. 1, 81; ibid., Det. S-Sergt. W. Mortimer report, 66; ibid., Sergt. W. Mulhall report, 39.

2 Tait to M.A. MacPherson, attorney general of Saskatchewan, 15 Sept. 1931, RCMP Estevan file, vol. 1, 43.

3 Inspector F.W. Schutz (secret) to Tait, 20 Sept. 1931, ibid., vol. 1, 73.

4 Ibid., vol. 1, 75, 73.

5 Tom Ewen, national secretary, WUL, 'Summary Report of Estevan Strike,' n.d, circa 20 Oct. 1931, MG28, IV.4, interim box 5, 51–25, NAC.

6 Ibid.

7 *Canadian Miner*, 12 Oct. 1931.

8 *Mercury*, 24 Sept. 1931.

9 Mortimer to Tait, 21 Sept. 1931, RCMP Estevan file, vol. 2,101; Tait to MacPherson, 3 Oct. 1931, ibid., vol. 3, 204; Mortimer to Tait, 4 Oct. 1931, ibid., 219; Inspector C. Rivett-Carnac report, 14 Oct. 1931, ibid., 293–301; Mulhall to Tait, 18 Oct. 1931, ibid., vol. 4, 338; Mulhall to Tait, 30 Oct. 1931, ibid., 427.

10 Mulhall to Tait, 17 Sept. 1931, ibid., vol. 1, 59; Sergt. C. Richardson to Tait, 18 Sept. 1931, ibid., 63.
11 Mulhall to Tait, 17 Sept. 1931, ibid., 59.
12 Molyneux to Tait, 21 Sept. 1931, ibid., vol. 2, 93–4; Schutz to Tait, 22 Sept. 1931, ibid., 111; Tait to MacPherson, 23 Sept. 1931, ibid., 116.
13 Schutz to Tait, 20 Sept. 1931, ibid., vol. 1, 74.
14 *Leader-Post*, 16 Sept. 1931.
15 CP telegram, 16 Sept. 1931, RCMP file 175p/2772 on Martin J. Forkin, vol. 4671–72, RG146, NAC.
16 Schutz to Tait, 20 Sept. 1931, RCMP Estevan file, vol. 1, 76–7.
17 Mayor David Bannatyne (personal and confidential) to Sergt. J. Metcalfe, Weyburn detachment, RCMP, 9 June 1931, ibid., 1.
18 Sergeant Wm. Mulhall, file 75.83, RCMP Museum, Regina.
19 Mulhall to Tait, 17 Sept. 1931, RCMP Estevan file, vol. 1, 58.
20 *Leader-Post*, 18 Sept. 1931.
21 Andrew King, *Estevan: The Power Centre*, 25.
22 Dr. James Creighton to Senator Gideon Robertson, minister of labour, 17 Sept. 1931, RCMP Estevan file, vol. 1, 50; Bannatyne to Colonel J.W. Spalding, RCMP, Regina, 17 Sept. 1931, ibid., 61.
23 Spalding to General MacBrien, commissioner, RCMP, Ottawa, 21 Sept. 1931, ibid., vol. 2, 99.
24 Spalding to Bannatyne, 20 Sept. 1931, ibid., vol. 1, 72.
25 Mortimer to Tait, 21 Sept. 1931, ibid., vol. 2, 102.
26 Molyneux to Metcalfe, 20 Sept. 1931, ibid., vol. 1, 81.
27 *Leader-Post*, 17 Sept. 1931.
28 Molyneux to Metcalfe, 20 Sept. 1931, RCMP Estevan file, vol. 1, 81; Mortimer to Tait, 21 Sept. 1931, ibid., vol. 2, 102; *Leader-Post*, 18 Sept. 1931; *Mercury*, 24 Sept. 1931.
29 Doris Shackleton, *Tommy Douglas* (Toronto: McClelland and Stewart 1975), 55.
30 Thomas H. McLeod and Ian McLeod, *Tommy Douglas: The Road to Jerusalem*, 35.
31 CBC documentary program: *Biography: Tommy Douglas*, aired in February 2000.
32 *Leader-Post*, 19 Sept. 1931.
33 Schutz to Tait, 26 Sept. 1931, vol. 2, 140.
34 Glen Makahonuk, *Class, State and Power: The Struggle for Trade Union Rights in Saskatchewan 1905–1997*, 14–15.

Chapter 6. Strikers versus the Strip Mine

1 *Mercury*, 18 Dec. 30. As listed in *The Financial Post Survey of Mines, 1933–34*,

vol. 8, 184, the capitalization of Truax-Traer Coal was only 10,000 common shares worth $10 each.

2 *Mercury*, 4 Sept. 30.

3 See Ovid Demaris, *Captive City*, 220ff.

4 *Wylie Commission*, vol. 11, testimony of Eleazer Garner, 69ff.

5 Glen Makahonuk, 'The Saskatchewan Coal Strikes of 1932: A Study in Class Relations,' 81.

6 *Wylie Commission*, vol. 11, testimony of Eleazer Garner, 70–1.

7 Ibid., exhibits, f.5, C68, J.R. Cox Report, 6.

8 Sergt. W. Mulhall (Estevan detachment) to R.R. Tait, commanding officer, Southern Saskatchewan District, RCMP, 5 Sept. 1931, RCMP Estevan file, vol. 1, 3–6.

9 Mulhall to Tait, 23 Sept. 1931, ibid., vol. 2, 119; W. Mortimer, criminal investigation branch, RCMP, Regina, to Tait, 27 Sept. 1931, ibid., 146.

10 *Wylie Commission*, vol. 10, testimony of Dan Moar, 44.

11 Mulhall to Tait, 25 Sept. 1931, RCMP Estevan file, vol. 2, 133–4.

12 Tait to MacPherson, 28 Sept. 1931, ibid., 147; ibid., 25 Sept. 1931, 135.

13 Mortimer to Tait, 25, 27 Sept. 1931, ibid., 137–9, 144–6; Special Constable J. Eberhardt to Tait, ibid., 137–9.

14 Telegram, Saskatchewan coal operators to MacPherson, 22 Sept. 1931, ibid., vol. 6, 637.

15 Mortimer to Tait, 27 Sept. 1931, ibid., vol. 2, 145.

16 Tom Ewen, 'Summary Report of Estevan Strike,' MG28.IV.4, interim box 5, 51–25, NAC.

17 Mortimer to Tait, 4 Oct. 1931, RCMP Estevan file, vol. 3, 220–1.

Chapter 7. The Parade

1 Larry Ward (New Democratic Party member of the provincial legislature for Estevan), *Our Times*, July/August 1997, 11.

2 Telegram from General J.H. MacBrien, commissioner, to assistant commissioner, RCMP, Ottawa, RCMP Estevan file, vol. 2, 153; Inspector W.J. Moorhead to R.R. Tait, commanding officer, Southern Saskatchewan District, RCMP, 1 Oct. 1931, ibid., 170–2.

3 Chris Higgenbotham, 'Defiant women aim missiles at police during hectic riot,' *Leader-Post*, 30 Sept. 1931.

4 Tait to M.A. MacPherson, attorney general of Saskatchewan, 5 Oct. 1931, RCMP Estevan file, vol. 3, 225.

5 A. McCutcheon, Estevan chief of police, to W.J. Moorhead 29 Sept. 1931, ibid., vol. 2, 151.

6 Exhibit P3 at the trial of Martin Day, 1 March 1932, R–95–53, *Rex vs. Scarlett*, SAB. A.B. Stuart, Estevan city clerk, to James Sloan, 29 Sept. 1931, 1931 Riot File, Estevan Municipal Archives.
7 *Wylie Commission*, vol. 11, 173, testimony of Dan Moar.
8 Testimony of Ella Katherine Carroll, 9 March 33, *Rex vs Buller*, SAB.
9 Tait to the Commissioner, Alberta Provincial Police, 9 Sept. 1931, RCMP Estevan file, vol. 1, 22.
10 Interview with Donald Doerr in Estevan, May 1998.
11 *Leader-Post*, 30 Sept. 1931.
12 Sergt. J. Metcalfe, Weyburn detachment, to Tait, 30 Sept. 1931, RCMP Estevan file, vol. 2, 158, 163.
13 Moorhead to Tait, 1 Oct. 1931, ibid., vol. 2, 173.

Chapter 8. Sticking with the Union

1 W.J. Moorhead, inspector, to R.R. Tait, commanding officer, Depot Division, Regina, 9 Nov. 1931, RCMP Estevan file, vol. 5, 452.
2 Moorhead to Tait, 1, 15 Oct. 1931, RCMP Estevan file, vol. 2, 170–2, vol. 3, 304–5; Thomas Hesketh, miner, interview taped in 1979, R-A1966, R-A1967, SAB; *Worker*, 10 Oct. 1931. The names of twenty-four men quickly arrested and accused of rioting were Peter Smarz, John Grycuik, Mike Paulowitch, Mike Palkoniuk, Charles Gregalis and Metro Uhryn of Taylorton, Joseph Bernotas, John Kolenkas, Joseph Leptak, R.W. Dixon, Martin Day, Andy Levie, Harry Michalowski, Tony Stankevitch, Mike Kyatick, Louis Revay and Fred Konopaki of Bienfait, Roy Buttozoni, William Cunnah, James McCool McLean, Chester McIllvenna of Estevan, Isadore Minster, Alex Petryk, and David Rowsen of Winnipeg. See *Leader-Post*, 1 Oct. 1931; for the results of their trials, see Staff-Sergt. W. Mortimer to Tait, 2 April 32, RCMP Estevan file, vol. 6, 676–8.
3 *Mercury*, 8 Oct. 1931; Inspector C. Rivett-Carnac (secret) to Tait, 15 Oct. 1931, RCMP Estevan file, vol. 3, 295; *Leader-Post*, 5 Oct. 1931; Interview with Steve Elchyson in Regina, May 1997.
4 Quoted in *Leader-Post*, 5 Oct. 1931. See also Louise Watson, *She Never Was Afraid*, 42. John Weir wrote a ballad called 'Estevan' to the music of the Irish rebel song 'Kevin Barry' to commemorate the miners' sacrifices. It was printed in *Canadian Miner*, 30 Jan. 1932, under the pseudonym of Cecil Boone. A shorter version is recorded by The Travellers, *A Century of Song* (CD) (Pointe-Claire, Que.: Unidisc Music, 1967/2001).
5 Annie Buller, 'The Estevan Massacre,' *National Affairs Monthly*, May 1949, 170.
6 Louise Watson, *She Never Was Afraid*, 42–6; RCMP, Manitoba District, 'Per-

sonal History File, Anna Buller,' 6 Oct. 1931, RG146, file 175/P1613; Interview with Mike and Elaine Baryluk in Bienfait, May 1995. Note: The Buller file is no. 68 in the ledger of documents released by CSIS and is held at the Solicitor General of Canada, Access Section, Ottawa.

7 *Mercury*, 8 Oct. 1931.
8 Moorhead to Tait, 15 Oct. 1931, RCMP Estevan file, vol. 3, 305.
9 Quoted in Annie Buller, 'The Estevan Massacre,' 171.
10 Moorhead to Tait, 15 Oct. 1931, RCMP Estevan file, vol. 3, 304; *Mercury*, 8 Oct. 1931.
11 Ibid.
12 Moorhead to Tait, 15 Oct. 1931, RCMP Estevan file, vol. 3, 304.
13 Rev. C.B. Lawson, address to Estevan Rotary Club, *Mercury*, 26 June 1930.
14 ibid., 15 Oct. 1931.
15 Tom Ewen, 'Summary Report of Estevan Strike,' MG28.IV.4, interim box 5, 51–25, NAC.
16 *Mercury*, 8, 15, 22 Oct. 1931; Bienfait Legion Branch 169, R–E312, SAB.
17 Ibid., 'Souvenir Programme, 15th Annual Banquet, 1931–1946,' Legion Branch 169, Bienfait.
18 Michelle Rohatyn taped interviews, 10 July 1979, with Thomas Hesketh, file R–A1966–1967, SAB.
19 Interview with Steve Elchyson, in Regina, May 1997.
20 *Mercury*, 22 Oct, 5 Nov. 1931; *Leader-Post*, 3 Oct. 1931.
21 *Canadian Miner*, 12 Dec. 1931.
22 J.G. Metcalfe, Det-Sergt, Weyburn criminal investigation branch, to Tait, 8 Dec. 1931, RCMP Estevan file, vol. 5, 531.
23 *Mercury*, 27 April 33.
24 Tom Ewen, 'Personal History file,' 175/P2459, 1 April 31, RG146, CSIS records public access, Box 17, NAC.
25 See chapter 10 for more on section 98.
26 Ewen, 'Summary Report of the Estevan Strike.'
27 Ewen, 'W.U.L. Muddlers in Estevan Strike,' *Workers' Unity*, vol. 1, no. 5 (30 Oct. 1931); Ewen, 'Summary Report of the Estevan Strike.'
28 Ibid.
29 *Workers' Unity*, 30 Oct. 1931.
30 Sergt. A.G. Beale, to Tait, 27 Oct. 1931, RCMP Estevan file, vol. 4, 406.
31 Mortimer to Tait, 26 Oct. 1931, RCMP Estevan file, vol. 4, 396a, 396b. When Bryson appealed his vagrancy conviction and showed that he was in the employ of the Mine Workers' Union of Canada, the Moose Jaw appeal court judge, F.A.G. Ouseley, denied the appeal saying such employment was illegal since the union was affiliated to the Workers' Unity League, which in turn

was affiliated to the Communist Party of Canada, an organization that had just been declared to be illegal by the Ontario courts. Although the MWUC was not on trial, the inference of Ouseley's 'opinion' was that it, too, was an illegal organization, a notion that was picked up by *Mercury* and the legionnaires in Bienfait to cause temporary confusion and worry among the union members. *Mercury*, 3 Dec. 1931, 11 Aug. 1932; *Rex vs. Bryson*, R95–53, SAB; M.A. MacPherson, attorney general of Saskatchewan, to Prime Minister R.B. Bennett, 14 Dec. 1931, *Bennett Papers*, 267407–9, NAC; Metcalfe to Tait, 8 Dec. 1931, RCMP Estevan file, vol. 5, 527–31.

32 *Mercury*, 22, 29 Oct. 1931.

33 Mortimer to Tait, 26 Oct. 1931, RCMP Estevan file, vol. 4, 396a.

34 Ibid., C.C. Morfit, general manager, Western Dominion Collieries, to MacPherson, 13 Nov. 1931, vol. 5, 465; J. Eberhardt, special constable, to Tait, 19 Oct. 1931, vol. 4, 353, 23 Oct. 1931, 485–6.

35 Ibid., Morfit to MacPherson, 13 Nov. 1931, vol. 5, 465.

36 Ibid., Metcalfe to Tait, 3 Dec. 1931, vol. 5, 508.

37 Ibid., A.H. Graham, Bienfait overseer, to MacPherson, 25 Nov. 1931, vol. 5, 496–7.

Chapter 9. The Trials

1 Quotations are from a pamphlet Smith published, *Workers' Self-defense in the Courts* (Toronto: Canadian Labor Defense League, n.d.), 8–9.

2 'Estevan Strike Riot Trials' (preliminary hearings), R-95-53, SAB.

3 A.E. Smith, *All My Life*, 125.

4 Inspector R.R. Tait, commanding officer of the Southern Saskatchewan District, RCMP, to M.A. MacPherson, attorney general of Saskatchewan, 5 Oct. 1931, RCMP Estevan file, vol. 3, 226.

5 Larry Warwaruk, *Red Finns on the Coteau*, 57.

6 *Mercury*, 22 Oct. 1931.

7 Det.-Sergt. W. Mortimer, criminal investigation branch, Regina, to Tait, 26 Oct. 1931, RCMP Estevan file, vol. 4, 398, 397.

8 J.G. Metcalfe, criminal investigation branch, Weyburn, to Tait, 29 Feb. 32, ibid., vol. 6, 664.

9 W.D. MacKay, city policeman, interviewed by Larry Johnston on 2 Sept. 1973, A-357, SAB, as cited in 'An Oral History of Industrial Unrest in the Estevan-Bienfait Coalfields,' *Towards a New Past*, vol. 3, 43.

10 Tait to W.J. Perkins, agent of the attorney general, Estevan, 17 Feb. 1932, RCMP Estevan file, vol. 6, 654.

11 W.D. MacKay interview, Tape A-357, SAB.

12 Sergt. J. Molyneux, Estevan detachment, RCMP, to Tait, 27 Feb. 1932, RCMP Estevan file, vol. 6, 663.

13 'Unity of All Workers – Native and Foreign-born – against Deportation!' Statement of national executive committee, Canadian Labour Defense League, n.d., circa December 1932, R.S. Kenny Collection, Fisher Library, University of Toronto.

14 Estevan History Book Committee, *A Tale Is Told: Estevan 1880–1980*, vol. 1, 40.

15 Metcalfe to Perkins, 25 Nov. 1931, RCMP Estevan file, vol. 5, 492.

16 RCMP personal history file on Annie Buller, 29 April 1930, file 175/P1613, RG146, NAC; 'Criminal Statistics, Individual Record of Annie Buller,' *Rex vs. Buller*, file R–95–53, SAB. Buller was not, in fact, a member of the party's political committee.

17 Mortimer to Tait, 4 Oct. 1931, RCMP Estevan file, vol. 3, 220; Tait to Mac-Pherson, 14 Oct. 1931, vol. 3, 302; Rivett-Carnac to Tait, 14 Oct. 1931, vol. 3, 299. Rivett-Carnac fitted an insertion into his summary of the text of the secret agent's report. It read as follows (italicized): '... She said "Your fight is the workers fight all over Canada, we are going to help you with ammunition in the way of men and food and see that you are well protected, the only thing I ask you is to be united, go over the top of Truax Mine and make those men quit working." *Then she continued referring to the Police. "There are only a handful of the Police, those yellow hireling of Bennet, [sic] why you can go through them like that (snapping her fingers in the air) they are nothing."* Forkin spoke next, announcing a further meeting to follow the one in session. Sloan also addressed a few words to the miners, saying, "They call me Red but comrade Buller is still Redder ..."'

18 Transcript of testimonies of Mortimer and Eberhardt in *Rex vs. Buller*, vol. 1, 64, 156, R–2.914, SAB; Judge Macdonald's charge to the jury, March 1932, ibid., 412.

19 Tait to deputy attorney general, Regina (copy to the commissioner, Ottawa), 4 Jan. 1932, RCMP 'Personal History File on Anna Buller,' file 175/P1613 in RG146, NAC.

20 Testimony of George Mathieson, March 1932, *Rex vs. Buller*, vol. 1, 151, R–2.914, SAB.

21 Metcalfe to Tait, copies to deputy attorney general (Regina) and to the commissioner (Ottawa), 21 Dec. 1931, file 175/P1613, RG146, NAC; preliminary hearing transcript: Thomas McLean, Jr., 38ff., George Mathieson, 63ff., R–95–53, SAB; transcript of Buller's trial, 17–22 March 1932: George Mathieson, 134–54, Thomas McLean, 188–200, Thomas Cronk, 200–9, vol. 1, mfm. R–2.914, SAB (also available in hard copy at the Saskatchewan Court of Appeal in Regina); transcript of Buller's appeal trial, 7–9 March 1933:

Thomas Cronk, 139–49, Thomas McLean, 150–66, George Mathieson, 166–75, R-1162.2, SAB.

22 Testimony of Constable Horace Taylor, *Rex vs. Buller*, vol. 1, 170ff., R–2.914, SAB.

23 23. RCMP Anna Buller file, 18 Dec. 1931, file 175/P1613, RG146, NAC.

24 Ibid., Molyneux to Metcalfe, 17 Dec. 1931.

25 Ibid., report of 21 Dec. 1931; 13, 21 Feb. 1932.

26 Ibid., This identification is tentative pending the complete declassification of Buller's file.

27 Ibid., A.E. Acland, superintendent commanding 'G' Division, Edmonton, to the commissioner, Ottawa, 10 Feb. 1932.

28 *Mercury*, 24 March 1932; *Rex vs. Buller*, 422.

29 *Rex vs. Buller*, vol. 2, 420, R–2.914; A.E. Smith, 'Annie Buller and Scarlett in the Estevan Trials,' *Worker*, 2 April 1932. The judge read a similar statement at the end of Scarlett's trial.

30 *Mercury*, 24 March 1932.

31 'Notice of Appeal,' and 'Amended Notice of Appeal,' *King vs. Anne Buller*, CA#52, Saskatchewan Court of Appeal (Regina).

32 Judge Embury's charge to the jury, 9 March 1933, 357ff., R-1162.2, SAB.

33 Ibid., Frank J.G. Cunningham to George King, 11 May 1933.

34 Ibid., Judge Embury's charge to the jury, 358–9.

Chapter 10. Spreading of Seeds

1 Letter from Ben Swankey, Burnaby, to the author, 23 Aug. 1997. The profound effect of the miners' strike on Tommy Douglas has already been referred to in chapter 5.

2 These benefits ranged from unemployment insurance and low-cost housing in urban centres, to free medical care, pensions for a secure old age, and marketing boards to stabilize agricultural production.

3 'The Trial of the Toronto Communists,' *Queen's Quarterly*, vol. 39 (August 1932), 512–13.

4 Interview with Tony Bachynski in Bienfait, May 1998.

5 'Constitution of the Workers' Unity League,' as amended by the Second National Congress, September 1933, MG28.IV 4, vol. 52–78, NAC.

6 At the height of its influence between 1933 and 1935, the Workers' Unity League claimed between 30,000 and 40,000 members, including a large contingent of unemployed workers. Although it was one of the smaller trade union centrals at the time, it led over half the strikes in those years. According to the Department of Labour, trade-union membership in Canada in

1934 totalled 281,000 and broke down as follows: Trades and Labour Congress: 120,000; All-Canadian Congress of Labour (including the One Big Union membership): 55,000; National Catholic Unions: 30,000; Workers' Unity League: 24,000; others: 52,000. See *Twenty-fourth Annual Report on Labour Organization in Canada* (Ottawa, 1935), 8.

7   'The Gains of the Estevan Miners' Strike,' *Canadian Miner*, 10 Feb. 1932.

8   Glen Makahonuk, 'The Saskatchewan Coal Strikes of 1932: A Study in Class Relations'; *Prairie Forum*, 1984, vol. 9, No. 1, 79–99; *Mercury*, 25 Feb, 3 March 32.

9   Interview with Peter Gemby, 1976, Tape R–1020, SAB.

10   Interview with Steve Elchyson in Regina, in May 1997.

11   Interview with William Baryluk in Estevan, in May 1998.

12   Interview with George Wozny at Stoney Creek, Ont, in December 1997.

13   *Wylie Commission*, vol. 12; extracts from 'Report of Royal Commission on the Industrial Dispute in the Coal Mines in the Estevan District, Sask.,' *Labour Gazette*, March 1932, 262ff.

14   *Mercury*, 31 March, 7 April 1932.

15   Among those deported (along with family members in most cases) were: Martin Day, Ludevit Revay, Jan Kolenkas, Jan Gryciuk, Joseph Bernotas, John Harris, and Fred Booth. See 'Communist Deports from September 1, 1932 to November 30, 1932,' RG26, vol. 16, file of 'Communist agitators 1931–1937 deported from Canada'; 'Unity of All Workers – Native and Foreign Born – against Deportation!' Canadian Labour Defense League, n.d., circa December 1932, R.S. Kenny Collection, Fisher Library, University of Toronto; Interview by the author with Steve Elchyson in Regina in May 1997; Interview with Harry Barker by Michelle Rohatyn, tape R–A1969, 1979, SAB.

16   RCMP, 'Personal History File on Forkin,' 5 July 1932, file 175/P2772 in vol. 4671–72, RG146, NAC; *Mercury*, 15 Sept. 1932.

17   *Mercury*, 4 May 1933.

18   Larry Ward, MLA for Estevan, 14 May 1997, from text given to the author.

19   *Minutes*, Bienfait village council, 5 Dec. 1932, by-law 30, section 9; Interview with Steve Elchyson, in Regina, May 1997.

20   RCMP, 'Personal History File on John Stokaluk,' 15 Oct. 1931, file 175/P2698 in vol. 879, RG146, NAC.

21   Verlee Dunnigan writing about her father in 'Histories,' *Black Diamond Reunion '88*, courtesy of Donald Doerr in Estevan.

22   Interview with Norvine Uhrich, in Estevan, in May 1998.

23   Interview with Tony Bachynski, in Bienfait, in May 1998.

24   Interviews with Donald Doerr, mining engineer, and Bob Leslie, member of the Estevan Labour Committee and the Saskatchewan Strip Miners Union, Local 1573, in Estevan, in May 1998.

25 'Coal miners choose UMWA,' *Leader-Post*, 26 Nov. 1998.
26 Clara Swityk, interview with Peter Gemby in Bienfait in 1976, R–1021, SAB.
27 Words on the plaque of the martyrs' tomb in Bienfait cemetery.
28 Larry Ward, MLA for Estevan, 14 May 1997, text given to the author after the meeting.
29 Our Times (Toronto), July/August 1997, 11.

Annotated Bibliography

For various reasons associated with the nature of coal mining – its importance to the economy, its dangers, its social upheavals and folk culture – there are a great many sources available to historians for the study of life and work in the south Saskatchewan coalfields in the twentieth century. The most useful ones in the preparation of this book are the following.

Archival Sources

Bienfait Village Office
  'Minutes of Council, 1931'

Bienfait Public Library and private holdings
  Bienfait, Saskatchewan (Community Economic Development Board 1985)
  Black Diamond Reunion '88 (Hilda Prescott Carlson and the Reunion Committee 1988)
  'History of Bienfait' (Bienfait High School Student Council, 1955)
  Pryznyk Family History 1888–1990 (courtesy of Helen Pryznyk/Hitchens Antoniuk)
  'Taylorton, 1955' (courtesy of Donald Doerr)

Estevan Court House
  Rex vs. Martin Day et al, and other related trials in 1932, KB#283–KB#291

Estevan Labour Committee
  Scrapbooks and copies of collective agreements (courtesy of Bob Leslie)

Estevan Municipal Archives
  'Strike of 1931, file'

National Archives of Canada, Ottawa
  R.B. Bennett Papers, MG26K
  Canadian Security Information Service (CSIS) records, RG146, including
    vol. 817, file H.V.7, parts 1 to 6, the Royal Canadian Mounted Police corre-
    spondence on the Saskatchewan coalminers' strike in 1931 [RCMP Estevan
    file]
  Comintern Fonds, MG10K3, K–281, files 117 and 120; K–282 file 128
  Communist Party of Canada records, MG28.IV.4

Archives of Ontario, Toronto
  *Agents of Revolution: A History of the Workers' Unity League, Setting Forth Its Origin
    and Aims* (Ontario, Attorney General 1931). See also Bennett Papers item
    no. 388406, National Archives of Canada.
  Microfilm records of the Communist Party of Canada, RG4. The *Worker*, the
    Western Miner/Canadian Miner, and *Workers' Unity* are on microfilm.

Regina Public Library
  Leader-Post (Regina)
  Overgard Southern Saskatchewan Directory (1939) lists the names and occupations
    of heads of households in Bienfait in 1939.

Rural Municipality of Coalfields, No. 4, Bienfait
  'Minutes of Council, 1931'

Saskatchewan Archives Board, Regina
  Bienfait Branch No. 169, Canadian Legion, 'Vimy Banquet of the British
    Empire Service League, April 1946'
  Cuddington, J.H. 'History of Bienfait'
  Estevan Strike File, 1931, Department of Labour, Deputy Minister's Office
  Harry Kaik et al vs. Nick Boraska et al, transcript of trial over the ownership of
    the Ukrainian Hall in Bienfait
  The *Mercury*, Estevan, on microfilm
  Records of the Royal Commission on the Estevan-Bienfait Mining Dispute, 1931
    (Wylie Commission)
  Records of the Royal Commission on Coal Mining, 1934 (Turgeon Commission)
  Rex vs. Anne Buller, microfilm and transcripts of preliminary hearing (1931),
    trial (1932), and appeal (1933)

Saskatchewan Court of Appeal, Regina
  King vs. Anne Buller, CA#52

King vs. Sam Scarlett, CA#53
King vs. Anne Buller (1933), transcript of trial proceedings, CA#75

United Church of Canada Archives, Toronto
   Board of Home Missions, files for 1931
   General Council, Executive and Subcommittee, Correspondence 1931 (July)

University of British Columbia, Special Collections, Vancouver
   Bill Bennett Collection
   Angus MacInnis Collection

Published Sources

Arnot, R. Page. *A History of the Scottish Miners from the Earliest Times.* London:
   George Allen and Unwin 1955. A pioneering study of the fluctuations of trade
   unionism and the growth of a strong socialist spirit among the Scottish miners, stressing the influence which the material conditions in which they
   worked exerted on their way of thinking.
Almanac of the Ukrainian Labour-Farmer Temple Association 1918–1929 [in Ukrain-
   ian]. Winnipeg: ULFTA 1930. Gives reports of membership and activities by
   the secretaries of the association's local organizations across Canada, including Bienfait.
Barry, Bill. *People Places: The Dictionary of Saskatchewan Place Names.* Regina: People Places Publishing 1998.
Bowen, Lynne. *Boss Whistle.* Lantzville, B.C.: Oolichan Books 1982. Based upon
   oral interviews, this is a colourful and enlightening memoir of day-to-day life
   in the mining camps and of the grim struggles of the Vancouver Island coalminers to build their union from 1900 to 1965.
Buller, Annie. 'The Estevan Massacre.' *National Affairs Monthly* (Toronto: May
   1949). A brief, informative memoir written eighteen years after the event.
Campbell, Alan B. *The Lanarkshire Miners: A Social History of Their Trade Unions,
   1775–1874.* Edinburgh: John Donald Publishers 1979. Examines the emergence of the Scottish miners from serfdom in the eighteenth century followed
   by the weaknesses of trade unionism owing to the colliers' 'independent'
   work culture, massive Irish immigration, and other sectoral divisions as well as
   frequent cyclical fluctuations in the coal market which gave the coal operators
   a strong hand.
Carr, E.H. *Twilight of the Comintern, 1930–1935.* New York: Pantheon Books 1982.
   This noted British historian analyses Comintern debates on building revolutionary trade unions. Contrary to many accounts written before and since,

Carr suggests that 'it would be misleading to depict Comintern and its compo-
nent parties in the early nineteen-thirties as a monolithic structure responding blindly to the dictates of a single supreme authority.'

Coal in Canada. Calgary: Coal Association of Canada 1985. Provides basic information on the Canadian coal industry.

Cochrane, Ken, ed. *Toil and Trouble: An Oral History of Industrial Unrest in the
Estevan-Bienfait Coalfields.* Vol. 3. *Towards a New Past.* Government of Saskatchewan: Department of Culture and Youth 1975.

Demaris Ovid. *Captive City.* New York: Lyle Stuart 1969. The captive city is Chicago in the early twentieth century where the Truax-Traer mining company
was connected to the criminal underworld for the purpose of winning coal
contracts.

Deverell, Rex. *Black Powder.* Moose Jaw: Coteau Books 1981. A play based upon
the transcripts of the Royal Commission on the Estevan-Bienfait mining dispute, 1931.

Dun, R.G. *The Mercantile Agency Reference Book for the Dominion of Canada*: 1929 to
1939. Printed and bound in Canada for R.G. Dun of New York City. Gives the
names and credit ratings of businesses operating in Bienfait, Taylorton, and
Estevan.

Estevan History Book Committee. *A Tale Is Told: Estevan, 1890–1980,* 2 vols. Estevan, 1981. A very valuable source of information on the community, with
chapters on coal mining, schools, churches, courts, business, and so on as well
as numerous photographs and biographies or autobiographies of many of the
families who lived in the area in the 1930s.

Frank, David. *J.B. McLachlan: A Biography.* Toronto: James Lorimer 1999. A magnificent account of the legendary Cape Breton miners' leader who was also
president of the Workers' Unity League.

Hanson, S.D. 'The Estevan Strike and Riot, 1931,' M.A. thesis, University of
Saskatchewan (Regina campus) 1971.

– 'Estevan 1931.' Pp. 33–77 in Irving Abella, ed., *On Strike: Six Key Labour Struggles in Canada, 1919–1949.* Toronto: James Lorimer 1975. For many years,
Hanson's writing has been the standard reference work on the strike of 1931.
Hanson seeks to apportion the responsibility for the strike and 'riot' among
the operators, the miners' leaders, and the state in an even-handed manner.
Although the royal commission made many recommendations (some later
translated into laws) substantiating the workers' grievances, Hanson believes
that the strike, the Mine Workers' Union of Canada, and 'the dramatic days'
of September 1931 had 'no permanent impact on the industry of the Souris
coal field.' He reaches this conclusion chiefly because the miners were denied
the right to have a union of their own choice.

Hewitt, Steve. 'September 1931: A Re-interpretation of the Royal Canadian Mounted Police's Handling of the 1931 Estevan Strike and Riot.' *Labour/Le Travail* 39 (spring 1997): 159–78. Proposes a somewhat novel interpretation of the relationship between the RCMP and labour. Drawing on the declassified RCMP documents on the 1931 strike, the author calls attention to the sympathy shown to the coalminers by some RCMP officers. He reaches the questionable conclusion that, in their handling of 'the Estevan Riot,' the Mounties 'were guilty more of incompetence than dishonesty.'

King, Andrew. *Estevan: The Power Centre.* Saskatoon: Modern Press 1967. Has an informative chapter on the mining of lignite coal in Saskatchewan in which the roles played by J.R. Brodie and Alex C. Wilson are highlighted.

– 'Glamour and Tragedy in Border History: The Miners' Riot of 1931,' in *Scarlett and Gold.* 51st ed., Vancouver: Royal Canadian Mounted Police Veterans Association 1969, 31–6. A largely fanciful account of the miners' strike sympathetic to the RCMP.

Krawchuk, Peter, ed. *Our Stage: Amateur Performing Arts of the Ukrainian Settlers in Canada.* Toronto: Kobzar Publishing, 1984. An account of the working-class cultural activities of a major immigrant group to Canada that was active in Bienfait from 1920 to the 1950s.

– *Women's Fate: Interviews with Ukrainian Canadian women* [in Ukrainian]. Toronto: Kobzar 1973. Two women from Bienfait in the 1930s are included in this collection.

Laslett, John H.M. *Colliers across the Sea.* Chicago: University of Illinois Press 2000. A comparative study of the growth of unionism among Scottish miners at home and when transplanted as immigrants in Illinois during the century after 1830. It demonstrates that on both sides of the Atlantic these miners developed similar militant visions of social progress.

Makahonuk, Glen. *Class, State and Power: The Struggle for Trade Union Rights in Saskatchewan, 1905–1997.* Regina: author 1997.

– 'The Saskatchewan Coal Strikes of 1932: A Study in Class Relations,' *Prairie Forum,* vol. 9, no. 1 (1984): 79–99.

– 'Trade Unions in the Saskatchewan Coal Industry, 1907–1945,' *Saskatchewan History,* vol. 31, no. 2 (spring 1978): 51–68.

– 'The Working and Living Conditions of the Saskatchewan Deep Seam Coal Miners, 1930–1939,' *Saskatchewan History,* vol. 33, no. 2, Spring 1980: 41–55. Three scholarly articles by a Saskatchewan trade unionist, flowing from his M.A. thesis, 'Labour Relations in the Saskatchewan Deep Seam Coal Mines During the 1930s,' University of Saskatchewan, 1976. The author recounts the early history of the coalminers' attempts to form a union and explores the social conditions and conflicts that arose in the course of these struggles.

Before his untimely death, the author completed an admirable short history
and guide to the struggle for trade-union rights in Saskatchewan during the
twentieth century.

Manley, John. 'Canadian Communists, Revolutionary Unionism and the "Third
Period": The Workers' Unity League 1929–1935,' *Journal of the Canadian Historical Association*, 1994, 167–94. This article presents the core of the author's
unpublished Dalhousie University Phd. dissertation of 1984. It is a clinical discussion of the life and role of the Workers' Unity League, with grudging
respect. Stressing the implications of its links to the Red International of
Labour Unions (being both 'in thrall to the Comintern' and having a 'degree
of autonomy'), the author argues that while the WUL was 'an unusually – but
not uniquely – militant brand of unionism,' it was never a revolutionary union
movement. He suggests that the league's leadership of the Bienfait coalminers' strike in 1931 offers strong support to its adventurist stereotype.

Maydonik, N. Allen. *The Luscar Story*. Edmonton: Jasper Printing 1985. The
official history of the corporation that eventually came to control the
Saskatchewan coal industry.

McEwen, Tom. *The Forge Glows Red*. Toronto: Progress Books, 1974. The autobiography of the national secretary of the Workers' Unity League. It includes
the constitutions of the Workers' Unity League (1933) and the Farmers' Unity
League (n.d., circa 1930).

McKay, Ian. 'Coal Miners and the Longue Durée: Learning from Decazeville,'
Labour/Le Travail, vol. 20 (fall 1987): 221–8. Gives a succinct review of recent
literature about coalminers and offers critical perspectives on the way historians interpret the miners' experience. The author sees strong parallels
between the history of coal mining in Canada, France, and other industrial-
ized countries.

McLeod, Thomas H., and Ian McLeod. *Tommy Douglas: The Road to Jerusalem*.
Edmonton: Hurtig Publishers 1987. An enlightening biography of Saskatchewan's famous socialist politician.

Mineral Statistics Yearbook, 1995. Regina: Department of Energy and Mines,
Saskatchewan, Miscellaneous Report 96–3.

Morier, Chris D. 'Families in the Souris Coalfields 1925–1935,' M.A. thesis,
University of Saskatchewan 1996. Highlights the productive, unpaid labour
of the women and children contributing to the livelihood of the coalmining
communities; the author does not dwell on the fact that this unpaid labour
allowed the mine operators to pay much of their labour force less than subsistence wages. The thesis has one chapter on the strike of 1931 in which the
role of the Workers' Unity League leaders (especially Annie Buller) is generally disparaged. The author strongly criticizes labour and social historians

who, he says, paint one-dimensional pictures of 'despair and wretchedness' when concentrating on the strike, an occurrence he characterizes as negative and anomalous. From the oral interviews he has conducted, the author is convinced that most mining camp families in the Bienfait area had 'a tolerable and acceptable standard of living' in the 1930s, with food on the tables that was 'sufficient and hearty.'

Pawson, Alice. *Memories of Shand: History of a Saskatchewan Coal Mining Community.* Self-published, 1992. Shand was one of the hamlets in the Estevan/Bienfait coalfield.

Richards, J.H., and K.I. Fung. *Atlas of Saskatchewan.* Saskatoon: University of Saskatchewan, 1969

Roberts, Barbara. 'Shoveling out the "mutinous": Political Deportation from Canada before 1936,' *Labour/Travail,* vol. 18 (fall 1986): 77–110. Documents how the threat of deportation was utilized by the government of Canada to discourage working-class protestors.

Robertson, Heather. *Grass Roots.* Toronto: James Lorimer 1973. Has a colourful but inadequately researched chapter on Bienfait including a semi-fictional account of the miners' strike and parade into Estevan in 1931. Drawing upon her interviews with local people, the author describes Bienfait as a tough, bleak little town, ashamed of its reputation for bootlegging and militant miners and held together by inertia.

Seager, Allen. 'A Proletariat in Wild Rose Country: The Alberta Coal Miners, 1905–1945,' Phd. dissertation, York University 1981. Analyses the different phases of working-class organization over four decades in one of the largest coalmining fields in Canada, and is mainly critical of the role of the Workers' Unity League and its national leadership.

Smith, A.E. *All My Life: An Autobiography.* Toronto: Progress Books 1949. Has a chapter on the 1931 strike and the subsequent court cases in which the author acted as an adviser to the defendants.

The 'Soo Line' and Its People. Regina: Overgard Saskatchewan Directories 1956. Has a chapter on the Souris valley coalfields which offers a concise account of the history, operations, and capital structure of the coalfields at the time when deep-seam mining was abandoned in favour of surface or strip mining. Especially valuable on North West Coal, started by the radical Konopaki and Bozak families who were blacklisted after the 1931 strike.

Warwaruk, Larry. *Red Finns on the Coteau.* Saskatoon: Core Communications 1982. A fascinating account of the rise and decline of a Finnish community in the area of Saskatchewan where the Workers' Unity League leaders sought refuge after the Bienfait strike of 1931.

Watson, Louise. *She Never Was Afraid: The Biography of Annie Buller.* Toronto:

Progress Books 1976. An appreciative, short biography of a woman who was one of Canada's most dedicated and accomplished labour leaders and union organizers and who played a part in the coalminers' struggles.

Whitaker, S.H., et al. *Coal Resources of Southern Saskatchewan.* Regina: Saskatchewan Research Council 1978. Indicates the extent of vast coal resources still available in Saskatchewan.

Wrigley's Saskatchewan Directory, vol. 1, 1921–2. Gives the names and occupations of heads of households in Bienfait in 1922.

Oral Histories

There are many taped interviews with people who lived and worked in the coalfields in the 1930s. These interviews were recorded in the 1970s and are kept at the Saskatchewan Archives Board, Regina. The ones consulted for this book include: Howard A. Babcock (camp cook), Peter Gemby (miner), Alex Konopaki (miner, small mine operator), Archibald MacQuarrie (miner), Jean Moroz (miner's wife), Harry Nicholson (town councillor, small mine operator, mayor of Estevan), Mervyn Enmark (miner, foreman), Thomas Hesketh (miner), Sarah Prescott (blacksmith's wife), Leslie Kingdon (miner), Joe Pryznyk (miner, policeman). I myself interviewed thirty-one people in or from Bienfait and Estevan over the years 1995–8 and most of these people are identified and thanked in the acknowledgments.

Illustration Credits

Almanac of the ULFTA, 1930: first-generation members of the Red Hall of ULFTA

Richard Anderson: large mines (map)

Mike Antoniuk: bar and saloon of King Edward Hotel; 'Green Hall'

Archives of Ontario: masthead of the Workers' Unity League paper; cartoon appearing in *Workers' Unity*

Mike Baryluk: Steve Baryluk

Stella Boruk Collection: 1924 Chevrolet touring car; King Edward Hotel; Bienfait village, ca. 1920; brick school house; Jim McLean; wedding picture of Alex Boruk and Tekla Scribialo; Boruk's Boarding House and Bakery; Stella Boruk; Matthew and Liza Popowich; orchestra and drama group of the Canadian Ukrainian Youth Federation; William and Eva Adler; household belongings of Martin Day; Day's wife and children evicted

Ann Elchyson Bozak: picketers' sod houses; Mounted Police to Bienfait

Amelia Billis Budris: wedding picture of Ursula and John Billis; Ursula Billis and her daughters Annie and Amelia; Bienfait miners; youth group at the UFLTA

Jim Buller: Joseph Forkin; Thomas Ewen; Annie Buller

Gene Choma: William Choma

Garnet Dishaw: plaque; Amelia Budris unveiling a plaque; 'Coal Miners' Corner' in Estevan

Sam Dzuba: M&S mine in the 1930s; M&S mining camp

Lena Wilson Endicott: CPR station, 1998

Stephen Endicott: marker at the foot of the grave

Rudy Fedorowich (retired miner): Bienfait miners in 1930 wait to descend in the cage

Peter Gemby: Peter Gemby

Stewart Giem: headframe and tipple of Eastern Collieries; open pit method of extracting

Ken Hesketh: Harry Hesketh

Maude Horrocks: Katherine Carroll

Land Survey Office, Regina: village of Bienfait, 1931

McKee Archives, John E. Robbins Library, Brandon University: John R. Brodie

Rae Murphy: conference of the Mine Workers' Union of Canada, 1932

National Archives of Canada: Sam Scarlett, C144260.

Adriane Paavo: Charles Pavo

Railway and Miners' Museum, Bienfait: miners assembling their cavalcade; Main Street, Bienfait

RCMP Museum, Regina: Sgt. Mulhall; Insp. Schutz; Insp. Rivett-Carnac; second picture on Fourth Street

Armand Roy: cover of the program and T-shirt

Saskatchewan Archives Board: loaded coal carts underground, R285; plan of Eastern Collieries, from folio 5, R-285 Wylie Commission; A.H. Graham and W.W. Lynd, R-E312; SK fuel market, Wylie Commission, folio 4; Annie Buller speaking to miners in Bienfait; J.T.M. Anderson, R-D656; Rev. T.C. Douglas, R-A7915; Major McPherson, R-E312; first picture on Fourth Street, R-A18332; Estevan town centre, R-95-53, Estevan Judicial District, Buller Trial, Exhibit D6; Peter Markunas, Nick Nargan, and Julian Gryshko; funeral procession for Peter Markunas, Nick Nargan, and Julian Gryshko, R-A18508; headstone of the martyrs' tomb, R-A6697-2

Index

(CLDL), 96; pamphlet, 126; purposes, 112
Canadian Manufacturers' Association, 77
Canadian Pacific Railway (CPR): Bienfait station, 34, 134; coal mining, 14; construction gang, 47; landowner, 9; recruiting immigrants, 9
Carr, Sam (Communist Party of Canada organizer), 27, 146n.2, 43; in Bienfait, 34–6, 46; on Harlan County miners, 42; on Soviet miners, 41–2
Christophers, P.M. (One Big Union organizer), 24
churches: Baptists, 51, 74, 147n.18 (see also Rev. H. Gordon Tolton); on drought conditions, 21–3; National Emergency Relief Committee, 23. *See also* United Church of Canada
class struggle, 43, 99, 132; Sam Scarlett on, 48–9
Coalfields: location, 9; population, 11
coal miners in Saskatchewan (deep seam): annual incomes, 50–2; boarding, housing, 55–6; company stores, 54–5, 63; dockage complaints 52; fines, 57; productivity, 16, 144n.19; short weights, 52; wage rates, 19–20, 23, 49–51
coal mining in Saskatchewan (deep seam, underground): coal zones, 13–14, 144n.6; early history, 14–15; 'gopher holes,' 17; inspectors, 23–4; lignite coal characteristics, 16–17; market, 17; mechanization, 16; methods, 15; output, 15; profitability, 17–19, 145n.23; reserves,

144n.13; ventilation, 15; water removal, 15, 52
coal mining in Saskatchewan (open pit, strip mining). *See* Truax-Traer strip mine
Communist Party of Canada: Bienfait unit, 27, 33, 43; nature of, 104; outlawed, 35; relation to Mine Workers' Union of Canada, 104; and section 98, 35, 129
company unions, 54, 133; Saskatchewan Coal Miners' Union, 4. *See also* Appendix 3
Congress of Industrial Organizations (CIO), 132–3
Conroy, Patrick (union leader), 133
Co-operative Commonwealth Federation (CCF): elected in Saskatchewan, 4, 76; labour legislation, 4, 76; Regina Manifesto, 43. *See also* T.C. Douglas
Cox, J. Raffles (mining engineer), 50, 51
Creighton, Dr James (Estevan doctor): enraged at police, 72; finances legion, 102; refuses to treat wounded miners, 94
Crescent Collieries: size, 21; strikes at, 47, 61, 130. *See also* Appendix 1
Criminal Code: section 98 (sedition), 35, 129; section 501 (watching and besetting), 66
Cronk, Thomas (witness), 120
Cuddington: James (merchant), 36, 135; Tom, 55
Cunningham, J.G., defence lawyer, 96

Dempsey, Irma, 74
deportations: reasons for, 4, 109–10;